paint effects
for the home

NORTH LIGHT BOOKS
CINCINNATI, OHIO

contents

introduction

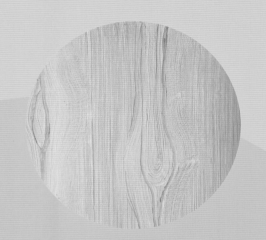

Discover how to trick the eye with trompe l'oeil designs and murals that will surprise, delight and intrigue!

You'll find this book an indispensible guide to creating trompe l'oeil designs, from preparing the surface and mixing paints to understanding scale and working out perspective. You'll also learn to paint trompe l'oeil using stencils, and get more than three dozen inspirational examples of spectacular interiors.

Whether you're a decorative painter looking for new challenges or an experienced muralist, whether your tastes are traditional or modern, this insightful guide will help you create fresh, fabulous looks for your home.

So why wait? Grab some brushes, set up your paints and get started!

Marvelous
MURALS
You Can Paint

Marvelous
MURALS
You Can Paint

NORTH LIGHT BOOKS
CINCINNATI, OHIO

www.nlbooks.com

GARY
LORD
&
DAVID
SCHMIDT

TABLE OF CONTENTS

3

Projects

Gallery *69*

2 2-D GRAPHIC AND SHADED MURALS *70*
Gallery *75*

3 DESIGNS FROM WALLPAPER AND FABRIC *78*
Gallery *84*

4 USING STENCILS *86*
Gallery *96*

5 PAINTING SKIES AND CLOUDS *98*
Gallery *107*

6 CREATING REALISTIC TEXTURES *110*
Gallery *122*

7 MOUNTAIN MURAL *124*
Gallery *140*

Introduction

We are very excited and pleased with what this book has to offer. Our goal was to write a concise but complete mural-painting book that would enable the reader to go from the most basic mural style to more advanced work. Each chapter builds upon the material in the previous chapters, so by the time you reach the more advanced projects, you will have a solid foundation for achieving the more challenging techniques.

In part 1 you will learn the importance of room preparation and the types of ladders and scaffolding that we as professionals feel are the best to use. We will also discuss drawing tools, spray equipment, brushes, rollers and paints. With the information in this section you will be able to select the right equipment and correct paints to paint any mural any size, anywhere.

In part 2 we explains how to choose the subject matter for your murals and how to acquire reference materials for developing your design from thumbnail sketches to full-color mockups. We will also cover color theory, how to make colors work for you and how colors create a mood. You will learn step by step how to use perspective drawing to add dimension to your work. We will also discuss composition and the uses of symmetrical, asymmetrical and radial balance. Following that, you will learn to enlarge and transfer your beautiful designs using four different methods that the professionals use. They are so easy to do and so quick, other people will think you are cheating.

In part 3 we will show you how to go from the most elementary style of mural painting to more complex and detailed murals. The first projects are two simple, but stunning, silhouette murals.

The next chapter builds on silhouette style often used in children's rooms. You will see how adding shadows and highlights gives more dimension and sophistication to your murals.

The next project shows you how to enhance a room by adapting designs from fabric, wallpaper, carpet and furniture. You can copy part of the design, alter it to please your eye and then match the colors. This technique will show you how to create flow, balance and harmony throughout the room you're decorating.

Project four will show you how stencils can be useful, either as an entire mural or as one component in a mural that uses hand-painting techniques as well.

Project five shows two ways to create beautiful sky murals. You can use the knowledge you gain in this chapter when you wish to advance to the next level and use the skies and cloud techniques with landscape painting.

Project six shows you how to create the illusion of dimensional textures in your murals. The demonstration features a wood-grained door, a fieldstone wall and a vine with leaves. Adding a drop shadow behind these elements adds to the feeling of realistic depth.

If you want to bring the great outdoors inside, you will enjoy the last project in which you will learn to paint realistic landscapes with mountains, grass, rocks, waterfalls and cloud-filled skies. These very detailed step-by-steps will allow you to proceed at your own pace to this more advanced level of mural painting.

We hope that you will enjoy the galleries at the end of the chapters and at the end of the book and that your creative process will be inspired by the wide variety of murals we have painted as professionals.

Equipment & Materials

BEFORE YOU BEGIN PAINTING A MURAL, YOU MUST FIRST PREPARE THE ROOM TO PROTECT THE THINGS IN IT FROM DAMAGE. NEXT, THE WALL MUST BE PREPARED BECAUSE A GOOD, SOUND PAINT SURFACE WILL NOT ONLY ALLOW YOUR MURALS TO LOOK BETTER, IT WILL ALSO ALLOW THEM TO LAST LONGER.

THE IMPORTANCE OF HAVING THE RIGHT TOOLS AND KNOWING HOW TO USE THEM SAFELY AND PROPERLY WILL ALSO BE ADDRESSED. WE WILL COVER THE USE OF LADDERS, SCAFFOLDING, DRAWING TOOLS, SPRAY EQUIP-MENT, BRUSHES AND ROLLERS AS WELL AS A VARIETY OF PAINTS. THIS KNOWLEDGE WILL HELP YOU FEEL COM-FORTABLE PAINTING ANY MURAL ANYWHERE.

St. John the Baptist Church in Middletown, Ohio, is a good example of a combination of a sprayed sky at the top of the half dome and a brushed sky by the windows. We also did all the general painting, gold gilding and marbelizing. The smaller altar mural is a mosaic that was done in the 1800s.

ROOM

$\mathcal{B}$ efore doing any painting, survey the area you are to be working in. Decide if any furniture, pictures, drapery, carpets or accessories should be removed from the room. The emptier a room is, the less likely anything will be damaged.

You will need to decide what type of ladders or scaffold, if any, will be required in the room.

We will only touch briefly on wall preparation, because many other books discuss in detail how to patch and repair walls before painting. (See *Recipes for Painted Surfaces: Decorative Paint Finishes Made Simple* by Mindy Drucker and Pierre Finkelstein.)

Look at all the walls closely with a bright light, preferably halogen, to see if there are any dings, dents, scratches or cracks that need to be patched, sanded and primed before

painting. Repairing any faults on your painting surface will ensure that they do not call attention away from your finished work. It is always best to fix problem areas first because correcting them after the fact would require repainting parts of the mural. Use a caulking gun to recaulk any trim that needs it before you mask out the trim. The caulk must be dry before taping out the trim.

Before fixing any wall imperfections, bring in dropcloths to protect the floor. Use a tape gun to mask around the baseboard and the tops of doors and windows to protect from paint spatters.

You can also use 2-inch (51mm) wide masking tape around your window and door edges to protect them from paint. Masking tape is useful, but can be left on the trim for only a

This room has been prepared for painting with a spray gun. The windows are covered in clear plastic, as is the fireplace, the door and the stairway banister. The floor is covered in drop cloths, and all other flat horizontal surfaces are also masked off. The outlet covers have been removed, and the vent has been closed.

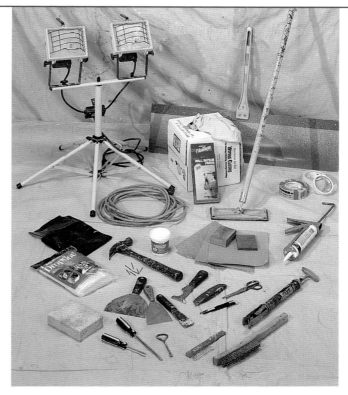

Some items useful in room prep are (from the upper left): halogen lights, spray shield, rags, wall repair kit, sanding pole, masking tape, electrical cord, garbage bags, spackle, sanding blocks and sandpaper, caulking gun, plastic dropcloths, hammer, finishing nails, hydrocellulose sponge, putty knives, utility knives, spinner (used for quickly drying paint brushes and rollers), screwdrivers, a paint opener and a wire brush.

few days or the adhesive may cause problems. If you are going to be on your project for a while, use blue tape, which will last seven to fourteen days even in direct sunlight.

If you are planning to spray paint in your room, you need to be a lot more careful than when using a brush or roller because of the overspray created by the spray gun. When masking out a room for a spray project, use 2-inch (51mm) wide masking tape and 4mil clear plastic to seal off the windows and doors. Cut the plastic to completely cover the door or window including the trim. Then use the masking tape to adhere the plastic to the trim, making sure the tape completely covers all the edges of the plastic and the outer edges of the trim.

A conventional cup gun creates a lot more overspray. If you are using a cup gun, cut a hole in the plastic in one window and put a fan in the window to evacuate the overspray as much as possible. Turn off or cover the heating and air conditioning vents in the room so the paint will not go through the HVAC system and get dispersed in other areas of the home. Finally, make sure that all the furniture and floor surfaces are totally protected before spraying.

PREPARATION

When you have removed everything possible, put down your dropcloths and masked out your trim, you can patch your walls if needed. Refer to the photograph on this page for a variety of tools to help you do this.

Your walls may just need a light sanding; use a pole sander for this. You may also need drywall mud to patch any dings or dents and sandpaper or sanding blocks to sand these patches smooth.

One note of caution: Any time you sand a drywall patch, a lot of dust is created. To keep this to a minimum, use sanding blocks wet with water. This keeps the volume of dust down tremendously.

Instead of a sanding block, you can use a slightly dampened hydrocellulose sponge. Rub it flat over the patched area in a

circular motion. Be careful not to rub too hard. The goal is to flatten out the patch so it is flush with the wall. If you rub too hard, you will remove too much of the patch itself and will wind up with a recessed area that you need to patch again.

You may find after using a damp sponge to smooth a patch that a "halo" of dried patching compound remains. To remove this, use a clean damp sponge to wipe the halo off right up to the edge of the patch.

After all the patches are sanded and all areas are caulked as needed, you are ready to apply a primer over your patches. If you have only a few patches, you can just prime those spots. However, if you have a lot of areas that have been patched, it is best to prime the whole wall.

Class III being the lightest and flimsiest and Class IA being very sturdy but heavy.

Ladders are made from aluminum, fiberglass or wood. Aluminum is the least sturdy and wood and fiberglass are of fairly equal strength. Aluminum ladders conduct electricity, so never, ever use them around electrical wiring, inside or outside. Wood ladders, if they have metal supports and brackets, can also conduct electricity. As time goes by, wood ladders will loosen up and get wobbly. They tend to collect moisture and swell or warp over time.

Fiberglass ladders, on the other hand, do not conduct electricity or warp. They are color coded for easy identification: red is for Class III

LADDERS

S ince most murals cover a wall from top to bottom, you will need to stand on something to reach the upper wall or ceiling areas. Painters use step stools, stepladders, articulated ladders, extension ladders, scaffolding, stretch boards and ladder jacks for this.

It is important to buy a good-quality ladder that has an industrial rating suited to your height and weight. There are four main classifications for all stepladders and extension ladders: Class III (rated household) can support up to 200 lb. (90kg); Class II (rated commercial) ladders can support up to 225 lb. (101kg); Class I is heavy duty; and Class IA is an extra heavy duty rating to 275 lb. (124kg). With each classification the sturdiness and structural strength of the ladder increases, with

household, green is for Class II commercial, blue is for Class I heavy duty, and orange is for Class IA extra heavy duty.

The chart shows 4-foot (1.2m) stepladders by classification and material and how much they weigh. Class III ladders are not recommended for a work environment because they simply aren't sturdy enough. We prefer either a Class II or Class I. The IA's get heavier as the ladder gets larger. On most jobs a 4- to 6-foot (1.2 to 1.8m) ladder is great. It can fit in most cars and trucks and is tall enough to reach most areas. Do not stand on the top step or platform. If you need to stand at a 4-foot (1.2m) height to reach something, you would need a 6-foot (1.8m) ladder.

If a stepladder will not reach your area, you may need scaf-

Specialty ladders used in a combination such as this one will allow you to paint safely in uneven areas. We are using a Little Giant ladder (left), an extension ladder (right, and a stretch board. Note how the extension ladder is braced against the bottom step so that the ladder cannot move.

folding or extension ladders with a stretch board. We have scaffolding that is 29 inches (73.6cm) wide, 6 feet (1.8m) high and 6 feet long. Two of these can be stacked a maximum platform height of 12 feet (3.6m). The scaffolding has a guardrail for safety. A small collapsible scaffold, 18 inches (46cm) wide, 4 feet (1.2m) high and 4 feet long, is also useful. Scaffolds are nice because they can hold a lot of materials and still have room for the painter to stand and move about.

Extension ladders have a classification rating exactly the same as stepladders. They usually start at 16 feet (4.8m) and extend to 40 feet (12m), with increments of 4 feet (1.2m). If you use extension ladders for high areas, you will find them difficult to use by themselves. Instead, use two extension ladders and ladder jacks to hold a stretch board between them to walk or sit on. Ladder jacks come in two sizes, one that can hold a 14-inch (35.5cm) wide plank and one that can hold up to a 20-inch

(51cm) wide plank. The stretch boards come in a variety of sizes and lengths. Aluminum is preferable because wood is springy, wobbly, and it warps. When you are standing on a 14-foot (4.2m) long plank 20 feet (6m) above the ground, you won't want to stand on a surface that wobbles.

Our favorite ladder is the Little Giant. It can do everything all the other ladders can, plus more. It can be an extension ladder, a stepladder, a stair ladder or an A-frame ladder. It is so versatile and sturdy, you probably won't need to buy anything more. We have abused this ladder for years and it keeps coming back every day for more. It's great!

LADDER WEIGHTS by type

Type	Aluminum	Fiberglass	Wood
II	9.5 lb.	10.5 lb.	15 lb.
I	10.5 lb.	13 lb.	19 lb.
IA	16 lb.	15 lb.	21 lb.

Giant and the extension ladder. The stretch board should be as level as possible. As you see, these can hold a lot of weight and are safe and sturdy to work on.

The photo on the left shows the scaffold we use most frequently in our work. Scaffolding, like ladders, comes in various sizes. The one that works for us 95 percent of the time is a system that has 29-inch (73.6cm) wide and 6-foot (1.8m) tall end frames. These are held erect by side rails that are 5 feet (1.5m) long. So, one scaffold rig is 29 inches (73.6cm) wide and 6 feet (1.8m) tall plus 8 inches (20cm) for the height of wheel casters and 5 feet (1.5m) in length. You can stack one system on top of another as shown in the photo to create a platform height of 12 feet (3.6m). When stacking scaffolding, it is required to have a guard rail system on the top section for additional protection.

One word of caution regarding scaffolding and stretch boards: Think! If people get hurt when using these systems, it's not because of system failure, but because of human error. People get hurt because they forget where they are after working six to eight hours and walk right off the stretch board. Sometimes people try

SCAFFOLDING

It seems that a lot of people want murals in areas difficult to access with a regular stepladder, such as stairways or high-ceilinged areas. Look at the murals of the White House Inn on this page and St. John the Baptist Church on page 15 and you will see that they could only have been done with special equipment.

In a stairwell, the Little Giant ladder is of great use. As you can see in the photo on page 19, the Little Giant ladder has expandable and retractable legs. This allows you to have a longer leg on a lower step of the stairway. For the next step, an extension ladder or tall stepladder can be used. In this case we used an extension ladder that braced against the lower step so the ladder could not kick out away from the wall. We used an aluminum stretch board to span between the Little

to use the system in ways it wasn't designed to be used. Do not walk on the outside of the scaffolding and use only the end frames to climb up and down. Brace ladders securely into steps as we have shown, or tie them into a handrail or something sturdy so that the ladder cannot slip. If used carefully, these systems are safe. If you do not wish to purchase these items, you can rent them at a local tool supply company.

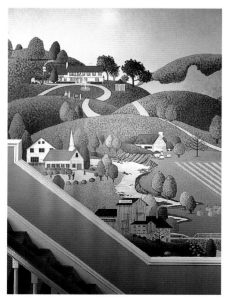

As you can see, this mural for the White House Inn in Cincinnati, Ohio was in a stairwell. We used the Little Giant ladder, a stretch board and an extension ladder here.

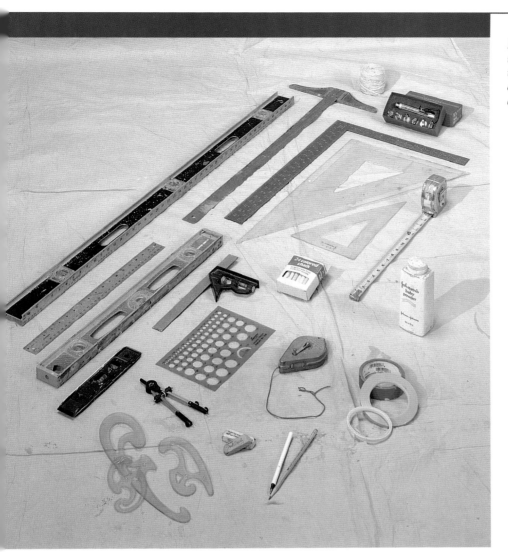

DRAWING
TOOLS

*Y*ou will need a variety of tools to help you through the process of designing and laying up your mural. A good pencil, various triangles, a compass, French curves, a circle guide, drafting tape and erasers (not that we ever need erasers, mind you) help in drawing the original design and enlarging it for your final mural.

We use three different sizes of levels, a 25-foot (7.5m) measuring tape, a yardstick and two different squares, all of which help make sure the objects in the mural are level and square and that the perspective is correct. (Refer to the section on perspective for more information on these tools.)

String and a chalk box are used to lay up the horizon line. Chalk and artist's charcoal are used to draw a design on a wall because they can be easily painted over or wiped off with a dry

or damp cloth. If you use a color of chalk close to the wall color, you won't be able to see it when the mural is finished. Pen, pencil and markers take many coats of paint to cover up, if they can be covered at all. This hinders you, especially if you want a loose, translucent, watercolor feeling in your final mural.

The Beugler striping tool is used to outline a graphic shape, such as the clown on page 70. See page 68 for a demonstration of using this handy tool. It is perfect for efficiently and neatly painting a long string of vines.

Spray equipment, clockwise from left: HVLP spray system, airbrush resting on a window fan, a conventional cup gun resting on a compressor, HVLP spray system, paint strainers, spray sock for your head, respirators, and in center, touch-up gun and auto cup gun.

The cup gun and touch-up gun require an air compressor. The one shown here is a 5 hp model, which can put 100 pounds per square inch (psi) of compressed air into the hose. You can then regulate this with a valve on your cup gun. We usually spray with about 40 psi of pressure. You can further adjust the amount of paint and air that is sprayed out of the gun in both the HVLP and the cup guns by attachments on the spray guns themselves.

SPRAY EQUIPMENT

*I*n the photograph above you can see a variety of the spray guns and accessories we use.

There are three main types of spray equipment used in painting murals: the HVLP, the artist airbrush and the conventional cup gun. HVLP stands for high velocity, low pressure. This type of spray equipment creates less overspray than the conventional cup gun, though you still need to protect all areas from overspray. With the HVLP you can work in the room for hours and not create a paint fog as you would with the cup gun. If there is a downside to the HVLP, it's that you cannot attain as fine a line of spray as with the cup gun, and the spray is slightly grainier than with a cup gun or touch-up gun. All HVLPs will come with a 25- to 50-foot (7.5 to 15m) hose, a spray gun and a turbine compressor, which is usually light in weight and easy to carry around. HVLP systems are also not as noisy as larger conventional compressors.

We use the airbrush when we want a much finer line than possible with the other sprayers. The airbrush is used in smaller areas because it does not have a very large spray fan and so covers a very small area at a time. Also it holds only a small amount of paint at a time. The others hold quarts of paint, but most airbrushes can hold only a few ounces.

When spraying in a room with a conventional cup gun, mask off the room to protect everything (see the section on room prep). Put a box fan in the window and seal around it with plastic to help vent the overspray to the outside. Always wear a respirator so you don't breathe in the overspray. When spraying a large area over your head, wear a pair of clear goggles to keep the paint from your eyes and a spray hood to protect your head.

Paint strainers are used to remove any large particles that may block your spray gun.

This is an auto touch-up gun, a type of cup gun. It sprays large areas with a fine (not grainy) spray. The bottle on the bottom holds paint, and a compressor forces air through the rubber tube into the spray nozzle. The paint and air mix and leave the nozzle in a fine spray. The trigger is at the top of the gun and is controlled with one finger.

When using a spray gun, dilute your paint with water by 10 to 20 percent to allow it to flow through your gun better. Strain this mixture with a paint strainer, a nylon hose or with doubled-up cheesecloth as shown here.

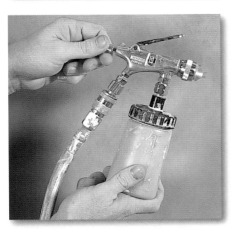

You can adjust the rate of airflow and paint flow to create a variety of spray patterns. Less air and less paint gives you a small spray area. More air and more paint enlarges the spray area.

Always hold your gun 6 to 12 inches (15 to 30cm) away from the surface you are painting. Be sure to keep the gun at a 90° angle to the wall so that the spray hits the surface evenly. Keeping your spray gun parallel to the surface will prevent an uneven coat. You can fade color using a spray gun by shooting a dense pattern on one end and a lighter pattern on the other.

The right tool for the right job makes painting much easier and faster. A wide variety of fine art brushes and standard paint brushes and rollers are needed when painting a large mural. We also use sponges, rags, cheesecloth, steel wool—and, to clean up, Goof Off and rubbing alcohol.

BRUSHES AND ROLLERS

arge-scale murals require a variety of tools with which to apply the paint. The first tools you will use are paint rollers and paint trays for painting a basecoat on the wall as well as for blocking in large areas of your mural. You can use various roller sizes to fit the area you are painting.

Choosing a tool to fit the area is also important when selecting paint brushes. Often people who paint have their favorite brushes and like to use them all the time no matter what size the area is that they are painting. It is okay to use a ¼-inch (6mm) flat shader brush when doing the small limb work on a tree, but don't use that same size brush when painting a 12-inch (30cm) tree trunk. Time is valuable, so use the right size tool for the right area.

There are so many different types of brushes and manufacturers that you will have to experiment and play on your own to see what you like for different areas and techniques. We will suggest brushes for each project throughout the book.

Rags, sponges, steel wool, cheesecloth and many more objects can also be used to create beautiful textures in murals.

All the paint products used in this book are waterbased, so they clean up with soap and water while the paint is still wet. Be sure to clean your tools as soon as you are finished with them to avoid having the paint dry hard. Wash the tools in warm, soapy water and then rinse them clean.

We use a paint spinner to help clean and remove the paint from larger brushes and rollers. After you have cleaned artist's brushes, you can shape the brush and then put a little soap on the bristles. This will allow the brush to harden a little in its natural shape. (When you buy the brush new, it has sizing in its bristles to maintain its shape.) Store all your brushes in a brush holder, or stand them with the bristles up in a container as shown in the photo.

If paint does harden in your brush, you can save it by using a brush cleaner. Denatured alcohol, Goof Off, rubbing alcohol, lacquer thinner or a chemical brush wash will soften the dried latex paint. You can use a wire brush to remove the paint once it is soft. Then clean the brush and store it as mentioned above.

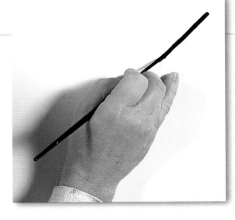

You can use a liner brush to create several different line widths by varying your pressure on the brush.

Light pressure with just the tip of the brush on the surface creates a thin line.

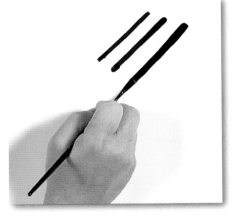

Heavy pressure, with almost the entire brush laying on the surface, creates the widest line.

By varying the pressure throughout one stroke, you can create a line that varies from thin to medium to heavy and back again. Use these techniques with a liner brush to outline shapes for 2-D graphics or when painting vines.

The acrylic paints are more brilliant in color and purity than latex emulsion paint, and they are also quite a bit more expensive than latex paints. A lot of the time we will use latex paints for larger areas (such as the sky, ground, etc.) and acrylics for details (such as animals or plants in the foreground).

Another way we use the latex paints is to buy what the paint manufacturers call a tinting base. Benjamin Moore makes five tinting bases for their paint. Each base is designed to enhance lighter or darker colors. This allows the manufacturer to mix up thousands of colors ranging from almost white to almost black. The difference between the bases is the amount of opaque white titanium dissolved in the clear base. The lighter the color you want, the greater the amount of titanium in the base. The darkest colors are mixed with the darkest base, which contains no titanium at all. The opacity and whiteness of the titanium allow colors with a very small amount of pigment to be applied with the same coverage as paints with a lot of pigment in them. More colorant is needed for darker colors, but the colors are more translucent because the base carries less titanium. The amount of titanium in the base also affects the drying time of the paint: high-titanium bases dry faster than titanium-free bases. Please note that you cannot use a pigment or colorant by itself as pure paint—or even in a mix containing 90 percent colorant. Pigments will not set or adhere to a surface unless mixed with sufficient binding material—in this case, the paint base.

The advantage to purchasing a paint base and separate universal colorants is flexibility. With your own tint base and several colors of pigment, you can mix any amount of any color for yourself—you don't have to buy a quart of every color in your mural.

We mix up most of our colors in 12-oz. (360ml) plastic cups and label them with the color name and where it is used. Dave uses a plastic glove to seal the mouth of the cup each night so the paint doesn't dry out.

PAINTS

Every paint used in this book is a water-based product. We almost never use oil-based paints for murals because they dry slowly, they cannot be disposed of easily and are not user-friendly in terms of odor and clean up.

All paints consist of two basic parts: a base, such as latex, acrylic, lacquer or oil; and a colorant, which is a natural or synthetic pigment. The paint base acts as a binding medium, keeping the pigments bound to each other and to the painted surface. The pigments can be added to any type of paint base and mixed to create custom colors. You can purchase a paint base with the pigments mixed into it, or you can buy the base and the pigments separately and mix them yourself.

Types of Paint

In this book we use two types of water-based paints: latex and acrylic. Latex paint is a generic term for a wide variety of water-based dispersions of powdered pigments into a base of rubber or resin. Latex paints are available in pints, quarts, gallons and 5-gallon containers. They are also available in different sheen levels, from flat, satin and semi-gloss to high gloss.

Artist acrylic colors are made from powdered pigments ground into acrylic polymer resins. They are packaged in tubes or jars from 2 oz. to 1 gallon (60ml to 3.8l) and often have a creamy consistency that can be thinned with water.

Mix small amounts of your paints in plastic cups and label each cup with what the paint was used for.

Large plastic buckets are good to hold water to rinse your brushes. A hair dryer is also great to use for drying down your wet color to see what the dry color looks like. All water-based colors are a little lighter in value when wet than when they dry. A rule of thumb is if the color matches perfectly when it is wet, it will be too dark when it is dry.

Glazes

In the chapter on creating realistic textures, we demonstrate methods of glazing, applying layers of opaque and transparent paint in succession. Glazes are transparent layers of darker colors applied over lighter ones, and scumbles are transparent layers of lighter colors applied over darker ones. Color resulting from this type of application has a greater luminosity than can be achieved with just opaque painting. This is because light is not only reflected from the surface of the paint film but also travels through the paint and is refracted and reflected from the paints underneath. Therefore a strong hue such as red-orange can be softened and made to appear cooler by glazing over it with a transparent blue.

Seal each cup with a plastic glove between uses.

When you are planning to use a glaze, paint your mural lighter and more sharply detailed than you intend it to be in the end. Glazing and scumbling will lower the value and brilliance of the color and obscure detail to a certain degree. There are three ways that we make glazes and scumbles in this book. The first is by adding water to the paint, which dilutes it, makes it more transparent, and lightens its value. The paint also loses some of its brilliance. (See the color theory section for a chart on this.)

Applying a glaze coat.

The second method is to add colorant to a translucent glazing medium, such as AquaCreme by Aqua Finishing Solutions. This is a glazing medium that you can tint with 100 percent acrylic or universal colorant. AquaCreme is also an extender, which means you will have a longer working time to blend your paints. Sometimes we will add it to our paint as a retarder and blending medium to help us create subtle shades of color. (Note the shading of the clown and the blended sky in the silhouette project.)

Applying scumble.

The third method of creating glazes and scumbles is to add latex or acrylic paint to a clear base. AquaGlaze by Aqua Finishing Solutions is a clear medium that is added to latex paint to create a translucent, slower-drying paint. We usually mix 75 percent AquaGlaze with 25 percent latex paint. This allows us a longer working time with our glazes or scumbles.

Preparing Your Design

THIS SECTION OF THE BOOK WILL GUIDE YOU THROUGH THE PROCESS OF CREATING A MURAL. YOU WILL LEARN HOW TO CHOOSE YOUR SUBJECT MATTER, OBTAIN REFERENCE MATERIAL, AND CREATE THUMBNAIL SKETCHES AND COLOR MOCK-UPS OF YOUR MURAL. YOU WILL ALSO FIND INSTRUCTION IN COLOR THEORY AND HOW HUE, VALUE, INTENSITY AND COLOR TEMPERATURE CAN HAVE A LARGE IMPACT ON YOUR FINAL MURAL. THE IMPORTANCE OF PERSPECTIVE WILL ALSO BE ADDRESSED. THE SECTION ON PERSPECTIVE WILL SHOW YOU HOW TO MAKE YOUR MURALS REALISTIC BY THE PROPER USE OF ONE- AND TWO-POINT PERSPECTIVE. YOU WILL ALSO DISCOVER HOW COMPOSITION CAN CREATE A MOOD OR FEELING IN A PAINTING BY THE ARRANGEMENT OF OBJECTS, COLOR, TEXTURE, SHAPE, SPACE, LIGHT AND LINE. THEN YOU WILL BE READY TO ENLARGE AND TRANSFER YOUR DESIGNS TO THE SURFACE OF YOUR CHOICE, USING ONE OF FOUR DIFFERENT METHODS.

WATER

SURFACE WATER

WATER

MID RANGE
AND OVER
SPRAY

WATER

ROCK BASE
SAND

SUN
AND
WAVES
BEFOR
DIESPRAY

SAND

SAND HIGH LITE

This is a small-scale, full-color mock-up of a mural. It's a good idea to make one of these prior to starting the full-scale project.

With the help of your reference photos or clip file, rough pencil drawings, known as thumbnails, can be drawn. Once you are pleased with the general idea and layout, it is extremely helpful to make a color mock-up before getting started on the full-scale mural.

CHOOSING A SUBJECT

he exciting thing about painting a mural is that it can be of anything you want. You can choose a cute whimsical theme for a child's room such as a collage of your child's favorite sports, animated characters, or rainbows and unicorns. You might want to have a soft, restful mural of one of your favorite vacation areas, which could be an ocean scene, mountains with waterfalls, a French countryside or a peaceful meadow with deer. The possibilities are endless. By looking through the many different murals and the variety of styles and themes in this book, you will have some help in deciding what type of mural you would like to have. Also, look

through other books, magazines or personal photographs to help you select your subject matter. The public library is a great reference source.

Once your major subject is selected, let's say a Northwestern mountain scene, you will need to narrow in on the details that you wish to include in the mural. You may love waterfalls and lakes, so let's include that somehow. Perhaps different types of rocks and their formations always captivate your soul. Don't forget the big, gorgeous skies with beautiful cumulus cloud formations. Northwestern ponderosa pine trees with various indigenous wildflowers and plants add a

When working on your mock-up, keep a record of every color you use. Although you may choose to change these colors later, keeping a record such as this one will save you hours in the long run.

good color balance. Animal life such as eagles, elk, mountain goats and raccoons give you a center of interest. Once you have decided which elements you want, it is time to combine them into a thumbnail sketch.

Not many people are able to draw all of these elements without some form of reference material. No matter if you want to paint one mural or ten, a reference file is essential. Shown here are pictures torn from magazines or personal photographs, broken down into categories. These are an invaluable resource, not only for composition, but also for different light sources, varying seasons, perspectives, values, colors and more. From the montage of resource material you can start to make your thumbnail sketches.

Thumbnail sketches are quick drawings that allow you to start to establish your composition, including color values and perspective. Once you are pleased with your sketch, you can move on to a color mock-up of the thumbnail design.

The color mock-up is where you really finalize your composition, your color palette (see the section on color theory), your color values, temperature and brilliance of your painting. If you do a color mock-up before you start your full-size mural, many potential problems will be resolved before starting the job. If you do the color mock-up first, you can keep a record of all the colors you used for each area of the mural as shown on this page. You will find that a color mock-up for a silhouette is not as essential as it is for a more detailed realistic mural. But it never hurts to have as much figured out as possible before beginning to paint your actual mural.

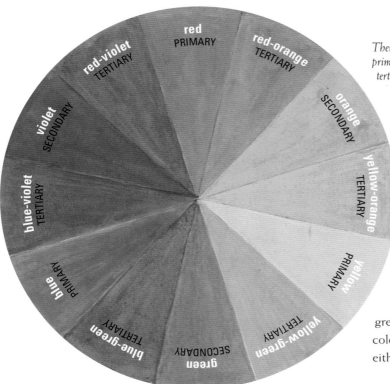

There are twelve hues on a color wheel: three primary colors, three secondary colors, and six tertiary colors.

Hue

Hue is the color name: red, yellow, blue, orange, etc. There are three primary colors that cannot be mixed from other colors. These are red, yellow and blue. These primary colors form the basis for the color wheel and from these three colors you can mix all other hues. The color wheel establishes logical relationships useful in color mixing and design, so get to know it well. As each color moves toward the next on the color wheel, it assumes the traits of its neighbors.

Between the primary colors are three secondary colors: green, violet and orange. These are mixed from the primary colors. By mixing any secondary color with the primary on either side of it on the color wheel, you get a tertiary color. Notice that the primary and secondary colors are described with one word: red, yellow, orange, etc. The tertiary colors are described with two words: blue-green, red-violet, etc. The first word is the adjective that describes the dominant hue of the color. Therefore, blue-green is a green color that's a little more blue than basic green. All of these colors make up the twelve hues on a color wheel. Understand that hue and color are general terms only and that pigment and paint names are very specific. Although there are only twelve hues on the color wheel, there are hundreds of pigment and paint variations of every hue. Colors will be described in this book by their hue name, pigment name, paint name or a number.

Be careful when using paints that have the same names but are made by different manufacturers, because there may be variations in the pigments used.

One last comment on hues—you may have noticed there is no mention of black, white or gray yet. These are considered to be colorless or achromatic. All other hues are called chromatic. When you mix a pure color with white, you get a tint; mix a color with gray, and you get a tone; mix a color with black, and you will get a shade.

COLOR THEORY

*C*olor is one of the most exciting art elements. It can create an entire mood, whether it be bright, bold and energetic, or quiet, somber and reflective. Color theory is very complex and to really understand it can be a lifelong endeavor. As in most things in life, there are guidelines in color theory that will help achieve better success more often than not, if followed correctly.

These few short pages could never begin to explain the depth of color theory, but perhaps your curiosity is piqued enough that you will practice some of these techniques and explore color for yourself.

Value

Value means the darkness or lightness of a color. A value scale is a ten-step gradation of any color that shows the color as it moves from light to dark. A tint moves toward white and a shade moves toward black. Yellow is the lightest color and violet is the darkest on a standard color wheel. Painter Jo Sonja Jansen once compared the value scale to a ten-step staircase coming up from a dark basement. At the top of the stairs the sun is shining, and at the bottom of the stairs it's completely dark. As you ascend from the basement you step on stair one or value one, and it gets a little lighter. Then you step on stair two or value two and it gets even lighter. As you continue to ascend the ten steps or values, you gradually go from dark to light.

Look at the ten-step value scale and note how soft and easy the transition of color is for your eye to follow. The five-step scale contains every other value from the ten-step scale. Even though it is missing every other color, your eye still makes an easy transition from values one to nine. This happens because values that are no farther apart than two values can be blended easily with the eye. The three-step value scale shows what happens if there's more than a two-value gap between colors. Your eye jumps across the colors for a much stronger contrast. If you get your values wrong in a painting, the elements will appear to jump out at you.

For example, say you are painting a beautiful landscape and you want the fox drinking from the stream to be the focal point, but the waterfall in the distance behind the fox is all that you see. Most likely you haven't stepped your values correctly. Graduating your values means a gradual transition. Your darkest values should be in the foreground, then mid values, and finally your lightest values in the background. This can all change, however, because of the placement of your light source—such as placing the moon behind the mountain in the wolf mural on page 35. Atmospheric perspective is the term for how the values of colors lighten up and turn blue as the objects recede further and further into the background.

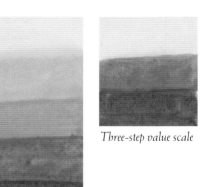

Three-step value scale

Five-step value scale

Ten-step value scale

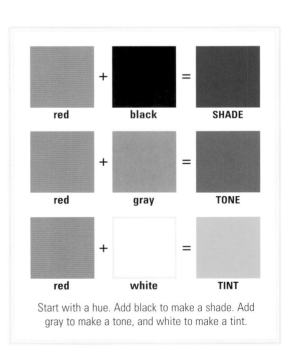

Start with a hue. Add black to make a shade. Add gray to make a tone, and white to make a tint.

How Hue and Value Relate

Here is a tip that many artists use to see values: squint your eyes when you look at a color. This allows you to see the value of the paint more than the exact hue. The scale on the right, below, shows that different hues can have the same value. The scale next to it shows that you can also change the value of a color by increasing its translucence. In this case watercolors were used, so water was added to the color. You can also do this with acrylic or latex paints. For oil-based paints, just add paint thinner to increase the translucence. The last scale shows a full value scale in green which was made by starting out with value five and adding white to values six, seven, eight and nine and black to values four, three, two and one.

Three hues of the same value

Decreasing value by increasing translucence

A full value scale made by adding black to values below five and white to values above five

The column of colors on the left is a value scale using a hue mixed with white. The value of each color across the rows is very similar. However, each column is of a lower intensity than the column to its left because it contains a higher proportion of gray.

According to the most general rules of atmospheric perspective, colors lighten and acquire a blue cast as they recede into the distance. Brighter and darker colors are used in the foreground (below). However, placement of your light source can affect the arrangement of values in your mural. In the wolf mural (left) the location of the moon behind the mountain determines that the darkest value be used in the background and the lightest in the foreground.

Intensity

Oftentimes people are confused by intensity and value. Remember that value is the lightness or darkness of a color. Intensity of a color, sometimes called brilliance or chroma, refers to a color's brightness or dullness. A pure bright color has a high intensity while a grayed color has a low intensity. The extreme of low intensity is a neutral gray.

By using color intensity in a variety of ways, you can control compositional emphasis and create a setting for beautiful color effects. For instance, when mixing two adjacent high intensity colors, the mixture will slightly lower in intensity than either color by itself. You will notice the greatest decline in intensity when the two colors are far apart on the color wheel. Lower a bright color's intensity by mixing in black, gray or an earth color. Note: It is very difficult, if not impossible, once you have lowered a color's intensity to turn it back into a pure hue again. In the color chart on page 34, there is a vertical value scale from light to dark on the left. Only white was used to change the value. In the next row a small amount of gray was added to the colors, matching the value level as closely as possible. For the next row more gray and less color was added, again matching the value as closely as possible. This continues across the rows until the final colors are mostly gray with only a hint of the original color.

Temperature

The fourth and final component of color is temperature. As you look at the color wheel on page 32, you can see that half of the colors are warm (red-violet to yellow) and half are cool (violet to yellow-green). Color temperature helps create mood, depth and movement, and thus adds to the realism of your painting. Warm colors advance and cool colors tend to recede. This can be seen in the mural on this page, which has a lot of cool colors in the background and foreground. The warm red flowers "pop" off the cooler colors.

Color temperature is relative. A color that appears warm in one place may look cool in another depending on how it is used with its surrounding colors. Every color has many temperature variations, so practice will help you see the differences. Highlights are places where there is the highest concentration of light on an object (such as sunlight on mountain tops). The sun is warm, as are most highlights. But there are also cool highlights, such as violet highlights on snow on an overcast wintry day. Colors in shady areas tend to be cool. But if objects are reflecting warm light into the shady area, the shadows may tend to be on the warm side.

To create a strong sense of depth in your paintings, carefully monitor color temperature. To warm up a color, you would add any color that's warmer than the initial color. It is best to add a relat-

Notice that the red flowers, which are warm colors, "pop" off the background of blues and greens, which are cool colors.

ed color. If you were using violet, you could add red to warm it up. To cool a color you would add a color that is cooler than what you were using. If you were using yellow-green, add more green. Red-orange is the warmest color and blue-green will be your coolest.

On the color wheel (page 32) the hues opposite each other are called color complements. One color is a warm color and the other one is a cool color. This is important to know because if you mix a little of a color's complement into itself, you will decrease or reduce its color intensity.

This mural is painted primarily in two values of blue, which is a monochromatic color scheme.

Color schemes

Color schemes are based on a dominant color. Monochromatic schemes are based upon one color in different values. Analogous schemes are based upon colors that are adjacent on the color wheel. Split complementary color schemes are composed of three colors: one color and the two on either side of its direct complement.

There is an enormous amount of information about color theory that has not been covered here. Further reading is advisable. Practice, practice, practice to understand the subject more clearly. If you want to learn to make colors, get a paint deck from your paint supplier that lists the formulas of the universal tints and the base color for each color. Then buy the universal tints and the base colors and custom-tint your colors to match the paint chips.

This mural shows an analogous color scheme.

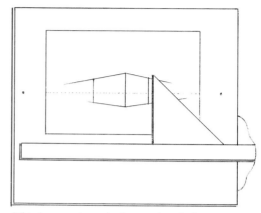

This drawing shows the drawing board of an artist with a triangle, T-square and paper. Note that the vanishing points are off the paper.

PERSPECTIVE

*P*erspective is a technical skill that has rules. Anyone can do a quality perspective drawing once the rules are learned. Perspective makes the objects we draw look solid and gives them dimension. Strong skills in perspective will improve your ability to paint excellent murals.

We will look at two types of perspective: one-point and two-point (based on the number of vanishing points in the drawing). Both are easily mastered and are the basic framework for drawing almost anything in perspective. All objects in a mural appear smaller as they approach the vanishing point, and larger the closer they get to the viewer.

One-point perspective works well when it is viewed from one specific spot. For example, if a hallway wall mural is going to be most often viewed from one end of the hallway, one-point perspective will work well.

Two-point perspective gives a more realistic dimensional quality to murals and requires more steps to complete. In one-point perspective the vanishing point is usually located on the drawing surface. In two-point perspective, the vanishing points are often located outside the bounds of the drawing, which makes it more challenging.

For these exercises in perspective, you will need: a large piece of paper, pushpins, a pencil, a T-square, an eraser, drafting tape and a clear plastic triangle. When drawing a horizontal line, rest a T-square firmly against the straight edge of your desk or table. When drawing a vertical line, rest a triangle firmly against your T-square. When connecting one line to another, such as the corner of a box, the lines must connect precisely. If not, your drawing will not line up properly.

When drawing in perspective on a wall, place your horizon line at the eye level of the viewer, 5'5" to 6' (1.6-1.8m). Measure this and snap a chalk line. Use pushpins or nails for vanishing points. Finding a straightedge long enough to reach the vanishing points is impossible. Instead, tie string to the nails at the vanishing points and pull tightly to create a straight line from the vanishing points to the line you're drawing. Make several marks along the line and connect them with a straightedge. Use a level for an accurate vertical line. When the mural is complete, the holes can be patched and painted.

If your vanishing points extend beyond the corners of the wall, do a drawing to scale and use an overhead projector to transfer the image. It works, but you will have to make adjustments by eye because the projector tends to distort the image slightly.

With your newfound knowledge of perspective, your murals will take on a whole new dimension, pulling the viewer into your work.

When you know how to use perspective, you can achieve some stunning effects with your murals.

FAR LEFT PANEL ①

Let's start with the horizon line. The horizon line is a horizontal line that divides the sky from the ground. Where things sit in relation to the horizon line determines how we see it. If we place a box in front of us at eye level, we see only the side or sides of the box, not the top or bottom. We see distance by the overall size of common objects. Things appear smaller the farther away they are from the viewer. This is also true of space and distance. The car parked in your driveway appears much larger than a car parked a block away. Look at the spacing of telephone poles when you are traveling down a straight highway. The farther the poles are from the viewer, the smaller the space appears between each pole. This also applies to the spacing between parallel horizontal lines. As they recede, the visual distance between them is reduced. But by how much? If you follow the lines all the way to the horizon line, you will see they all meet at one point, the vanishing point

Now let's get started with an exercise in creating one-point perspective—that is, perspective using one vanishing point.

Where an object sits in relation to the horizon line determines how we see that object.

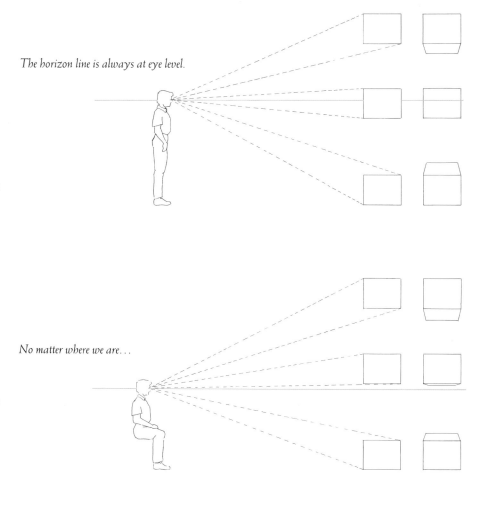

The horizon line is always at eye level.

No matter where we are...

...the horizon line is always at eye level.

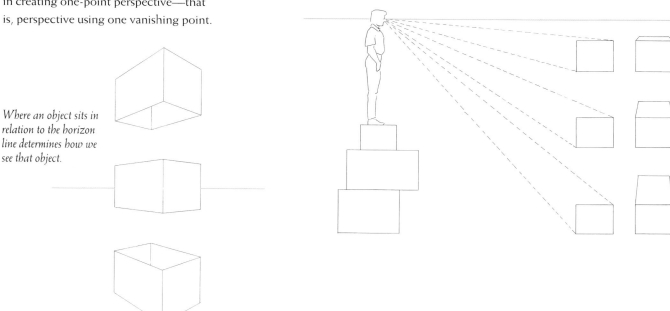

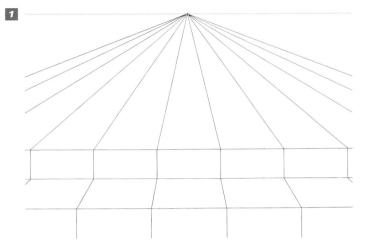

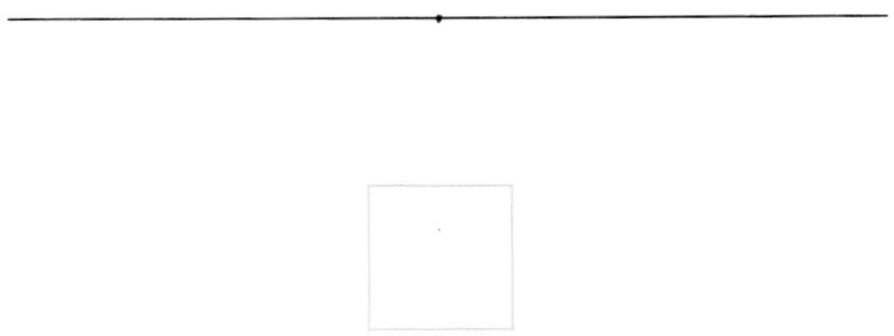

Figure 1 › As parallel lines recede, the distance between them is reduced.

Figure 2 › First and always first, place your horizon line. Since this is just a practice exercise, place your horizon line in the center of your paper. This is done using your T-square.

Figure 3 › Next, on the center of your horizon line, place a small dot. This is your vanishing point. The vanishing point is where receding parallel lines meet on the horizon line.

Figure 4 › With the base of your triangle set firmly against your T-square, draw a light center line down from your vanishing point. Use the vertical side of the triangle to draw the sides of a box, and slide the T-square to make the top and bottom.

5

Figure 5 › Next, draw a line from the lower left and right corners of your square to your vanishing point. You can slide your T-square out of the way and use a straightedge to draw these lines.

Figure 6 › Now draw two more lines from the vanishing point to the top two corners of your box.

Figure 7 › You can see the square is taking on some dimension. To draw the back end of the box, another square is drawn with each corner touching the receding parallel lines. That's it! You have a box drawn in one-point perspective.

6

7

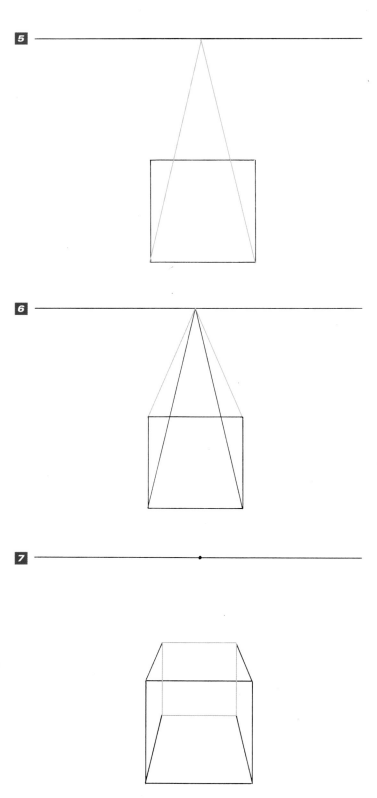

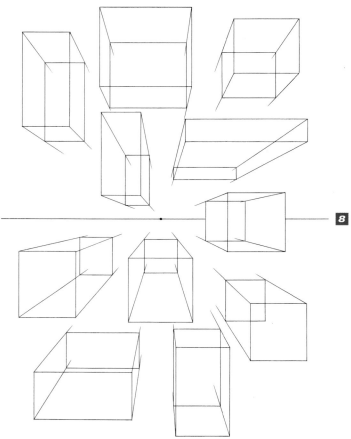

8

Figure 8 › From that one vanishing point, other boxes can be drawn. Notice the boxes above the horizon line. You can now see the bottom of these boxes. That's because any object above the horizon line is above our eye level. Practice one-point perspective by drawing boxes of different sizes and shapes using only one vanishing point.

Figure 9 › All the boxes in one-point perspective have something in common. They all face directly at you. To turn the box or angle it slightly, you need to use two-point perspective. To start, draw the horizon line.

Figure 10 › Next, draw the front vertical edge closest to the viewer. This is done using your triangle and T-square. It is important to remember that all vertical lines in one- and two-point perspective are just that: vertical. Vertical lines are not altered by perspective.

Figure 11 › Mark the horizon line directly above the vertical edge and measure out an equal distance from that point to locate your left and right vanishing points. Although you can put your vanishing points anywhere on the horizon, following these instructions will ensure that your drawing looks like mine.

Figure 12 › In two-point perspective, every line you draw will extend to either your left or right vanishing point, except for your vertical lines. › Now that the height of the box has been determined by the front corner (the vertical line) drawn earlier, draw a line from the top and bottom corners to your vanishing point right (v.p.r.). Repeat to vanishing point left (v.p.l.). › Hint: It will be easier and help your lines "click" if you use pushpins for your vanishing points. Your T-square can rest against them for a more accurate line.

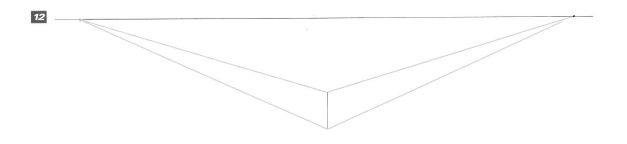

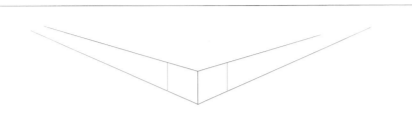

Figure 13 › To establish the width and length of your box, draw a vertical line on each side of the front corner, inside the lines extending to the vanishing points.

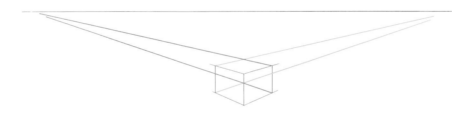

Figure 14 › Draw a line from the top and bottom of these two outside edges to the opposite vanishing point. Lines from the right vertical edge are drawn to vanishing point left; lines from the left vertical edge are drawn to vanishing point right. Where these two lines intersect on top and bottom determines the back vertical edge. Two sides of the box are now complete!

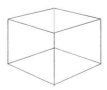

Figure 15 › Where the top and bottom lines intersect indicates where the back corner is located. This is a vertical line drawn in with your triangle and T-square. Now you will find out if all your lines click. (If your lines drawn earlier are off just a little, your back corner will not line up top to bottom.) Your box is complete.

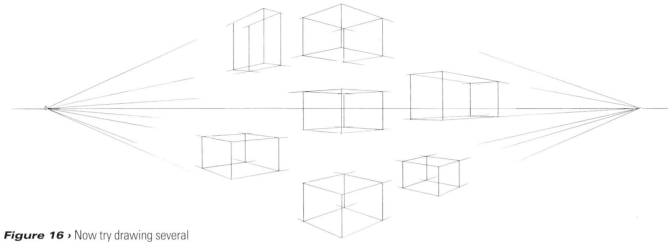

Figure 16 › Now try drawing several boxes using two-point perspective. You will notice the back corner changes depending on the position of the box in relation to the vanishing points.

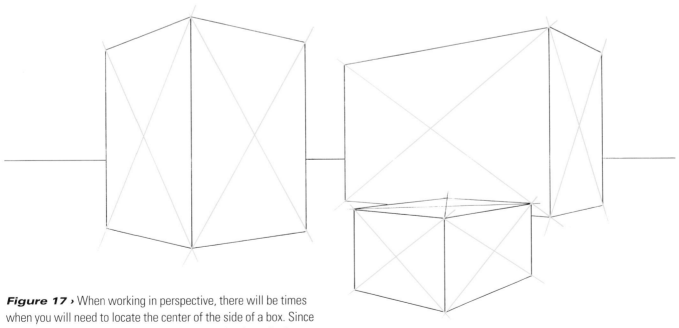

Figure 17 › When working in perspective, there will be times when you will need to locate the center of the side of a box. Since the box is drawn in perspective, simply measuring from the front corner to the back corner and dividing by two will not work. To accurately and easily find the center, draw diagonal lines from corner to corner. The center location of the side of the box will be where the two lines intersect.

Figure 18 › The key to drawing circles in perspective, such as the top of a wine glass, is to first draw a cube and locate its center. › Next, draw a vertical line intersecting the center. Then draw a line from v.p.r. through the center point as well. (If the circle faces right, draw the horizontal center line from v.p.r. If it faces left, draw it from v.p.l.) The side is now divided into eight equal parts. Do the same to the opposite side of the cube.

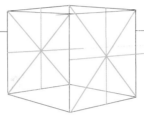

Figure 19 › To start your circle, draw a smooth arc in one quarter of the cube face. Use the intersection of the arc with the diagonal line as a starting point for a smaller square set inside the first. Use the vanishing point to establish the top and bottom of the square. The distance from the top line of the square to the middle line equals the distance from the middle to the bottom line. You can make the back square proportional to the front square by using the opposite vanishing point (in this case, v.p.l.) to draw lines from the corners of the smaller front square to intersect with the diagonals on the back cube face. The corners of the smaller back box are located where the lines intersect.

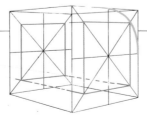

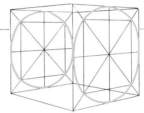

Figure 20 › Use these smaller squares as a reference point for drawing the rest of your circles. Now you have two circles drawn in proper perspective.

Figure 21 › Using v.p.l., connect the top of the back circle to the top of the front circle. Repeat for the bottom of the circles, using the same vanishing point. You have drawn a cylinder. You will probably need to practice this exercise to master it.

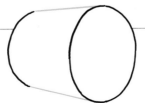

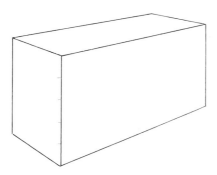

Figure 22 › You may need equal horizontal measurements in some drawings. For instance, you may want to draw a row of books. Start by determining how many equal horizontal segments you will need. Draw an extended box shape to the visual length you would like. Then mark the vertical front edge of your box with the number of horizontal segments you need, spacing them equally. Note: In this exercise, as will be the case with many murals, my vanishing points are located off the edges of the drawing surface.

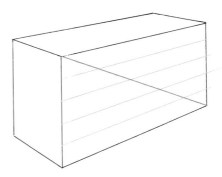

Figure 23 › Once again, remember that if you want your segments to face right, draw lines from v.p.r. If you want it to face left, draw from v.p.l. In this case, I want my segments to face right. Draw horizontal lines from the vanishing point through the tic marks you made on the front edge of the box. Then draw a diagonal line from corner to corner so that each line is intersected by the diagonal line.

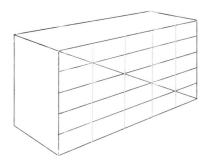

Figure 24 › Next draw a vertical line through each intersection, using your T-square to keep the lines vertical. Now you have equal segments drawn in perspective.

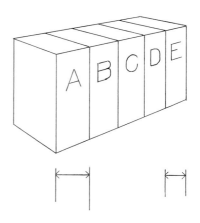

Figure 25 › Notice the difference between the width of the first box (A) and the last box (E), which is farther away.

Figure 26 › This living room scene was drawn using basic box shapes and circles in perspective.

Figure 28 › These round objects were drawn with box bases, circles, and cylinders.

Figure 27 › You can now see how each item was constructed from basic box shapes.

Figure 29 › Now you can see how each object started out as a box.

COMPOSITION

omposition is everything to a painting. It is the arrangement of objects, color, texture, shape, space, light and line. This arrangement can create a mood or feeling in a painting. Visit your local art museum and study the masters. Do you find the painting soothing and relaxing, happy or sad, exciting or frightening? Composition plays a part in all these emotions. A painting with poor composition will not hold the viewer's attention.

Liking or not liking a certain composition is a matter of taste, and as with anything in the world of art, nothing is written in stone. However, there are certain factors that affect how your eye travels through an image. This chapter will show you options in compositional design.

Let's start with how you see a painting. As you read the text in this book, you read from left to right. We read paintings the same way. We start at the left, if only for a split second, then begin to travel to the main focal point. The eye can be pulled quickly to the subject, or the composition can slowly pull us in. Once the eye locates the main focal point of the painting, it tends to wander. A good composition will direct the eye through the painting and back to the main focal point, locking the eyes of the viewer inside the picture.

As an artist works, you may notice him stop and stare at his painting. He may tilt his head, close one eye, and step back a distance. Why? Balance. You don't have to be an artist to see or feel it. If the painting has no balance, both the artist and viewer will sense something is not quite right.

There are three types of balance: symmetrical, asymmetrical and radial. When arranging your composition, keep it simple. Use only the elements that support your original idea. Unnecessary elements add nothing but confusion. Finally, use thumbnails—and lots of them—to work out any problems you may have with the composition.

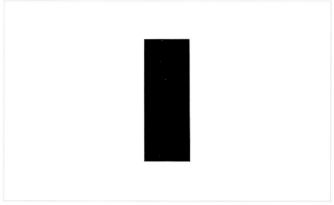

An object placed in the center of a painting with equal distance on each side is a good example of symmetrical balance. If the painting were divided in half, vertically, each side would have an equal amount of design as the other half.

Any object placed left or right of center will be balanced by the open or negative space across from the subject.

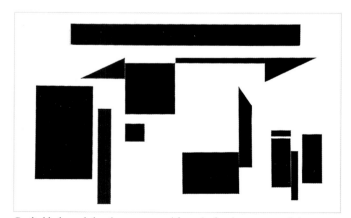

Radial balance helps the eye to travel from the focal point around the painting in a circular motion, returning again to the main focal point. The eye never leaves the picture.

Most compositions use both negative and positive space. Positive space is usually occupied by objects, the subjects of the composition. Negative space surrounds and balances the positive space.

Use of negative space is one way to pull the eye to the subject. The positive space in this composition is taken up by the tree and the owl.

Notice how the negative space creates "pointers" that go directly to the subject.

Contrast in color is a great way to pull the eye into the subject. Any dark color on light, or light color on dark, will quickly grab the attention of the viewer.

Shadows can also pull the eye into the subject. Even though the value of the tree is close to the value of the stormy sky, the shadow traveling across the foreground pulls you to it.

Compositions are vertical if they are taller than they are wide and horizontal if they are wider than they are tall. Don't fight the format. If your painting is in a vertical format, it requires a vertical composition.

Here there are more verticals than just the trees. The reflections in the water are vertical, as is the graduation in the sky. Even the positive and negative spaces create a vertical flow.

Various shapes can be used to draw the eye from one area of a composition to another. One good trick is to use letters of the alphabet. Here the letter U was used to guide the eye down and then up to the subject.

The letter Z was used here. The viewer enters the picture by following the shadows across the grass, up the strong vertical of the tree trunks, then follows the Z shape down and across the picture. The shadow from the rock carries the eye back to the vertical tree trunks.

Repeating or "echoing" shapes is a good way to harmonize composition and create flow. The S shape in the bird's neck was repeated throughout this composition. The flow of the stream bank, the ripples off the water and the branches in the foreground all echo the curve of the bird's neck.

ENLARGING AND TRANSFERRING

There are four different ways to enlarge your designs to their finished size and transfer them. As professionals, we have used all four of these techniques at one time or another, but the one we use most frequently is the overhead projector. The other three methods are using an opaque projector, using a slide projector, or enlarging the pattern using the grid method.

Finished Scale Drawing

We begin by doing small "thumbnail" sketches to work out the composition and values of the mural before making a final drawing. The final drawing is smaller in scale than the final work of art will be, so it must be enlarged. To do this you need to make your finished drawing to the scale that your actual mural will be. First you must measure the area where your mural will go. Many times we will work in what is called a 1-inch scale (1 inch equals 1 foot), (2.5cm equals 30cm) though you can work in any scale such as ¼-inch (6mm), ⅛-inch (3mm), ½-inch (12mm), etc. If you are using 1-inch scale and you have a wall that is 8 feet (2.4m) tall by 12 feet (3.6m) long, you would need to make your final drawing 8 inches by 12 inches (2.4cm by 3.6cm) so that it stays proportionately the same as the wall when you enlarge it. This scale drawing is important in each of the enlarging processes.

Enlarging With a Grid Pattern

To enlarge by the grid technique shown on page 56, you need to overlay a square grid pattern on top of your finished design. Each 1-inch (2.5cm) square, when enlarged to full size, will equal 1 foot (30cm). Sometimes you will want to use a smaller grid, such as ¼-inch (6mm) squares, which would equal 3-inch (7.6cm) squares when enlarged. The size of grid you use depends upon how much detail is in the drawing. The more detail the drawing has, the smaller the grid should be.

Once you have established your grid size, you can draw a grid pattern directly on the wall using something you can easily paint over, such as chalk or light pencil.

Transferring a Cartoon

This is the technique that Michelangelo used to transfer his drawings for the Sistine Chapel. The grid is drawn on large pieces of craft paper or newsprint. Once the grid is drawn, sketch the image inside of each corresponding square from the original finished drawing to the enlarged drawing. The finished enlarged drawing is now called a cartoon.

The next step is to transfer the cartoon onto the wall itself. First the design is perforated with a pounce wheel, which is pictured on page 57. Then tape up each piece of paper on the wall in its appropriate area and use a chalk bag (a piece of cotton rag with powdered chalk in it) and pounce over the perforated holes. The chalk will go through the holes and recreate your pattern underneath. The color of the chalk must contrast with the wall color so you can easily see it, but do not use the red or yellow ground chalk found in hardware stores because it is a permanent chalk. Use the blue or white chalk or baby powder by itself or mixed with the chalk.

Once the cartoon is transferred, the image is easily smeared, so lightly draw over the chalk lines with a pencil. Michelangelo would trace right over his cartoon onto the plaster wall, slightly indenting the wall with his knife to etch the lines into the plaster.

Although these methods are time-consuming, you will need to use grids and cartoons when you do not have enough distance to use a projector or if the light in the room is too bright for a projected image to show up. When conditions are right, using a projector is a quick and easy way to transfer your drawing to the wall. Michelangelo would have been envious.

At this high school, the walls were 30 feet (9m) tall and 300 feet (90m) long. The surface was too large to project the original designs, so we used the grid system, which worked perfectly.

Overhead Projector

The overhead projector is designed to be used with a transparency to enlarge a line drawing by projecting the image onto a vertical surface. You must still make your line drawing to scale for the space you are working on. Once you have drawn your design, you can photocopy it onto a clear transparency.

There are two ways to adjust the size of your image: One is a control knob on the projector and the other is by varying the distance you have the projector from the wall. The farther away from the wall the projector is, the larger your image. If you try to enlarge a very small image to a great size, your lines will become blurred and very thick. To correct this, you need to make adjustments with the projector or start with a larger transparency design.

Sometimes the projector can't be used in certain rooms because there is not enough distance back from the wall to enlarge your design to the required height. If this is the case, then you can project your image up onto sheets of craft paper, working in a space that will give you the required distance, such as your basement or garage. Then you can use the pounce pattern technique to transfer it to your walls.

Using the overhead projector requires a low level of light in the area where you are projecting the image. In the daytime, turn off all the lights and close the curtains or put a sheet over the windows and doors. We sometimes use the overhead just to enlarge certain detail elements in the mural, such as the animals, people or buildings.

Opaque Projectors

Opaque projectors are used like overhead projectors, but they can project directly from a photograph, a magazine clipping, a transparency, or a picture out of a book. This allows you to enlarge a copyright-free design or a personal photograph. Opaque projectors require lower light levels than overhead projectors.

Slide Projector

Like the opaque projector, a slide projector requires a darkened room. The benefit of using a slide projector is that you can use all the wonderful slides you've taken for mural design ideas. Keeping a loaded camera in the car is handy when you come across the perfect clouds, trees, animals, stone wall, buildings or other subject matter for your murals.

Opaque projector (left) and overhead projector (right)

At the same high school as shown on the previous page, we were able to use the overhead projector for the large detailed panels.

Enlarging Your Design

Grid Method

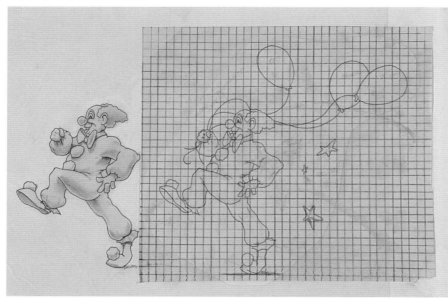

1 › Start your grid enlargement process by drawing a grid pattern over your original design. This grid uses ¼-inch (6mm) squares.

2 › Enlarge your pattern by transferring the line work inside each ¼-inch (6mm) grid block to its corresponding 6-inch (15cm) grid block on the wall. Use chalk because it is easy to erase. Only a portion of the design is shown here. Continue the process for the entire image. Then follow the directions for painting the image.

This is a pounce wheel, which perforates the craft paper so that the lines of your drawing can be transferred to the wall.

Cartoon Method

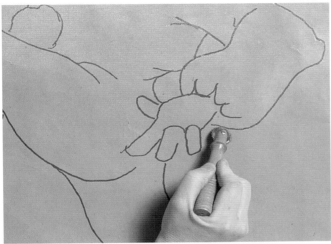

1 › To create the cartoon, project the drawing onto one or more sheets of craft paper and trace over the lines. Use the pounce wheel to perforate the paper on the lines you have drawn. The wheel will make better holes if you first place the craft paper on a soft surface, such as carpet or corrugated cardboard.

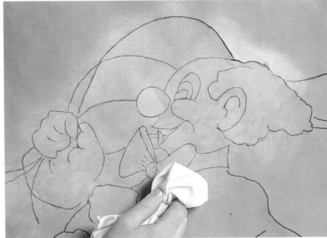

2 › Fill a cloth bag with chalk or baby powder and tie shut. Position your cartoon where you want it, and tape it securely to the wall. Now pat the pounce bag over the perforated holes to transfer the design.

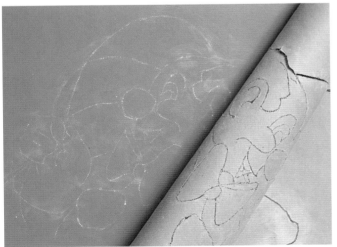

3 › Very carefully remove the cartoon, taking care not to smear the chalk on the wall. The image is fragile at this point, so you will want to trace over it immediately.

4 › Trace over the powder lines with a pencil, colored pencil or stick of chalk. Choose something that you will be able to see, yet that will easily be covered by the paint.

Projects

THIS IS THE PART OF THE BOOK WE ARE SURE YOU WILL FIND THE MOST ENJOYABLE. IT IS IN THESE NEXT PROJECTS THAT WE WILL GUIDE YOU THROUGH THE ART OF MURAL PAINTING. IF YOU FOLLOW THE PROJECTS IN THE ORDER IN WHICH THEY ARE WRITTEN, YOU WILL PROGRESS FROM THE MOST BASIC STYLE OF MURAL PAINTING TO MORE ADVANCED TECHNIQUES. EACH PROJECT HAS ITS OWN BEAUTY AND STYLE AND SHOWS YOU WONDERFUL WAYS TO PAINT A VARIETY OF MURALS. LEARN EACH STYLE SO THAT YOU CAN USE THAT STYLE WITH YOUR OWN DESIGNS. EVENTUALLY YOU WILL BE ABLE TO CREATE YOUR OWN UNIQUE STYLE. THE MURALS FROM THIS BOOK MAY CERTAINLY BE REPRODUCED, BUT WHAT WE REALLY WANT IS FOR YOU TO USE THIS SECTION AS A REFERENCE BOOK AND A TEXTBOOK THAT WILL HELP YOU LEARN TO PAINT MURALS AT MANY DIFFERENT LEVELS OF DIFFICULTY.

ALWAYS PHOTOGRAPH YOUR COMPLETED PROJECTS. IT WON'T TAKE LONG FOR YOU TO HAVE YOUR OWN PORTFOLIO OF MURALS. WE WOULD LOVE TO SEE THE WORK YOU WERE ABLE TO DO WITH THE HELP FROM OUR BOOK. PLEASE SEND ANY PHOTOS YOU WISH TO GARY LORD AND DAVE SCHMIDT, C/O PRISMATIC PAINTING STUDIO, 935 W. GALBRAITH RD., CINCINNATI, OHIO 45231.

Silhouettes

Materials

- design of your own or a copyright-free design
- transparency of design
- overhead projector
- pencil
- 9"-wide (22cm) paint roller and frame
- paint tray
- paint colors of your choice
- AquaCreme
- 2" (51mm) latex sash brush
- ½", ¾", and 1" (12, 19, 25mm) flat brushes
- softening brush to blend colors
- Beugler striping tool
- 4'-long (1.2m) level

Project One

One of the nicest and easiest ways to introduce yourself to mural painting is by doing silhouettes. If you can paint inside the line, you can paint silhouettes. Commercial artists, illustrators and muralists frequently turn to this eye-catching technique for its highly decorative quality and its ability to capture a theme subtly. In this chapter you will learn how to design silhouettes, enlarge them to the size you wish and paint them.

Anywhere you think a mural might work, you can consider a silhouette as an option. You can create the silhouettes in any motif: a sports theme for a child's room or recreational room, fitness characters for your exercise room, movie stars for a theater room, animals for a child's room or a landscape mural for a powder room. With these step-by-step instructions and your own creativity, the options are unlimited.

Our pattern for this project came from Elegant Silhouettes of the Twenties, *edited by Bonnie Welch and printed by Dover Publications in 1987. Dover books are inexpensive and they provide great reference material for mural art.*

1 START THE SKY BACKGROUND

For this mural the background will be painted before the silhouette is projected and drawn. This mural was done in a latex low-luster paint applied with a brush. The image should be projected on the wall first to establish placement. Begin the faded evening sky by blocking in the colors starting at the ceiling line, using your darkest blue color. Use two shades of blue and blend them together while they are still wet, creating horizontal cloud shapes as you blend. Then bring the lighter blue downward and create a lavender tone by mixing in a little red and white.

2 CONTINUE WITH THE SKY REFLECTION

Fade the lavender color into an orange yellow toward the horizon line. From the horizon line, reverse the same colors, fading into the darkest blue at the base of the picture. While the paint is wet, add a yellow sun and blend the color down into the water as a reflection. Let this dry. Now go back and do a smoother blend and make the colors more opaque by first applying AquaCreme, which acts as a retarder and blending agent. Then follow the same steps as above to make the colors more opaque.

3 REFINE THE SKY

Keep blending the colors, working from top to bottom until you are satisfied. You'll notice that the AquaCreme makes the paint easier to blend.

4 TRACE SILHOUETTE ON BACKGROUND

Once the background dries, project the silhouette image onto it and trace the outline. You may also use any of the other transfer techniques discussed on pages 54 to 57.

5 FILL IN THE SILHOUETTE

To paint the silhouettes themselves, use a 2-inch (51mm) latex sash brush to define the larger contour shapes and a small flat artist's brush to paint the more detailed contour shapes. Because of the scale of this piece, most of the work was done with artist's brushes. On larger work, once the silhouette is outlined, you can use either a 3-inch, 7-inch or 9-inch (7.6, 17.8, or 22cm) roller handle and paint sleeve to roll the remaining areas with the latex paint. If the silhouette color doesn't cover in one coat, apply a second coat. We intentionally made the outside border of this silhouette irregular. You will see from the pictures of other silhouettes that sometimes there are no borders at all.

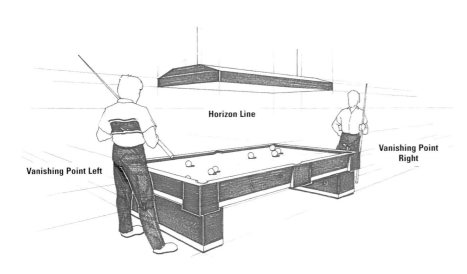

Horizon Line

Vanishing Point Right

Vanishing Point Left

1 PROJECT DRAWING ON WALL

This project shows red colored pencil lines indicating the perspective lines used in the drawing, which is in blue pencil. You can use an overhead projector to enlarge your drawing up to wall size. You need to be sure all of your perspective lines "click" before enlarging. A small error will be magnified tremendously when the drawing is enlarged.

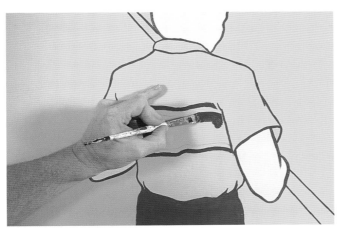

2 OUTLINE THE IMAGE

When you are painting over the existing wall color, all you need to do is select a color that harmonizes with the colors in the room and paint inside the lines you have drawn. An artist's brush is handy for outlining solid areas before filling them in with a larger brush.

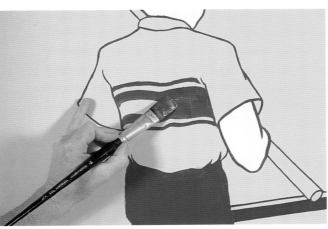

3 FILL IN THE SOLID AREAS

Save time by filling in the larger areas with a wider brush. See the next page for tips on making perfectly straight lines using a Beugler striping tool.

Using a Beugler Striping Tool

The Beugler striping tool comes with various size heads for different size stripes.

1 › Do not thin your paint. Thinned paint can cause your lines to bleed.

2 › Apply the striping head and slightly depress the plunger until a small amount of paint saturates the wheel.

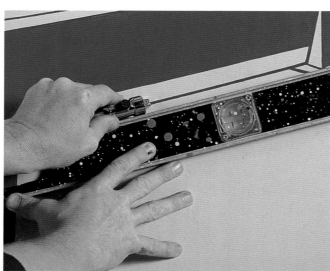

Use this tool instead of a liner brush when you want to create straight, even lines.

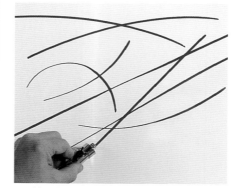

3 › Use the striping tool by pulling it toward you with a firm, even pressure. Various size lines can be executed with the same head depending on the angle at which you hold the head to the wall.

TOP › *Painting an interesting background behind your silhouette is a simple way to add drama and impact.*

BOTTOM › *Note how the black lion, column, and Statue of Liberty appear to come forward; that's because dark colors advance and light colors recede. Also note how multiple colors on the bridge and stonework add extra dimension. Use of positive and negative space also creates a feeling of dimension and interest.*

2-D Graphic & Shaded Murals

Materials

- design of your own or a copyright-free design
- pencil
- chalk
- pounce bag
- paint colors of your choice (we used blue-violet, yellow-orange, red, green, orange, blue, white and black)
- AquaCreme
- two rulers, 12" and 3' (30cm and 1m) for enlarging by the grid method
- various art brushes
- craft paper
- pounce wheel
- clear polyurethane

Project Two

In this chapter you will go to the next level of mural painting by adding a more dimensional aspect to your work. This will be accomplished by using a line drawing with multiple colors. By juxtaposing different color values and hues, you will achieve a sense of depth.

This clown can be left as solid colored shapes, which we call a 2-D graphic mural. This type of mural is especially suitable for a child's wall. You can also go one step further by adding shading and highlights to give the image a more substantial and solid appearance. The final step is to outline the shapes, which really makes the image seem to pop right off of the wall surface. We call this a 2-D shaded mural. By following the steps in creating the clown mural, you will see for yourself how each step helps create the finished dimensional effect. Then you can get inspiration from our gallery of 2-D graphic and 2-D shaded murals.

See pages 56 and 57 for information on enlarging this image using the grid and cartoon methods. However, if you have an opaque projector, you could simply project the image of the finished clown mural from this book and trace the outlines directly on your wall.

1 BEGIN PAINTING

For graphic painting you can just butt up color to color using a brush or roller. You can see in this color scheme the use of complementary (blue-violet background and yellow-orange stars; red and green; orange and blue) and analogous colors (blue and blue-violet; orange and yellow-orange). If you have a Beugler striping tool, use it for the balloon strings.

2 FILL IN ALL THE COLOR AREAS

Notice how the background color is left to define where the clown's legs and arms have folds in the fabric. You will probably need to paint two or more coats to completely cover the background color. The paints were used without thinning to achieve a nice, opaque appearance. You may like the look of the mural at this point and want to leave it as a 2-D graphic mural. That is one choice you can make.

3 ADD HIGHLIGHTS

If you want to take your mural one step further, add highlights, shading and outlines. First, be sure that the paint is completely dry. The highlights go on first. The light source is from the top right, so put the highlights on top of the hair, shoulder, knees, shoes and tops of the balloons. In the areas you are going to highlight, paint an undercoat of AquaCreme the way you did for the silhouette sky; only this time, when you paint in your highlight color, blend it out with a dry brush into the dry base color. This gives nice, soft transitions in your highlight areas.

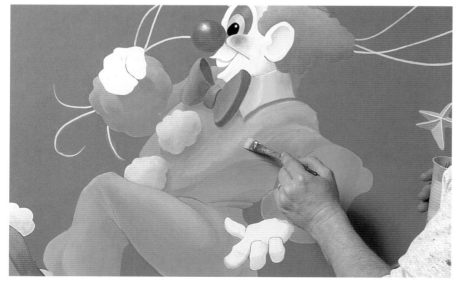

4 ADD SHADING
Add shading to the bottom of the balloons, legs, arms and feet the same way you did the highlights. Use AquaCreme and blend out the shading color for a smooth transition. Notice that the shadows on the stars are created with orange and the highlights are white lines.

5 COMPLETE THE HIGHLIGHTS AND SHADING
Use this photo as a reference for your highlights and shadows. Compare this to the flat graphic style in step 2, and you will see the extra dimension added to the work. The next step will make the image "pop."

6 ADD BLACK OUTLINES
Use a liner brush to add outlines. Note that the paint can is securely taped to the top of the ladder. This will help avoid a catastrophe!

7 SEAL THE MURAL

If you want the surface to be protected for extra durability, coat it with clear polyurethane after the paint is thoroughly dry. The best way is to spray this on using a spray gun (spray polyurethane works too, but it will take several cans). You can also use a brush or roller.

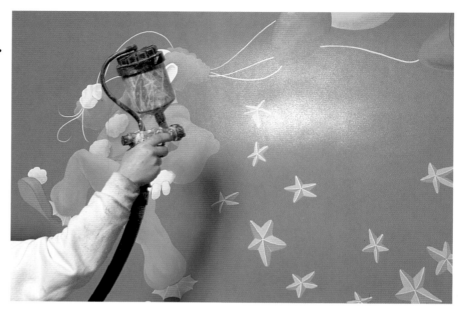

Now step back and admire your work. Although the clown would have been acceptable with flat colors, you can see how adding the extras contributes to its appearance.

The addition of shading creates the illusion that this boy's room is really a space station.

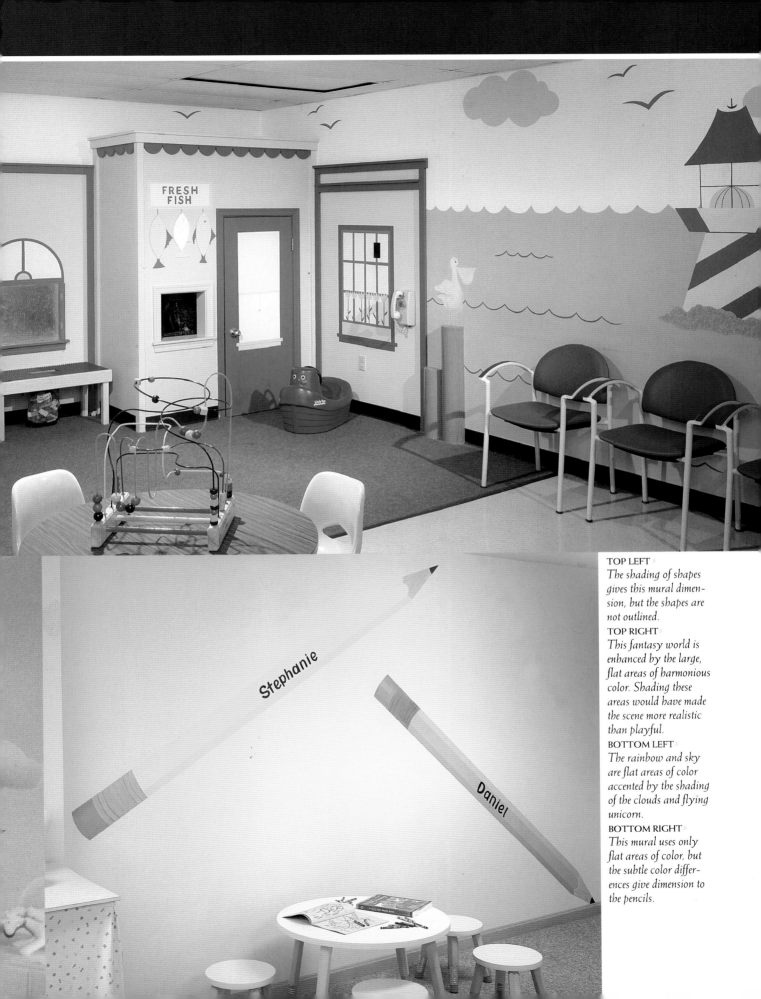

TOP LEFT
The shading of shapes gives this mural dimension, but the shapes are not outlined.

TOP RIGHT
This fantasy world is enhanced by the large, flat areas of harmonious color. Shading these areas would have made the scene more realistic than playful.

BOTTOM LEFT
The rainbow and sky are flat areas of color accented by the shading of the clouds and flying unicorn.

BOTTOM RIGHT
This mural uses only flat areas of color, but the subtle color differences give dimension to the pencils.

Designs From Wallpaper & Fabric

Materials
+ design of your own choice
+ tracing paper
+ pencil
+ chalk line
+ blue masking tape
+ paint colors to go with your pattern
+ tape measure
+ various artist's brushes
+ transfer paper or graphite paper

A muralist can pick and choose from design elements that are already in a home to accent other areas just as a music arranger rearranges a composer's score to fit his needs or a chef combines ingredients in a unique way for a marvelous new taste. In this chapter you will learn how to pick out design elements from fabrics, carpet, draperies, wallpaper or furniture and adapt them to your wall decorating needs. You can either copy a part of a design element and repeat it on the walls, or you can use a design as a foundation and embellish it.

When selecting a design, you must consider the area you are decorating. Look at the other elements in the room, such as furniture, cabinets, floor treatment and curtains. For example, you may have a new kitchen with nice cabinets, a contemporary hardwood floor and window treatments, but the walls seem plain. You could pull a border design from the curtain fabric and use it in accent areas above the sink, doorways, stove and around windows. Although you may not want to duplicate this project exactly, you can see how to use this process to fit your own individual needs.

1 CHOOSE YOUR DESIGN

A copy machine can be used to enlarge or reduce a pattern. If you are doing a continuous border, you will need to measure the wall and create the design so it divides evenly in the given space. For example, if the wall is 12 feet (3.6m) long, you could make each design 12 inches (30cm) long and repeat it twelve times. If you want the design to be a certain size, but it won't fit evenly in the given space, a space between the designs will make up for the odd measurements. For example, if you have 155 inches (393.7cm) of wall space and the design is 12 inches (30cm) long, you could put eleven spaces between the twelve designs with each space measuring 1 inch (2.5cm).

In this example, the design is taken from fabric.

2 TRACE THE DESIGN

Use tracing paper and trace the design from the fabric.

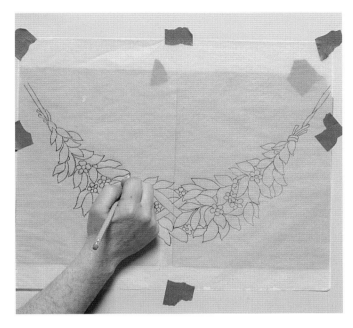

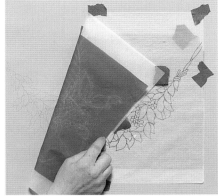

3 TRANSFER THE DESIGN TO THE WALL

Use transfer paper or graphite paper to transfer the design to the area you wish to work on. If you use a piece of transfer paper that is close to the paint color, it will be easier to hide the lines when painting. When transferring a design, you need to have a registration line to ensure that your pattern stays in correct alignment. You can make a registration mark by snapping a level chalk line to connect with the top of the design so that it will stay consistent and level.

4 BLOCK IN THE COLORS

To paint the swag in this design, match the paint colors to those in the fabric as closely as possible. Start out by blocking in the solid colors of the leaves and berries, alternating the lights and darks next to each other.

5 SHADE AND HIGHLIGHT
In areas based in a light color, add dark accents; add light accents for areas based in a dark color.

6 ADD DETAILS
Use a little liner brush to add the small details.

Now connect as many swags as you wish to create your design around the room.

OPPOSITE PAGE *The main rose floral element from the draperies was repeated to accent this corner cabinet.*
TOP *The design from the wallpaper border was extended to the wall itself in this playful, yet pretty girl's room.*
BOTTOM *This kitchen border was adapted from the curtains.*

Using Stencils

Materials

- AquaBond Off White latex paint in Yellow Ochre
- Delta Creamcoat paint: English Yew, Boston Fern, Burnt Umber, Misty Mauve, Rose Mist, Raw Sienna, Palomino Tan, Spice Tan, and Sonoma Wine
- AquaGlaze
- stencil (We used Dee-Signs, Ltd. #502 Aubusson)
- 3 stencil brushes of each of the following sizes: ½" (12mm); ¾" (19mm) ; ¼" (6mm)
- 4" (10cm) paint brush
- coarse steel wool
- spray adhesive
- tape measure
- level for making vertical lines

You can paint either part of or an entire mural using ready-made stencils from today's wonderful stencil designers and manufacturers. Using stencils for a repetitive pattern is more efficient than tracing a design over and over. The room shown on this and the previous page was stenciled in less than one day (although it took part of the previous day to glaze the walls before stenciling). Stencils can be used with other techniques as a time-saver. If you want to paint a border of flowers and leaves, you can cut stencils for the basic leaf and flower shapes, use highlighting and shading to give the shapes more dimension, then paint the stems and vines.

If you are using a design in multiple applications around the room, stencil that design everywhere it belongs before moving on to the next stencil. This is a faster, more organized way to approach the project. When stenciling, use only a little bit of paint on the tip of your stencil brush and remove any excess paint on a paper towel before painting inside the stencil. You can either pounce or swirl the brush to transfer the paint to the wall.

The repetition of this stenciled design around the room gives the room a feeling of harmony.

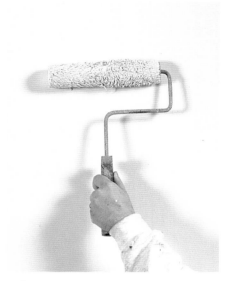

1 BASECOAT THE WALL
Basecoat the wall in AquaBond Off White, then let it dry.

2 GLAZE THE WALL
Mix a glaze of four parts AquaGlaze and one part Yellow Ochre latex paint. Working in a 2'- to 3'-wide (60.9 to 91cm) strip from ceiling to floor, brush glaze on the wall. Paint a light coat with a 4-inch (10cm) brush in a vertical pattern. The trick is to be sure you have enough glaze on so that it stays wet while you are working, but not so much that you will spend a lot of time removing the excess.

3 REMOVE THE EXCESS GLAZE
While the glaze is still wet, drag a piece of coarse steel wool vertically through it several times to get the desired effect. Repeat the process of step 2 and step 3 until you have glazed all of the walls. Let dry 24 hours.

4 POSITION THE LEFT OVERLAY
Determine the placement for the design. This design is centered inside the panels, starting 3 inches (7.6cm) down from the top. The center of each panel is marked in chalk with a vertical line, which is used to line up each stencil.

5 STENCIL THE FIRST COLOR
Select the colors and have one brush for each color you are using. Spray adhesive on the back of the stencils to help them adhere to the wall. This stencil consists of eight individual parts called overlays, four for the left side, and four for the right. Although they are numbered by the manufacturer, it is wise to number them in marker LF1 for the first left front side, LF2 for the second one, and so forth. Also highlight the center vertical line on all the overlays so you won't have any trouble identifying which one goes on which side.

6 STENCIL THE OTHER COLORS
Be sure paint does not get underneath the edge of the overlay. Smudges will be difficult to repair because of the glazing. Pounce or swirl the colors in the stencil, using a separate brush for each color.

7 COMPLETED LEFT SIDE
Carefully lift off the overlay to avoid smudging the wet paint. Now the first overlay, LF1, is finished.

8 USE FIRST OVERLAY ON RIGHT SIDE

Line up the right side the same way you did the left. This will be the overlay marked RF1. Stencil in the colors for this overlay.

This shows the design after the first two overlays have been completed.

9 USE SECOND OVERLAY, LEFT SIDE AND RIGHT SIDE

Stencil in all colors one at a time. When LF2 is complete, stencil the colors for RF2.

The second overlay on the left side is completed.

This shows overlay RF2 being stenciled.

10 USE THE THIRD OVERLAYS

This will be the overlay marked LF3. Stencil the colors one at a time, as you did before. Then position RF3 and stencil those colors.

This shows the design after the third overlay left side has been painted.

This shows the design after the third overlays have been completed.

11 USE THE FOURTH OVERLAYS

This will be the overlay marked LF4.
Stencil the colors, and remove the overlay.
Position RF4 and stencil those colors.

This shows the design after completion of the fourth overlay left side.

This shows stenciling overlay RF4.

This shows the completed design.

OPPOSITE PAGE › *The leaves were stencils, and the trees were drawn and painted.*
TOP › *The leaves and grapes were stencils, and the vines were handpainted.*
BOTTOM LEFT › *The flower pattern in this painted stair runner was stenciled.*
BOTTOM RIGHT › *This wall and ceiling shows a combination of stencils and handwork.*

Painting Skies & Clouds

Materials for Brushing Clouds

- plant mister spray bottle
- sea sponge
- 2" (5cm) chip brush
- 3" (7.6cm) sash brush
- 4" (10cm) sash brush
- paint roller
- 4" (10cm) foam roller
- paint tray
- Benjamin Moore latex satin paints (sold by number, not by name) 769, 788, 890, 804

Materials for Spraying Clouds

- airbrush or automobile touch-up gun
- compressor
- Benjamin Moore latex satin paints: 038, 370, 769, 890

What better way to add subtle warmth and openness to a room than with a beautiful sky mural? On walls or ceilings, in dining rooms, nurseries or studies, sky murals can add life and a sense of movement to a room. Skies don't have to be just a large blue mass with white fluffy clouds. To create drama in your sky, a storm cloud can be added to the corner of the mural. This is also a great way to add movement to your sky, as the viewer wonders if the storm is moving in or out. For more interest, consider adding birds, butterflies or a few fall leaves.

Clouds can be sprayed, ragged, sponged, brushed or a combination of all four. Spraying clouds with an airbrush or touch-up gun is fast and a great way to achieve soft, subtle effects. Check tool rental shops for compressors and spray equipment if spraying your sky mural is the direction you want to go. The results can be well worth the effort.

Before starting, keep in mind that if you paint your clouds on the ceiling, the viewing point is different from those on walls. Look overhead at the clouds on a nice day. You are seeing mainly the bottom of the clouds, the shaded area. Now look out toward the horizon and notice that the stronger highlights are seen on top because of the viewing angle.

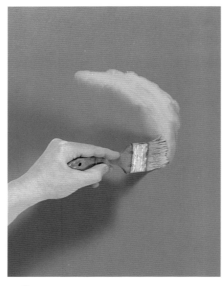

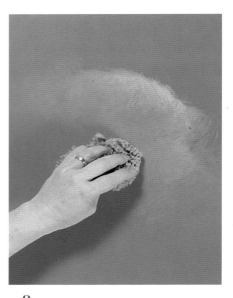

1 BASECOAT THE WALL

Paint your wall in the sky color, Benjamin Moore 769, and let dry. Use a spray bottle to mist the area where you want to place your first cloud. Roll over the water with a 4-inch (10cm) foam roller to even it out. The water will slow down the drying time of the latex paint, giving you more time to work with it.

2 LAY IN THE CLOUDS

Using your 2-inch (6cm) brush, form the outside edge of your cloud with the cloud base color, Benjamin Moore 788 latex satin.

3 SPONGE THE CLOUDS

While the paint is still wet, soften the color toward the inside of the cloud with a damp sea sponge.

4 BUILD UP LAYERS OF WHITE

Build your edges up in layers like rolling hills to add dimension to the clouds. After this has dried, step back and look at the clouds and decide where you want to beef up the shapes. This will be done by repeating the first step. As you apply the same color again in select areas, the color will become more opaque, giving the cloud a fuller, denser look, while leaving the other areas with a lighter, airy look.

As you are doing this, keep in mind where your imaginary light source (the sun) is. The edge of the clouds facing the light source is where the strongest highlight will be placed.

6 HIGHLIGHT

Add highlights in Benjamin Moore 890 using your sash brush. Thin your color slightly with water and stipple the highlight on. (Remember your light source.)

7 REMOVE EXTRA PAINT
Knock off the excess paint on a piece of board or paper.

8 BLEND
Blend the highlight areas with the same brush in a circular motion toward the center of the cloud.

9 ADD SHADOWS

To create greater dimension within the clouds, add shadows. The first shadow color will be the same color we used for the blue sky, Benjamin Moore 769. When you built your clouds up by layering the edges, you created hills and valleys. The valleys are the areas for the shadows. Dilute your color to turn it into a transparent wash, brush it into the valleys and fade it out toward the highlighted area of the cloud. Be careful not to cover the highlighted ridge of the cloud in front of the shadow. The color can also be used to push back any areas you feel are too strong. After diluting it further, brush over those areas and soften with a damp sponge. A second shadow color, Benjamin Moore 804, can be added to each cloud on top of the first in areas furthest from your light source. Now step back to see if any additional highlights or shadows are needed.

The finished brushed sky.

2 TEST THE SPRAY

Have a piece of cardboard handy to test your spray. This paint is too thick. If it appears grainy and it is hard to spray, the paint is too thick.

If the paint is too thin, it will be runny and will bead on the wall. Keep the spray gun at a 90° angle to the wall, about 6 to 12 inches (15 to 30cm) away.

1 PREPARE THE PAINT

This time, instead of adding white clouds to a blue background, blue will be sprayed onto a cloud-colored background. Apply the base color with a paint roller and allow to dry. This wall was painted with Benjamin Moore 890 latex paint. Use a flat latex paint for a ceiling, but use a satin or eggshell base for walls so they can be cleaned if soiled. A cup gun was used for this demonstration. Thin some Benjamin Moore 769 with water to the consistency of light cream and strain the paint through a nylon panty hose to remove any lumps. Fill the spray cup about three-quarters full and fasten it to the gun. Make sure it is securely fastened! For this gun, set the pressure between 30 and 40 psi.

3 BEGIN SPRAYING THE SKY

The first color is the sky color, Benjamin Moore 769. Pull the trigger about halfway and lightly spray to establish the size, shape and location of your clouds. Make the first pass very light so corrections will be simple. Large blue sky areas can quickly be filled in by pulling back on the trigger all the way. To prevent runs and buildup, start moving the gun before you pull the trigger, and release the trigger before you stop.

4 STOP AND STEP BACK

Now that your clouds are roughed in, step back and see if you are satisfied with the overall composition. If so, shape your clouds with the same sky blue color and fill in any thin areas. Depending on the look you are going for, this could be a completed sky. Note that diagonal drifts to your sky work better than horizontal or vertical.

5 FURTHER DEFINE THE CLOUDS

To add further shape and definition to your clouds, shade with Benjamin Moore 038 flat latex paint.

6 ADD HIGHLIGHTS

Highlight the areas closest to your imaginary light source with Benjamin Moore 370. To finish the mural, load the gun with the base color, Benjamin Moore 890, and lightly mist over the clouds and into the blue. This will soften the clouds and the sky together. Hold the gun back farther from the surface to mist the area.

The completed sprayed sky.

This night sky was painted with a cup gun and airbrush. The sky accurately depicts the stars in the Northern hemisphere at the Summer Solstice.

OPPOSITE PAGE *This sky was sprayed with a cup gun and airbrush.*
TOP *The wall behind the bed does have a recessed alcove, but the windows on either side of it are painted, as are the stones.*
BOTTOM *This very dramatic sky shows that clouds don't have to be just white, fluffy masses on a blue background.*

Creating Realistic Textures

Materials

- Benjamin Moore latex paint: 105, 232, 242, 433, 441, 518, 525, 546, 700, 1225, 1531, 1538, 1552, 1577, 1595, 1601, HC-70
- AquaColor in Earth Green and Earth Brown
- latex paint in black and red
- AquaCreme
- 3" (7.6cm) and regular size paint roller
- various artist's brushes
- chalk
- level and straightedges
- blue masking tape
- spray bottle

The earth tones and varied textures in this project are relaxing and pleasing. This mural adds a certain richness to a room, and it would be a great backdrop for the aged Southwestern furniture that is so popular today.

The variety of textures makes this rather simple composition interesting. The soft, rounded edges of the stones and subtle shading create a very calming effect. It's easy to "get lost" in the nooks and crannies between the stones. The aged, weather-beaten wooden door adds contrast with its strong horizontal and vertical lines and textured woodgrain, yet its gentle curving lines echo the shapes of the stones.

The vine adds to the composition by creating a stronger sense of depth. The vine casts shadows onto the wall, giving the feeling that it's closer to the viewer. The tangled branches of the vine repeat the shapes of the dark areas between the stones. The green of the vine is complementary to the reddish color of the stones, and the vine is essential for breaking up the hard edge of the header above the door.

The textures in this mural were a great deal of fun to paint, and this project pulls together everything you have learned in this book. We hope you enjoy painting this as much as we did.

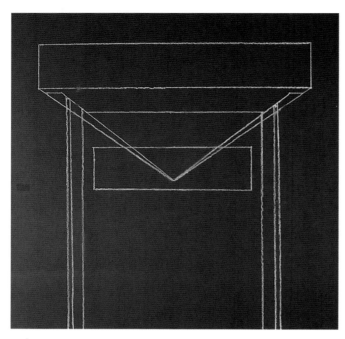

1 BASECOAT THE WALL

Paint the wall with black paint that has a touch of red to make the color richer. After the paint dries, draw the door using one-point perspective and a level. Since the stone wall will be painted first, use blue tape to tape off the inside edges of the door, including the door frame and header. (See step 11 for a photo of this.)

2 ADD FIRST SCUMBLE

Next, add the first of three scumbles to the rock area. With a 3-inch (7.6cm) roller, roll on a coat of B.M. 700 in a small patch about the size of a dinner plate. Immediately soften the edge with a soft, damp cotton rag. Then move on to the area next to it, roll on the paint, then soften with a rag. Continue until the entire rock area is scumbled.

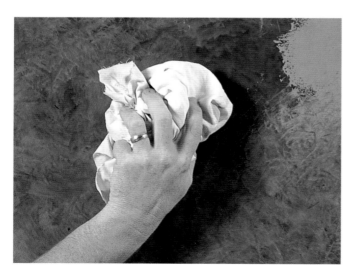

3 ADD SECOND SCUMBLE

Add another scumble over the first one. Roll on a coat of B.M. 1538 about the size of a dinner plate, then soften with a rag. If you try to do more than a dinner plate-size area at one time, the paint will dry too quickly and you won't be able to soften it. Continue until the entire rock area is scumbled.

4 ADD THIRD SCUMBLE

Roll on a coat of B.M. 1531 and repeat the scumbling process. The three scumbles combined will be the background for the stone blocks.

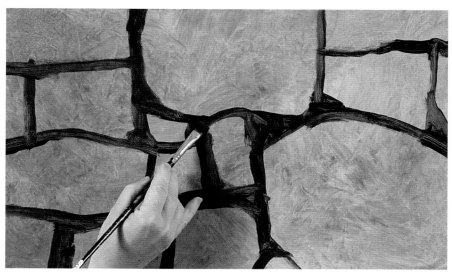

5 BEGIN DEFINING ROCKS

Draw in the stones with chalk. Then use the same black paint you used for the basecoat to paint the shadow areas between the stones with a ¾- or ½-inch (19 or 12mm) brush. Notice how the line varies from thick to thin.

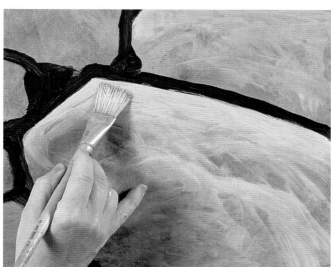

6 HIGHLIGHT STONES

Thin B.M. 242 with water to make a wash and use a 2-inch (5cm) chip brush in a scrubbing motion to highlight each stone. The top and right sides of the stones will be highlighted.

7 PUT FIRST WASH ON STONES

Thin B.M. 105 to make a wash, then lightly spray the stone area with water. Roll over the surface with a clean paint roller to break up the water droplets. While the surface is still wet, apply the wash with a brush. Using a synthetic sponge, blot the area to remove excess paint and brushstrokes. Your highlights should still show through. Let dry.

8 APPLY THE SECOND WASH

Apply B.M. HC-70 the same way as in step 7, using the water bottle to spray the wall first. The only difference is that you will only apply the wash to the lower left areas of the stones.

9 BLOT THE WASH

Before the wash dries, blot and blend it with the sponge.

10 SPATTER THE STONES

Spatter the stones with the black paint, then with one of the scumble colors. Thin the paint with water to get smaller spatter. Use a 2-inch (5cm) chip brush for a spatter tool.

11 TAPE AND PAINT THE DOOR

Next, tape off every other plank of the door. Thin B.M. 1595 slightly with water. Using a 2-inch (5cm) chip brush, apply color in one continuous stroke from top to bottom. Use very little pressure. This is how the woodgrain pattern is established. Use the final photograph to see where to add waves in the grain.

12 ADD MORE WOODGRAIN

The second woodgrain color is B.M. 1225 thinned with water and applied as in the previous step.

13 APPLY THIRD WOOD COLOR

Thin B.M. 441 and repeat the woodgrain process as above. It is not important to cover the whole area. Skip some areas to add interest.

14 HIGHLIGHT THE WOOD

Use B.M. 232 as a highlight color on the wood. This should be applied randomly. Be careful not to overdo this step. After the paint dries, remove the tape and tape off the planks you just painted. Start with step 11 and paint the remaining planks the same way.

15 CREATE CRACKS

When all the planks are woodgrained, use a liner brush to paint the cracks between the planks. Also paint small holes and splits in the wood. Be sure to follow the direction of the grain.

16 STAIN THE WOOD

Mix AquaColor Earth Green, Earth Brown and AquaCreme. Use this slow-drying mix to create a dirty stain for the door. Paint one plank at a time, then wipe off the glaze with cheesecloth, following the direction of the grain. Leave some areas of glaze a little heavier than others to create interesting light and dark values.

17 HIGHLIGHT THE CRACKS

After the wash has dried, use B.M. 232 to highlight the cracks in the planks and the gaps between them. Since the light is coming from the upper right, the highlights will fall on the left side of the black cracks and gaps in the door. Use the black base color to pump up any dark area that may have been lost when the wash was applied.

18 ADD SHADOWS

Use the dirty stain color from step 16 and a ¾-inch (19mm) brush to add shadows to the door, such as shown here. Soften the shadow with a dry chip brush to remove brushstrokes. Nail heads can be created by dipping a pencil eraser in black paint.

19 BEGIN LAYING IN THE VINE

Draw the vine with chalk. Use the black base color to paint the vines with a ¾- or 1-inch (19 or 25mm) brush.

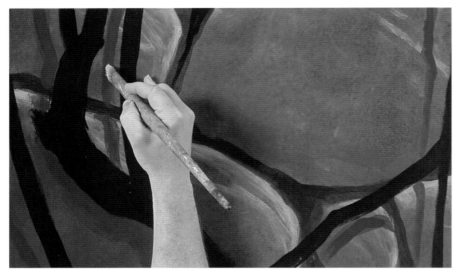

20 PAINT THE SHADOW

After the base color has dried, paint the shadow cast on the wall by the vine using a touch of black and B.M. HC-70. Use a ¾- or 1-inch (19 or 25mm) brush, and keep in mind where your light source is.

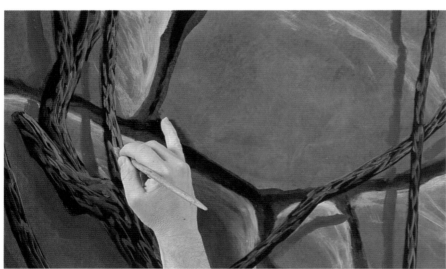

21 APPLY FIRST VINE HIGHLIGHTS

The highlights for the vine will be added in three stages. Use B.M. 1601 to lay in the texture of the bark. Use a side-to-side motion with the flat side of the brush, allowing it to bounce on and off the surface. This will give you a series of short, random dashes of color. Follow the direction and contour of the vine when applying the color.

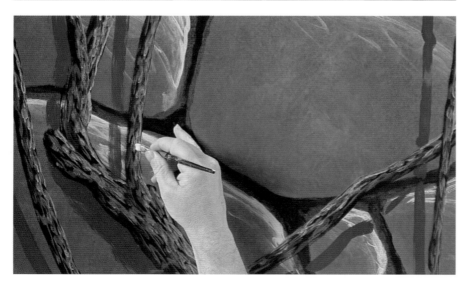

22 APPLY SECOND VINE HIGHLIGHTS

Apply the next color, B.M. 1552 in the same way, only this time start on the highlighted edge of the vine and work the color only three-quarters of the way around the vine. Slowly taper off the color as you approach that point.

23 APPLY FINAL HIGHLIGHTS
Apply the strongest highlight color, B.M. 1577, on only one-quarter of the vine, starting on the highlighted side. Be careful not to overdo it.

24 ADD A WASH
Now you may add a wash of B.M. 525 to any areas of the vine that you feel are too strong. Selected areas can be wiped with cheesecloth to bring out some of the highlights.

25 LAY IN THE LEAF CLUSTERS
Sketch in the leaf clusters with chalk. Start with the shadow color from step 20 and paint in the areas that will be shadows cast by the leaves. Then paint the leaves with black and purple in a quick one-step stroke. Start with the ¾-inch (19mm) brush vertical to the wall, then pull it along its narrow edge while slowly twisting the brush. This makes a line that starts thin and slowly widens. Then reverse the twist, slowly bringing the brush back to a narrow point. Place your leaves according to the shadows you painted first.

26 ADD GREEN LEAF COLOR

Next, lay in B.M. 518. This needs to be painted with more care. Paint the leaves in clusters of three, and let these clusters overlap each other.

27 ADD FIRST HIGHLIGHTS

The next leaf color is B.M. 546, and it should be painted keeping the light source in mind. Begin to work from the highlighted edge toward the shadowed side of the entire leaf cluster. Carry the color about three-quarters of the way across each leaf.

28 ADD SECOND HIGHLIGHTS

Apply B.M. 433 next, working from the highlight edge and carrying the color over only about halfway across each leaf.

29 ADD FINAL HIGHLIGHTS
Finally, use B.M. 430 sparingly for sparkle.

Now the mural is complete!

TOP LEFT ▶ *A butler's pantry door was painted with dishes, tiles, cups and a shelf; the cabinet doors and drawer fronts are real and are mounted over the painted door.*
TOP MIDDLE ▶ *The use of shadows enhances the realistic effect of this delightfully playful mural.*
TOP RIGHT ▶ *A good reference photograph was essential in recreating this moon-scape.*
BOTTOM LEFT ▶ *The floor is painted masonite; stucco was added to the walls and shaded; the shutters, thatched roof and door are real.*
BOTTOM MIDDLE ▶ *The lighting and use of shadows make this mural appear 3-D.*
BOTTOM RIGHT ▶ *A real sign is "hung" with a painted wire to the painted tree. Adding a real birdhouse further develops the play between what is 3-D and what is painted illusion.*

The paint used in this mural was latex interior house paint, and the colors were mixed on-site using universal tints. These colorants are similar to what is used in paint stores to tint paint. The tints are extremely concentrated, and it takes very little to make a color by mixing it with white or another color. You can't use tints directly from the bottle; they must be mixed with paint.

Mountain Mural

Materials

- 2" (5cm) chip brush
- 1", ¾", ½", ¼" (25, 19, 12, 6mm) flat brushes
- chalk line
- paint tray
- paint roller
- charcoal pencil or chalk
- rags
- plastic cups
- blue masking tape
- cup gun and air compressor
- sea sponge
- dropcloths

The project detailed in this section was for a client who enjoyed the wide open spaces of the American West. The area for the mural was an eight-sided tray ceiling approximately 15 feet (4.5m) from the floor, 17 feet (5.1m) long and 15 feet (4.5m) wide. The mural was a complete wraparound panoramic mountain scene with the sky trailing across the ceiling. After a drawing of the scene was made, it was transferred to the wall. With a large project such as this, it is essential to make a full-color mock-up to work out any problems beforehand.

Remember, a small dot of color on a mock-up can represent an entire boulder or side of a building when it is enlarged to the size of your wall. Be aware of these things when painting your mock-up.

1 BASECOAT THE WALL

The techniques on pages 104 to 106 can be used here for painting the sky and clouds. Roll on the sky blue color first. Then mix a slightly darker shade by adding purple and spray lightly in random areas to add depth to the sky. Make sure the two colors melt together. Refer to your clip file or photos of mountains to get an idea of the correct size for the clouds in relation to the mountain. Once the sky is dry, you can lay your clouds in.

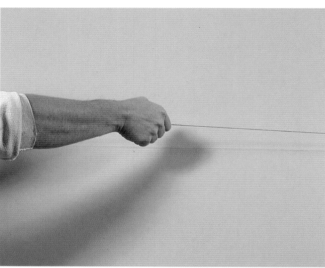

2 SNAP THE HORIZON LINE

Remember that when painting a wall mural—whether it's an architectural scene or landscape—you need to start with a horizon line. This should be at eye level to the viewer, between 5 and 6 feet (1.5 and 1.8m) from the floor. This line can be snapped in using a chalk line.

3 TRANSFER THE DESIGN TO THE WALL

Lightly draw your pattern using a charcoal pencil or chalk. An overhead projector can also be used. Mix your first colors in plastic cups and label each color according to what it will be used for (mountain highlights, grass, etc.). You may very well end up with twenty to forty cups of paint by the time your mural is finished.

4 PAINT DISTANT MOUNTAINS
To create distant mountains, you must keep details to a minimum. The colors should be lighter, softer and cooler.

5 SPRAY MOUNTAIN
When the mountain is finished, lightly spray over it with the spray gun, using the same color as the sky. This gives the mountain a realistic sense of atmospheric perspective.

6 KEEP COLORS LIGHT
Don't worry that the mountains seem unfinished and pale; these mountains will look just right when the darker and richer colors are applied later to the foreground.

7 OUTLINE THE MOUNTAIN

Mix dark blue, red and raw umber to create a dark purple. Use this color and loose, free-flowing strokes with the edge of a 2-inch (51mm) brush to lay in the basic lines of your mountain. Allow to dry.

8 ADD A THIN WASH OF COLOR

Dilute some of the color from step 1 with an equal amount of water. This mixture is known as a wash and will be transparent when applied. Cover the entire mountain with this wash using a scrubbing motion and the flat side of a 2-inch (51mm) flat brush. Blot with a rag or damp sea sponge to remove excess color.

9 CHECK YOUR WORK

When dry, the lines brushed on in step 7 should still be visible.

10 APPLY FIRST HIGHLIGHTS

Mix raw umber, yellow ochre and white to make your first highlight color. You will be building up your highlights slowly with each step, so this color should have a slightly lighter value than the base color used in your mountain. Thinning the colors a little with water will help them to flow. With the edge of your ½-inch (12mm) flat brush, follow the contour of your mountain and lay in highlights. Remember to use the same imaginary light source you used for your clouds.

11 STEP BACK AND LOOK

It is very important to stand back from your work as you are painting. This helps you to see how the mural is progressing and prevents you from overworking any one area with details that will not be visible from the normal viewing distance. With your first highlight complete, your mountain should be taking shape.

12 APPLY SECOND HIGHLIGHTS

Add more yellow ochre and white to your first highlight color. Highlight the areas that will receive full sun from your imaginary light source. Begin by highlighting the areas where you're sure light will hit, then stand back to see if you've missed anything. Do not cover your first highlight 100 percent; instead it should be 75 percent coverage, then 25 percent on your next highlight. Allowing each highlight color to show next to the preceding color will create a fade from dark to light.

13 APPLY THIRD HIGHLIGHTS

Add red and a little white to the second highlight color to make a slightly more orange color. Mix this in a separate cup using part of your second highlight color in case you need more of your second highlight color later. Apply it along the ridges of your mountain.

14 APPLY FINAL HIGHLIGHT

Adding a light color brings out points of interest and, when applied against a dark background, helps pull the ridge closer to the viewer, creating depth. Notice the much lighter highlights on the tops of the ridges. White was added to the previous color to make this highlight.

15 CREATE DISTANCE

At this point, it is time to create some distance between the mountain and the viewer. With the same wash used in step 8 and a 2-inch (51mm) flat brush, scrub in color following the contour of the mountain. Work quickly and cover about 75 percent of the mountain, letting some true color show through. Add water if your wash is too opaque.

16 CHECK YOUR WORK

Stop! Stand back and study your mountain. Look for areas you want to play with or areas where you can create some interest with cracks and crevices.

17 APPLY FINAL HIGHLIGHTS

Mix blue, white, red and raw umber to add a final highlight to the places on the mountain where the light is strongest.

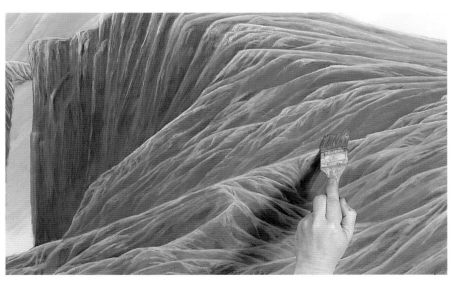

18 ADD SHADOWS

Use more of the wash from step 8 to deepen the existing shadowed areas. Notice how the shadowed area directly above the highlight ridge helps to separate and pull the ridge closer to the viewer.

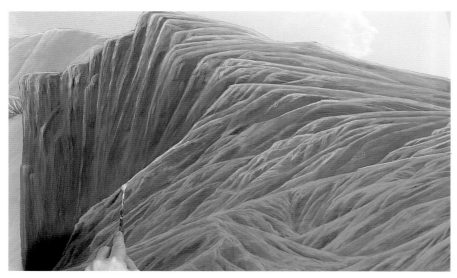

19 ADD ADDITIONAL HIGHLIGHTS

A touch of white can be added to your first highlight color for additional highlights, if necessary.

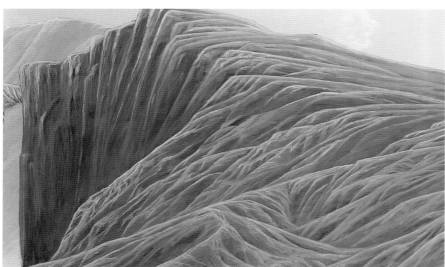

20 WARM UP THE MOUNTAIN

With your last highlight complete, the mountain has somewhat of a cold and lifeless appearance. You can warm it up with some greenery.

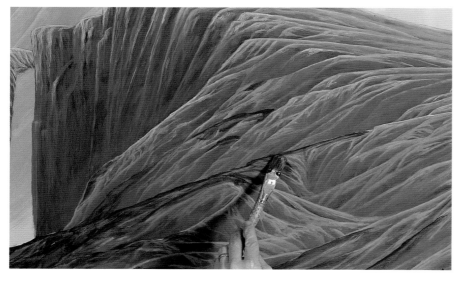

21 BEGIN DEFINING GREEN AREAS

Mix dark blue, raw umber and black to create a rich, dark color that is almost black (pure black is never used because it's too dull and flat). Thin slightly with water so it's somewhat transparent. Lay in this color with a ½-inch (12mm) flat brush, following the contour of the land. This color will be the foundation for the grass.

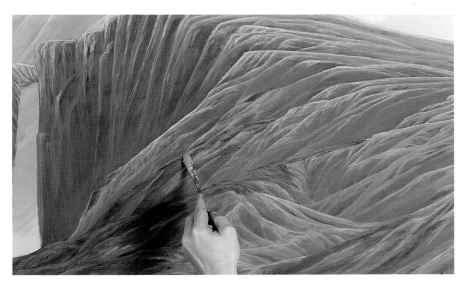

22 PAINT FIRST LAYER OF GRASS

Mix phthalo green and white with your foundation color for the grass color. Be careful not to make it too bright. Using a side-to-side scrubbing motion, lay in color with a ¼-inch (6mm) flat brush following the landscape contours. Allow some of the dark foundation to show. This gives the feel of rough, uneven terrain.

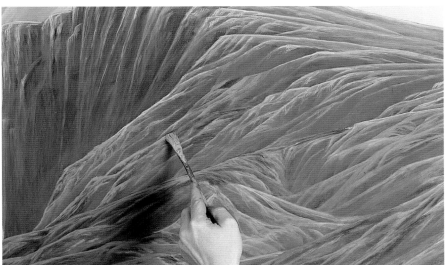

23 HIGHLIGHT GRASS

Highlight again with a mixture of green, raw umber and yellow ochre. If you have too much yellow ochre, the highlight color will be too bright. Knock it down a bit with raw umber.

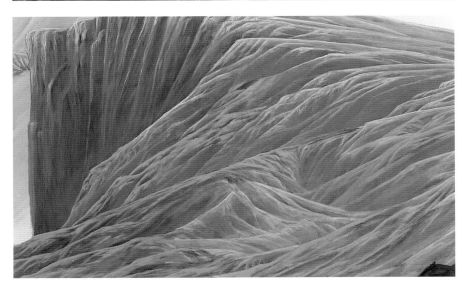

24 ADD MORE HIGHLIGHTS

An additional highlight can be added if needed by using the second highlight you used on the mountain. Be careful not to overdo it.

25 PAINT THE WATERFALL

If you want to add a waterfall, first paint the blue area for the water. The back of the gorge is where the waterfall will be placed.

26 PAINT REFLECTIONS

Using the same color as the rocks, paint reflections of the rocks in the water, blending the colors and keeping them lower in value than the rocks.

27 ADD THE WATERFALL

Begin laying in the waterfall by mixing a light blue color and warming it up a little with raw umber. Apply this color in long, vertical strokes following the direction and flow of the water. Give the water some movement by painting in some ripples.

28 FINISH THE WATERFALL

Finally, mix a very pale blue, almost white, and use it to highlight the waterfall and ripples in the water. This adds sparkle.

29 PAINT FOREGROUND ROCKS

The foreground in this mural will be rocky terrain with grasses and flowers. When you painted the mountain, you used washes to mute and dull the colors and push them back into the distance. You will want to do the opposite with the foreground. Here the colors will be darker, bolder and brighter because they are closer to the viewer. After drawing in the rocks, base them in with 100 percent coverage using a mix of dark blue, raw umber and a touch of black.

30 SHAPE THE ROCKS

Add enough white to the base mixture to separate the colors and rough in the general shape of the rocks using a ½-inch (12mm) brush. This is similar to step 7.

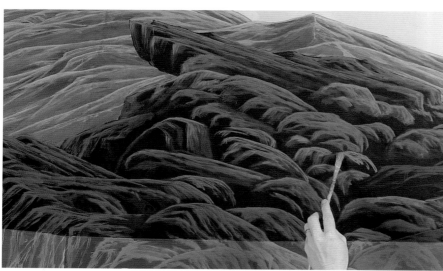

31 CREATE VARIETY IN THE ROCKS

Using a variety of color mixtures, begin laying in your rocks. Since the rocks are sitting one in front of the other, some rocks are not entirely visible. Starting at the bottom of the mural and working up will make this step easier.

32 ADD HIGHLIGHTS

Highlight your rocks with lighter versions of the color mixtures used for each rock. Build from dark to light as you did for the mountain. Remember your imaginary light source.

33 ADD FOREGROUND GRASS

This rocky terrain is somewhat cold and uninviting. Painting grass between the rocks will add a bit of life and warmth. Because this grass is much closer to the viewer, it will not be painted like the grass you painted earlier. Mix black and red for the base, paint it in and let it dry. Mix black, yellow and a bit of green to make a forest green. Apply in long, sweeping, drybrush strokes using a 2-inch (51mm) chip brush.

34 LAY IN GRASS BLADES

Using the same color and a large liner brush, lay in individual blades of grass, again using quick, sweeping strokes.

35 DEFINE THE GRASS

Mix a grassy green color and use the same liner brush to define the grass blades. Use short, quick strokes in different directions to create the look of clumps of grass.

36 ADD A SPLASH OF COLOR

Mix a brownish orange with yellow, red and brown. Use this color with the liner brush to represent dried blades of grass. This adds an interesting color to the area.

37 APPLY A WASH

To create a sense of depth and a separation between the rows and clumps of grass, make a wash by adding water to the dark base color. Apply the wash to the base of the grass clusters.

38 DEFINE FOREGROUND GRASS

The wash just applied will knock back the taller blades of grass in the clumps closer to the foreground. These areas need to be pumped up again by reapplying the grassy green color that was used earlier.

39 SHARPEN DETAILS
Use the brownish orange color to re-define the dead blades of grass.

The grass is complete. A well-done area of grass with some wildflowers can accent and create interest in a mural.

OPPOSITE PAGE › *This is a flat wall, but a vast sense of depth was created using perspective.*
TOP › *The rocks in the extreme foreground are "real" (three-dimensional replicas). Can you tell where they end and the painted ones begin?*
BOTTOM LEFT › *All the elements in this mural are covered in the step-by-step instructions. Mountain scenes are always a challenge, but satisfying to do.*
BOTTOM RIGHT › *The foreground tree enhances the feeling of depth in this winter scene.*

141

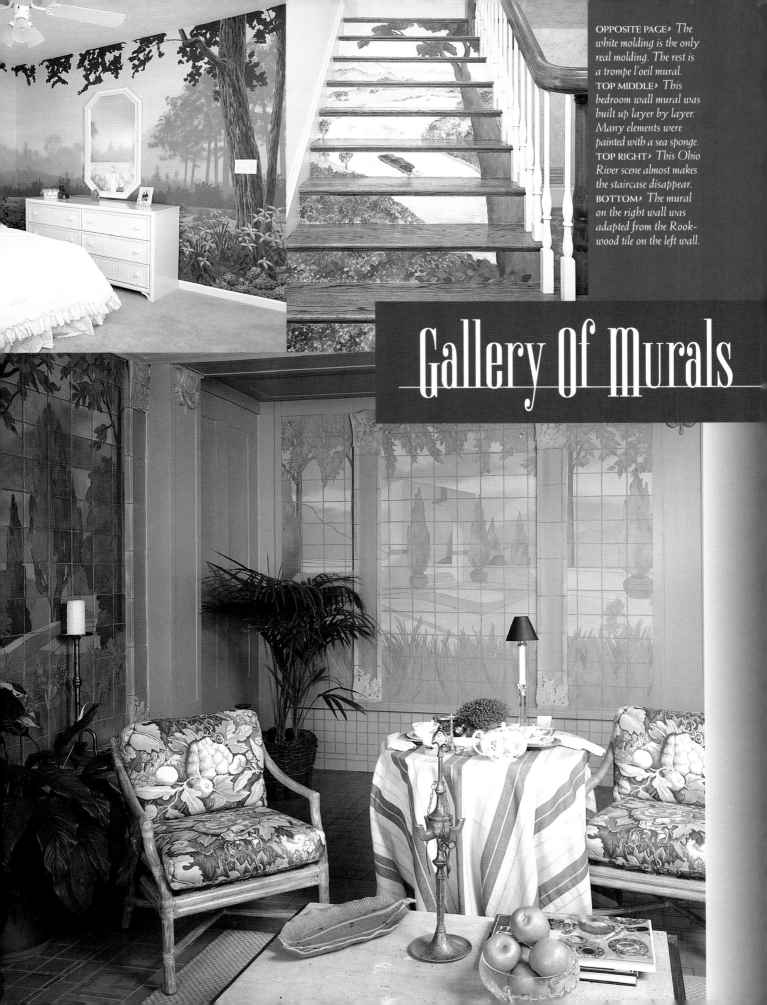

OPPOSITE PAGE> The white molding is the only real molding. The rest is a trompe l'oeil mural.
TOP MIDDLE> This bedroom wall mural was built up layer by layer. Many elements were painted with a sea sponge.
TOP RIGHT> This Ohio River scene almost makes the staircase disappear.
BOTTOM> The mural on the right wall was adapted from the Rookwood tile on the left wall.

Gallery Of Murals

Resources

Books for Further Reading

Exploring Color by Nita Leland, North Light Books, 1998

Perspective Drawing by Ernest Norling, Walter T. Foster Art Books, 1987

Recipes for Surfaces: Decorative Paint Finishes Made Simple by Mindy Drucker and Pierre Finkelstein, Fireside, 1990

Schools

Prismatic Painting Studio
935 W. Galbraith Rd.
Cincinnati, OH 45231
(513) 931-5520
www.prismaticpaintingstudio.com

Faux Effects, Inc.
3435 Aviation Blvd.
Vero Beach, FL 32960
(800) 270-8871
www.fauxfx.com

Sarasota School of Decorative Arts
5376 Catalyst Ave.
Sarasota, FL 34233
(888) 454-3289
www.ssda1.com

Chicago Institute of Fine Finishes
504 E. St. Charles Rd.
Carol Stream, IL 60188
(800) 797-4305
www.fauxbykathy.com

The Finishing School
50 Carnation Ave., Bldg. 2
Floral Park, NY 11001
(516) 327-4850
www.thefinishing school.com

Definitive School of Decorative Arts
6010 Washington Ave.
Houston, TX 77007
(713) 802-9022
www.definitivefaux.com

Ritins Studio, Inc.
170 Wicksteed Ave.
Toronto, Ontario M4G 2B6 Canada
(866) 467-8920

Paints

Delta Technical Coatings, Inc.
2550 Pellissier Place
Whittier, CA 90601
(800) 423-4135
www.deltacrafts.com

Benjamin Moore & Co.
51 Chestnut Ridge Rd.
Montvale, NJ 07645
(800) 344-0400
www.benjaminmoore.com

Aqua Finishing Solutions
3435 Aviation Blvd., A4
Vero Beach, FL 32960
(800) 270-8871
www.aquafinishing.com

Brushes

Daler-Rowney USA
Robert Simmons Brushes
2 Corporate Dr.
Cranbury, NJ 08512
(609) 655-5252
www.daler-rowney.com

Loew-Cornell, Inc.
563 Chestnut Ave.
Teaneck, NJ 07666
(201) 836-7070
www.loew-cornell.com

Stencils

Royal Design Studios
2504 Transportation Ave., Ste. H
National City, CA 91950
(800) 747-9767
www.royaldesignstudio.com

Deesigns Decorative Stencils
107 Jefferson St.
Newnan, GA 30264
(888) 656-4515
www.deesigns.com

Dressler Stencil Co.
253 SW 41st St.
Renton, WA 98059
(888) 656-4515
www.dresslerstencils.com

The Mad Stencilist
P.O. Box 219, Dept. N
Diamond Springs, CA 95619
(888) 882-6232
www.madstencilist.com

Organizations

Society of Decorative Painters (SDP)
393 N. McLean
Wichita, KS 67203
(316) 269-9300
www.decorativepainters.com

Stencil Artisans League, Inc.
P.O. Box 3109
Los Lunas, NM 87031
(505) 865-9119
www.sali.org

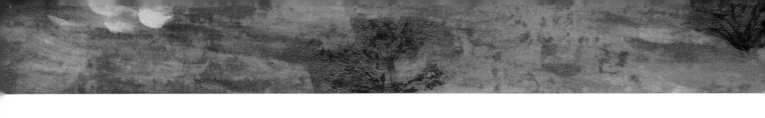

TROMPE L'OEIL MURALS using stencils

Melanie Royals

NORTH LIGHT BOOKS
CINCINNATI, OHIO
www.nlbooks.com

TABLE OF CONTENTS

INTRODUCTION

Trompe l'oeil, a painting technique that involves the use of visual devices and tricks that are designed to literally "fool the eye" of the viewer and (for an instant) make him believe that he is seeing something real and dimensional, has been practiced by artists for centuries.

This art form has been used through the ages to adorn churches, castles and the homes of nobility. Most often, it was used to represent classical forms in architecture, such as moldings, bas-relief, columns and capitals. The effective use of light and shadow combined with texture and a believable perspective (point of view) create the illusion of a three-dimensional object or mural on a two-dimensional surface.

The use of trompe l'oeil painting reached its peak during the Renaissance. Changes in taste led to a gradual decline in its use. Impressionistic and contemporary art, which gained momentum in the late nineteenth and early twentieth centuries, represented objects in more non-specific ways.

All things being cyclical, trompe l'oeil painting has enjoyed a resurgence of late, along with other forms of decorative painting and art. It is seen extensively today in commercial applica-

tions and in public art, as well as in homes both stately and simple.

In addition to a renewed appreciation for decorative art, there is growing interest among artists and nonartists to develop painting skills that will enable them to create their own masterpieces using trompe l'oeil and decorative painting.

This book focuses on skills and techniques that can be learned, used and adapted by anyone with an interest in developing her artistic talents. Whether you plan to use them in your own home or as a professional, whether you are a skilled artist already or you have never taken pencil to paper or paint to a wall, you will find the inspiration, instruction and encouragement here to transform ordinary surfaces into artistic illusions. Learning freehand painting skills and mastering proper brush and blending techniques can take years of

study and practice! Fortunately, you have a variety of tools at your disposal that can simplify the application of your great ideas and creativity to transform surfaces in your environment into works of art.

In fact, if you are prone to call yourself a nonartist, and find yourself saying, "But I can't draw or paint," then this book is definitely for you! Through the use of stencils, shields and tape, the creation of trompe l'oeil illusions becomes easy and accessible to potential artists of all skill levels. We will take the basic concepts of using simple tools to control and limit the application of paint and use them to define space, create three-dimensional looks easily and develop the shadows and highlights that make painted illusions come to life.

My goal with this book is to give you the basic information, simple techniques and tools that will allow you to easily develop the skills that will enable you to

- create believable textures with painted effects
- utilize correct perspective and define space
- visually represent the values and contrast necessary to create the illusion and dimension and trompe l'oeil art

These three things—texture, perspective and value contrast—done correctly will lend realism and polish to your painting, whatever your skill level.

By combining these techniques with the rules of layout and composition, architectural elements and simple decorative painting treatments, we will create *trompe l'oeil murals*!

LEFT
This trompe l'oeil mural was created entirely with stencils. What looks to be an incredible amount of painted work is actually very simple and easy to execute by simply using the edge of the stencil to develop the shading and contrasting values that create the illusion of a three-dimensional surface.

chapter one
STENCILS

One of the most versatile and useful tools available to artists is the stencil. Stencils have been used as a tool to create surface decoration for thousands of years and have many unique qualities. A stencil, in its simplest form, is nothing more than a shape that is cut out of a semirigid surface. When the shape is in the form of a specific design and paint is applied through it to a hard surface, a print is made.

It is the complexity of the stencil design and the technique that is used to apply the paint that determines what the finished result will look like. A heavy, uniform application of paint through a simple, single-overlay stencil design will result in a very graphic or primitive look. Using a multiple-overlay stencil design with a studied approach to color application and careful attention to creating contrast and detailed shading will result in a print that appears sophisticated, dimensional and hand-painted.

The basic concept behind the use of stencils, and what makes them so unique and useful to artists (and potential artists) like us, is that they control and limit the application of paint on a surface. The uncut areas of the stencil form a barrier between the paint and the surface. The paint is limited only to those areas that are cut out and exposed. When we use the edges of the cutout areas to build up layers of paint and shading, a dimensional look results. We will extend that concept—the controlled and limited application of paint—to our use of shields and tape as well. Once you start working with this concept, you will undoubtedly begin to find and develop your own applications

for these marvelous tools as you realize what time-savers they are!

Artists employ a variety of techniques and materials for stenciling. We will examine all our options here and when each might be most useful for our trompe l'oeil mural work. Please remember: there is no right way, and the "no rules" rule rules! In the fifteen years I've been stenciling, I have definitely developed my own shortcuts, techniques and

preferences (and I'm very happy to share them). You will develop your own favorite techniques and preferences as well. You will find the most success with using and perfecting techniques with mediums that are comfortable for you at your own taste and skill level. We'll discuss those options shortly. First, though, let's start with some useful tools and supplies you will need.

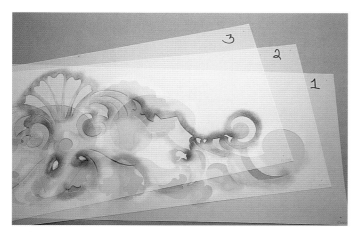

Multi-overlay designs are stenciled one after the other. Each piece contains separate elements of the design that interlock, much like a jigsaw puzzle, to form the whole design.

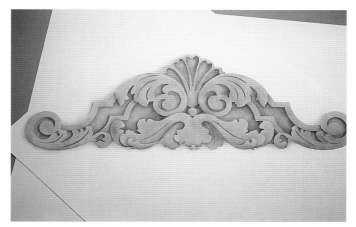

The use of a multi-overlay stencil allows you to work with contrasting values, building up areas of both dark values and lighter highlights, which creates a realistic dimensional look. Notice that because there are no bridges or unpainted areas, it is difficult to tell that a stencil has been used at all when viewing the completed design.

A solid application of paint through a simple but beautiful design produces a look that is very graphic and mechanical, similar to block printing or silk screening.

Tools and Supplies

STENCIL BRUSHES

The quality of your work will depend greatly on the quality of your tools and materials, and no tools are more important than the brushes you use. Natural-hair brushes with long, soft bristles will yield the best results for the stencil method that is featured in this book. Short, stiff-bristled brushes will not only make it hard to achieve the soft, blended effect that a firm, swirling motion produces, they will be hard on your wrist and arm as well!

Brushes come in a wide variety of sizes, from ¼" (6mm) up to 1½" (4cm). The size of brush you use will depend on the size of the area you are stenciling. For large open areas, such as pots or sizable architectural elements, you will want a larger brush that fills in the space quickly. Using a small brush will take longer, and you will most likely end up with a blotchy, uneven effect.

FOAM STENCIL ROLLERS

A dense foam roller is another option for stenciling large areas that don't require varied depth of color, such as large architectural elements. Foam rollers allow you to cover a lot of ground quickly and are indispensable for large mural work. Where necessary, additional shading can also be added with a stencil brush after the roller work is complete.

Here's a selection of stencil brushes.

Use a foam roller to quickly fill in a large area.

TAPES AND ADHESIVES

Blue tape. Most professionals use blue painter's tape. It is more expensive than masking tape but retains its tack much longer (so it can be used repeatedly). It also has less of a tendency to harm or remove paint from the work surface when pulled off.

Easy Mask paper tape. This tape resembles a Post-it Note and is sticky on just one edge. It allows for straight, clean lines on a smooth surface and is ideal for creating and building architectural elements. Like the blue tape, it also can be used repeatedly.

Other tapes. For masking off curved areas, use thin masking or pinstriping tape. These will flex easily enough to protect curved areas, such as elongated leaves, and to create arches and rounded objects.

Repositionable stencil adhesive spray. For large stencils and weak stencils (meaning that a large portion of the material is cut away) and for any situation in which you desire a more secure seal, spray adhesive can be very useful. Lay your stencil right side down on newsprint or scrap paper and lightly mist with adhesive. Hold the can at least 12" (30cm) away from the surface and don't overapply. Allow the adhesive to dry briefly before pressing the stencil onto the surface. The stencil may be moved and used repeatedly before reap-

An assortment of tape includes from left to right, ¼" masking tape, Easy Mask paper tape and blue painter's tape.

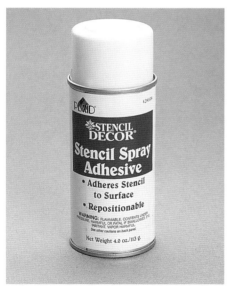

Repositionable spray adhesive provides a secure seal.

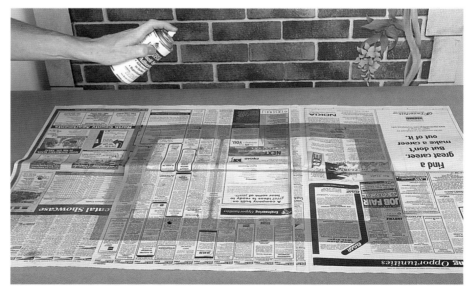

Hold the spray adhesive approximately 12" (30cm) away from the stencil as you apply a light misting.

PAPER TOWELS

I highly encourage all of my students to use Bounty paper towels or something similar of high quality. The primary purpose of the paper towels is to remove almost all of the paint from your brushes after you load them by "off-loading" with a hard pressure, so the towels need to be strong and absorbent. Another purpose of off-loading is to be sure that your paint is distributed evenly on the brush to produce an even print. Lower-quality towels will not take enough paint off the brush and will shred under the pressure.

CONTAINERS

Small plastic cups work well for keeping colors separated and for keeping thinned paint in one place. They are available at restaurant supply stores in a variety of sizes.

You're thinking either I'm insane or those paper towel people are paying me off! No, neither, but after many years of practicing and teaching stenciling, I've found that the most important step to achieving a wonderfully blended, soft stencil print is to properly off-load the brush on very good quality paper towels, and Bounty fits the bill every time. Bounty paper towels are shown on the left and some bargain brand on the right. No bargain there. Save them for drying your hands!

Small plastic cups are handy for keeping thinned paint separated. To keep extra paint from drying out, use plastic lids or store in airtight containers.

MEASURING AND MARKING TOOLS

Measuring up to the job requires tools for creating straight and level lines. Here are some items you will find very useful for stenciled mural work.

Pencils and artist's erasers. Use soft lead pencils and keep marks and lines light so they are easy to erase and to paint over.

Watercolor pencils. A damp cloth or sponge easily removes watercolor pencils, or they dissolve and blend in with the paint. Choose a light color when drawing or marking over a dark background, and a light, neutral color (such as soft gray) for a light background.

Bubble level. Levels are mandatory tools to be used when creating or "building" architectural elements. Use them to mark truly level (horizontal) lines and perfectly plumb (vertical) lines.

Chalk line. When laying out long lines, use a chalk line. Pull the line taught between two predetermined points and snap it by pulling slightly away from the surface and letting go. The chalk on the line will transfer to the surface. An alternative to using colored chalk (especially when marking dark surfaces) is using baby powder, which doesn't leave any residue or color your painting.

Clear grid ruler. I find clear grid rulers indispensable for all kinds of measuring and marking. You can easily draw right angles and parallel lines by lining up the grid lines on the transparent ruler.

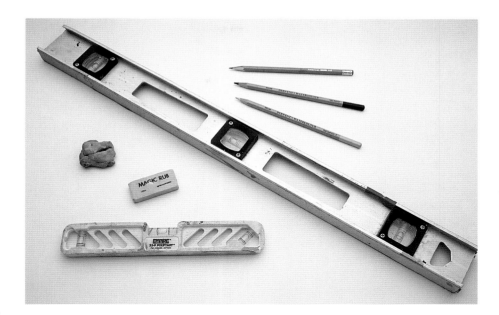

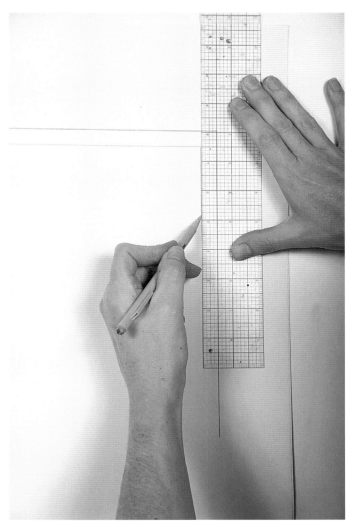

Use a transparent grid ruler for quick, accurate measurements. You can easily create parallel lines by lining up the first line with the measurement on the ruler that is the thickness you desire, then drawing the second line along the edge of the ruler.

Paint Mediums

ACRYLIC PAINT

The majority of the projects and techniques in this book call for craft acrylic paints. These offer many advantages: They are readily available in a wide range of premixed colors. With the addition of water or FolkArt Extender they can be made translucent to create a glazelike or watercolor effect. Unthinned, they can be used opaque and will cover previous colors well. They dry quickly, so multiple coats and colors can be layered quickly without muddying.

EXTENDER

For creating soft, blended, translucent effects, and for making acrylics easier to paint with, we will be adding FolkArt Extender to the acrylic paint. Undiluted, acrylic paint is very heavy and builds up quickly and excessively on both stencils and brushes, making it difficult to stencil effectively. The addition of extender completely changes these properties, making the paint flow easier for softer, blended prints. It also makes cleanup of stencils and brushes much easier—*a big plus!*

OIL-BASED STENCIL PAINT

Many artists prefer to work with stencil cremes, which are oil-based paints in a solid, cakelike form. These are available both as crayons and in pots. Many beginning stencil artists find these very easy to work with because they naturally produce a soft effect beginning artists find it easy to control the buildup of paint. The disadvantages for mural work are that the cremes come in a limited color range, don't layer well (because they are not opaque and they muddy when multiple colors are used together) and do not completely dry for days.

Because they do stay soft and blend easily, I have found them to be most useful for creating softly gradated shadows and architectural elements with tape. Because you are putting on such a thin layer of paint, it is possible to paint over these with water-based paints, so you can feel free to mix both mediums in mural work.

The addition of extender to ordinary craft acrylics creates an entirely different medium that is ideal for trompe l'oeil stenciling because it allows for easy shading and color blending.

Paint cremes allow for easy shading and blending and work wonderfully for creating shadows.

LATEX PAINT

Latex paints can be used for stenciling in large areas and creating architectural elements such as columns and block walls. Latex paint builds up very quickly on the stencil, is tacky and is hard to clean, so it is definitely not recommended for intricate designs. It does not dry as quickly as acrylic paint, so you will have to wait a bit between building up coats of paint. Latex paints can be thinned and made more translucent by adding water and glazing mediums.

GLAZE

Waterbased glazing mediums can be added to latex paint to make it more translucent and easier to work with. We will be using glazes and a variety of manipulative tools to create trompe l'oeil surface textures on our stenciled elements.

PAINT FOR EXTERIOR SURFACES

For painting murals on exterior surfaces, several companies have developed lines of waterbased paints that will bond to concrete, terra cotta and stucco, and will not fade, peel or crack under adverse weather conditions and strong sunlight.

Latex paints are extremely useful and cost-effective when your stenciling and painting will cover large areas. I recommend using a flat finish in a 100 percent acrylic, exterior grade.

Just a little glaze medium added to latex paint will make it more suitable for brush stenciling. A larger ratio of glaze to paint will create a translucent medium that can be manipulated with tools over large areas to produce a variety of effects. Note: The more glaze that is added, the "wetter" the medium becomes, and longer drying and curing times will be required.

Two good lines of paints that are widely available and created specifically for painting outdoors are Plaid's Durable Colors and Patio Paints from DecoArt.

Cleaning Brushes and Stencils

STENCIL BRUSHES

Stencil brushes are sturdy little guys and will last many years with some basic care. The most important things to remember: Do not allow paint to dry in the brush. Brushes are much more sensitive when wet, so be sure they are not pressing up against something as they are drying or they will dry with a permanent bend. Be sure the brush is completely dry before attempting to stencil with it again.

Take care of brushes by cleaning well after each use and you will find that they last for years. I like to keep handy a brush soak container, filled with a mixture of one part concentrated Murphy Oil Soap and two parts water. As I finish with a particular color and brush, I drop it in to soak until I am ready to clean up at the end of the day.

For oil-based cleanup, work out as much excess oil-based paint as possible on paper towels. If you are going to reuse the brush soon, paper towel cleanup should be sufficient. Otherwise, clean brushes with Murphy Oil Soap and water, or rub across paper towels that have a few drops of baby oil on them.

Follow up by working out all paint with a good brush cleaner. A small plastic brush scrubber will get in between bristles to easily remove traces of paint. The paint may stain the bristles and leave them slightly colored, but you will know when you have removed all traces because the water will run clear.

STENCILS

I am pretty fanatical about cleaning stencils. Stencils with layers of paint built up on them are harder to work with. The dried paint creates more drag on the brush. Additionally, the paint will build in on the stencil, throwing the registration off on multi-overlay designs. Without proper cleaning, you will lose the benefit of the translucency of the plastic, which allows you to see previous prints and more easily line up subsequent overlays.

Stencils cut from Mylar should last through many uses and years with some care. The amount of elbow grease that will go into cleaning them will depend on the paint medium used.

Acrylic and latex paints that have been thinned with either extender or glaze will clean up easily with warm water and a kitchen scrubber sponge.

Spray on a little cleaner, such as Murphy Oil Soap, Simple Green or Formula 409, for even easier cleanup.

If you are using oil-based paint cremes, clean your stencils immediately after use by simply wiping with a clean paper towel. If you've allowed the paint to dry and cure you will need to use mineral spirits and a little pressure to get your stencils clean.

For thick, dried paint, you may want to let your stencils soak. Lay out a plastic garbage bag and layer stencils with healthy squirts of any of the above cleaners. Fold up completely in the plastic and allow to sit for several hours to overnight. The paint should almost slide off at this point.

When cleaning stencils, always take care not to bend back pointy areas or tear at delicate bridges. Stencils should be allowed to lie flat for cleaning, so if it is a very large stencil, you will need to put it in the bathtub. You may or may not want to clean the tub while you're there!

Inadvertent tears in the stencil can be fixed by placing clear tape over the damaged seam on both sides. Carefully cut any excess tape away from the edges with a sharp craft knife.

Stenciling Techniques

The stencil is simply a tool that is used to easily define the shape and form of the design by allowing paint only into limited areas. It is the techniques used by the artist while stenciling, (color selection, shading, highlighting, value contrast, etc.) that will bring the design to life and give it dimension and realism. Stenciling techniques are easy to learn and master; all that is required is some good, basic instruction, quality tools and practice, practice, practice!

STENCILING 101

Always hold the brush perpendicular (straight up and down) to the surface while stenciling, and while loading and off-loading the paint.

To properly off-load the brush, rub with a very firm circular motion on paper towels. The size of paint circles that you make should be at least twice the diameter of the stencil brush. This ensures that you are removing excess paint as well as distributing paint evenly on the brush.

Keep this concept in mind: You are building up thin, translucent layers of color. It is much better to apply two thin layers of paint than one thick one. If you try to build up too much color too quickly, paint may seep under your stencil.

Each time you reload the brush, you are beginning again with more paint, so lessen your pressure on the brush to avoid starting too dark.

Adding extender will make your paint more translucent. If you need your paint color to cover or hide something that has been painted underneath, or just wish to create a more solid effect, don't add extender.

If you want even more opacity to the color, add some white to it.

If you can see brush marks in your print, you have too much paint on the brush. A sufficiently dry brush allows you to place nice, firm pressure on the brush, which will give you a soft, smooth, completely blended effect.

The most common mistake made is leaving too much paint on the brush. When you are beginning and getting a feel for it, take off more paint than you think necessary. You can always add more layers and build up more color.

It is the amount of pressure placed on the brush that affects the depth of color on the print. A good warm-up practice (shown below) is to load the brush and do a value study. Start with a firm but light pressure to create a soft blush of color. Then, without reloading your brush, increase your pressure (this comes through the shoulder) to create a medium value. Finally, press very hard to create a dark solid value. Now go back to the light pressure again, trying to feel the difference.

As a rule, it is hard for most people to believe what a small amount of paint is necessary for stenciling. If you are unsure about how much paint on the brush is too much, here's a simple test: Lightly brush across the back of your hand with the loaded stencil brush. If you see paint there, you have too much!

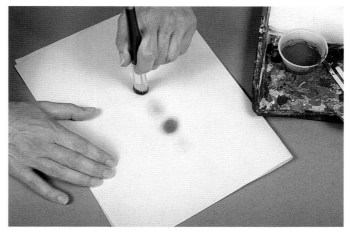

Making a value study

SWIRLING

Swirling is the stenciling technique I prefer because it produces a softly blended, refined, hand-painted look. With some practice, you will find that it is very easy to achieve the shaded, dimensional look that is essential to trompe l'oeil painting. Simply concentrate paint along the edges of the stencil and control the amount of pressure you are putting on the brush. More pressure, more paint.

1 Correctly load the brush
For a translucent effect and easier shading, thin paint with FolkArt Extender to the consistency of melted ice cream, generally a few drops of extender per teaspoon of paint. Stir well. Load just the tip of the brush by dipping straight into the stencil paint, and remove excess by rubbing in a firm circular motion on the paper towels. I have found that most students do not press hard enough or off-load enough paint at first because they can't believe that you can treat a brush that way. They also think that they need more paint on the brush than they actually do! A good technique for off-loading is to create three circles of paint that become progressively lighter. Also notice the circles of paint are more than twice the diameter of the brush. This means you are pressing firmly enough to remove the correct amount of paint.

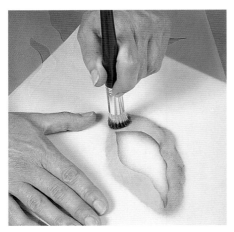

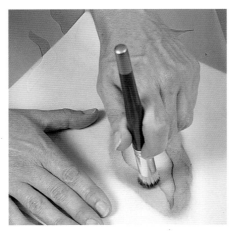

2 The stenciling technique
Begin stenciling by first concentrating paint around the edges of the cutout areas of the design, constantly moving the brush in small, firm circles as you continue around the outer portion of the exposed areas of the design. Notice that the majority of the stencil brush is on the Mylar at this point. This serves to define the edge of the design cleanly and clearly with a deeper color that naturally fades away in value toward the center. I like to push the brush into the edge to achieve a nice clean, crisp edge. Remember to build up color slowly! You can always go back and add more.

3 Filling in
Gradually blend in the color toward the middle of the exposed area by using a lighter pressure and a dryer brush. The fade out of color should be gradual, not abrupt. This will take some practice as you learn to adjust your pressure.

4 The completed print
By using a very dry brush held perpendicular to the surface, and maintaining a nice even pressure while building up translucent color, I was able to create this soft, powdery print with a dimensional look.

STIPPLING

Stippling, which is sometimes referred to as pouncing, is an alternative brush-stroke used for applying paint through the stencil. A stippled print has a more textural, grainy quality to it. Stippling deposits and builds up the paint more quickly and heavily, so it is useful when you are trying to cover over a background color or trying to bring back a lighter color over a darker one, as in the creation of highlights.

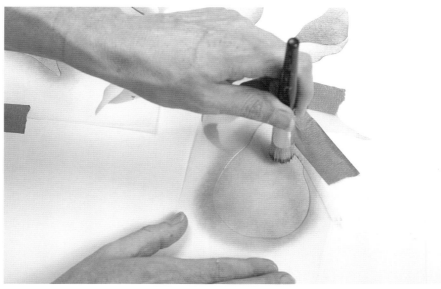

Stippling is a straight up-and-down, tapping motion with the brush. Because you are not pushing into the edges of the stencil as in the dry-brush method, you may leave a little more paint on the brush. If your brush is too heavily loaded with paint, you can still experience some seepage under the stencil, so don't forget to off-load paint!

STENCILING WITH ROLLERS

When you want to cover a large area quickly and evenly, roller stenciling is the way to go. It is very important to still work dry, so that you don't have excess paint seeping under the edges. A light misting with spray adhesive will help hold the edges of large stencils securely. A firm, even pressure with the roller will give a smoother look. As always, it is best to build up the paint slowly, and two (or more) thin layers with nice clean edges are better that one thick sloppy one. Note: It is important to allow the first layer of paint to dry completely before adding additional coats. It the paint underneath is still slightly wet, you will lift that layer off as you try to apply more paint onto it.

For quick even coverage, use a stencil roller. Keep in mind that you are still working dry, and off-load excess paint on absorbent paper towels or clean newsprint. Just as with a brush, it is important to have the paint distributed evenly on the roller. In a situation where you are going for a uniform look, start from the center and work out to the edges. This way, you are removing more excess paint from the roller before you work toward the edges.

STENCILING WITH OIL-BASED PAINT CREMES

Cremes are excellent for creating very soft, blended looks because they stay wet. This allows you to go back and rework areas, softening and blending them further. You can even remove excess buildup of paint by rubbing gently with a paper towel. Cremes come in a limited color range and can't be premixed, so you must create new colors by blending two or three colors together as you work. This allows for a very painterly look, with the colors blending easily into each other. The downside to this is that you can't layer colors without them blending and muddying, because they don't dry instantly on the surface like acrylics do.

The technique for stenciling with cremes is similar to that of using extended acrylics, however, you will load the brush a little differently.

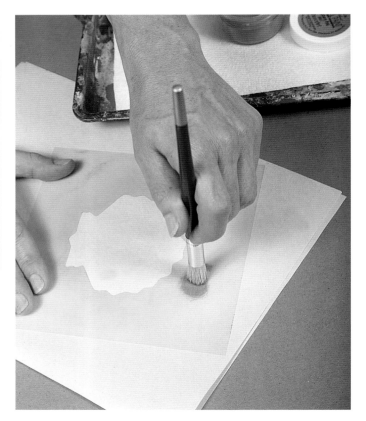

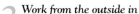
1 Load and off-load the brush
Load the brush by rubbing directly into the paint. Remember that a little goes a long way. You can always come back and get more paint if you need it. It is not necessary to off-load excess color to nearly the extent that using acrylics requires. I do like to make sure that the paint is blended evenly on the brush, however, and always rub a little circle first on paper towels or a portion of the Mylar. Off-loading the excess on the mylar allows you to go back and pick up additional paint from there as you need it.

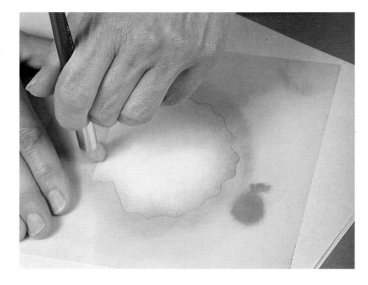
2 Work from the outside in
Just as with the swirling technique done with acrylics, you will want to develop the color slowly. Begin by working the color around the edges of the design, and then blend toward the center, adjusting your pressure as you go.

3 *Paint Creme Considerations*

Because the paint does not dry completely right away you will want to be careful of paint on your hands and excess paint on the Mylar that could be messy. If you are using a dry brush and not depositing excessive amounts of paint on the surface, your print will be dry enough to immediately place another overlay on top of it without worry. If you want to flip your stencil over to get the mirror image, you will need to clean it off first to avoid transferring paint to places you don't want it.

PROOFING YOUR STENCILS

I always recommend to my students to stencil practice proofs on newsprint. It is inexpensive and easy to get and will give you a wonderful surface to stencil on. Whenever you are working with a new, unfamiliar design, it will be to your benefit to play around with it a bit. Try out various color combinations and techniques. Study how the elements of the design relate to each other to determine how to shade properly and effectively. Use your proofs to determine where you will position those elements in your mural and to see how they relate to the rest of the composition and your design space.

Other good materials for stenciling proofs are frosted Mylar and acetate, especially when you are planning free-form designs and murals. The paint adheres and blends well on the frosted side of the material, and you then have a translucent proof that you can place over previously painted areas and see how the new elements will fit in. You can even flip the proof over to see the reverse effect.

Use stenciled proofs to determine color selections and shading patterns. You then will have a useful tool for planning positioning of elements in your mural.

chapter two

TROMPE L'OEIL STENCILING

Now that you are familiar with the basic tools and techniques that are inherent to the art of stenciling, we will focus on some more-detailed techniques that go beyond merely filling in the blanks and allow us to create true trompe l'oeil: the painted illusion of a three-dimensional object on a flat, two-dimensional surface.

What is it that separates trompe l'oeil stenciling from ordinary stenciling? With trompe l'oeil stenciling we are not simply creating pretty patterns; we are focusing on realistic-looking objects and architectural features. As with any type of trompe l'oeil work, we will concentrate on four important basic elements. The first element involves establishing a well-defined light source and shading appropriately. We will also focus on creating surface textures that correspond to the object we are trying to represent (this aspect will be demonstrated in chapter four). Developing contrasting values is the third element. This contrast in values will occur between the object and background, and within elements of the object itself. Contrasting values draw the viewer into the illusion and help define spatial relationships. It defines where one element ends and another one begins. Value contrasts can be subtle or very sharp and well defined, depending on the desired effect and the quality of light being represented. Lastly, we will concentrate on using shading and highlighting correctly to effectively create and model the effect of a three-dimensional form. Shading tells the viewer what shape the object takes, which areas come forward and which recede, and also where the object sits in relationship to the light source.

This mural detail illustrates the use of the elements that are necessary for achieving realistic-looking illusions in trompe l'oeil stenciling and painting. Note the effective use of a well-defined light source and the differences in the variety of surface textures on the objects themselves. Also notice how the shading and highlights follow and conform to the shape of the objects and how contrasts in values help to separate and define space. The velvet drapery will be seen again on page 228 as a step-by-step technique.

You can see the effect that shading and highlighting have on these stenciled, basic shapes: A circle becomes a sphere, a rectangle becomes a column, a triangle becomes a cone and a square becomes a raised panel. By reversing the application of light and shadow, we can create an entirely different illᵢ ion—that of a concave, rather that convex, surface.

Successful Theorem Stenciling

The term theorem stenciling originally referred to the 18th-century art of painting on light-colored cotton velvet that was taught to young women as a "polite occupation," along with other types of painting and handiwork. The theorems most commonly took the form of still-life paintings: realistic bowls and baskets filled with fruits, and floral motifs. They were executed with oil paints in bright, vivid colors and embellished with hand-painting.

This style of painting is also sometimes referred to as bridgeless, or multi-overlay, stenciling. The process involves using a series of overlays (separate pieces of Mylar) to complete the print. Each overlay has different elements of the design cut into it with spaces in between so that the elements are separated from each other by areas of uncut Mylar. This allows you to shade and color each portion of the design individually.

When the overlays are precisely cut, you should be able to stencil them one after the other, with the elements of the design fitting together snugly, like pieces of a jigsaw puzzle. With proper shading, the result is more of a hand-painted look than a stenciled one because you do not see unpainted areas or lines between the painted portions that are present in single-overlay stencils.

ONE STEP AT A TIME

Theorem stenciling is done in layers. Each layer, or overlay, contains only portions of the completed design. As each overlay is completed, the design begins to develop as the elements lock in and come together.

The first time you work with a new stencil design, the various cutout portions will just look like a series of odd shapes. At this point, you don't know where you want shading and highlight-ing because it is impossible to see how each element relates to the others. The best approach I've found is to go through and stencil each overlay lightly at first. Once the whole design is in place you can study it to determine how to shade correctly. Note: Many precut stencil designs for trompe l'oeil work come with detailed instructions and pictures of finished examples that you can refer to. Also, be aware that once you become more familiar with a design through use and practice, the painting and shading process becomes much quicker.

The following demonstration uses a two-overlay leaf design. This group of leaves is part of a free-form set of leaves that can be used and combined with some simple hand-painting to create the tree featured in the mural on page 150.

These fleur-de-lis designs demonstrate how effective multi-overlay stencils are at creating a hand-painted look. While the stencil on the left has a decidedly stenciled look to it, the stencil on the right looks carved and dimensional, thanks to proper shading and an absence of tell-tale bridges.

1 Position the first overlay. If there are pinpoint registration marks, you will transfer them lightly at this point using a soft lead pencil. If you want to avoid marking your surface, you can place small pieces of tape underneath the Mylar and mark the registration points directly on the tape. This allows you to make nice dark marks that are removed along with the tape. Stencil using the dry-brush method, building up color along the edges of the design and fade toward the middle. Keep your color light at this point, because you want to give yourself somewhere to go, valuewise, with your shading later.

2 Align the second overlay using the registration marks. There is an even more important place for your registration to match up, however, and that is where the edges of the elements meet. Each piece fits into the next, similar to a jigsaw puzzle. You should not be able to see anything you have previously stenciled showing through the exposed areas, because what you will stencil now will lie right next to it. This means that it is important to have well-defined edges of stenciling. Don't allow your edges to fade out. This photograph shows the second overlay positioned correctly. Laser-cut stencils are highly accurate, and there is one spot where the whole design locks into place. Move the stencil around slightly until you can see that all of the connecting edges of the design match up.

This photograph shows misalignment, which should be apparent because there are portions of previous stenciling visible. This will cause overlapping in some places and gaps in others.

3 Once the design is based in with color, replace the stencil overlays one at a time and go back and add more depth and dimension with deeper shading. Study the layering of the leaves. Some are in front and fully visible, and some are partially obscured by other leaves. The areas where the overlapping occurs need to be visually separated by creating contrast. If everything is painted in the same value, the look remains flat.

FIXING GAPS IN YOUR STENCILING

Without proper alignment and registration, you will end up with unpainted gaps between the stenciled areas. Like anything else you do with paint, they can be fixed. Simply nudge the stencil over to accommodate the error, and fill in with paint. It is best to do this repair work on the side that will be getting darker shading anyway, so that you don't end up building up additional color in an area you wanted to leave lighter.

4 Contrast in values causes the eye to see some elements as coming forward and others receding. The lighter values will naturally appear to come forward, while the darker areas will seem to recede.

TOP LEFT

The darker shading will occur on areas where they appear to go behind elements that are overlapping them. This is an interpretation of how light affects how we view an object. Darkness occurs in the absence of light, so where the light would be blocked from hitting an object by something that is shielding it, it will be darker. Where an object is getting unobstructed light, it will be lighter.

TOP RIGHT

In the case of this leaf grouping, some of the leaves are meant to appear as if they are curled up in front of themselves. The portion that is curled up in front will be lighter, but note how I have shaded along the edge where it curves back away from view to soften it and give it a rounded effect.

Here's the completed shading.

VISUAL LAYERING: TROMPE L'OEIL POT PROJECT

Visual layering is key to creating successful illusions with stencils. When you begin working with a stencil, the outline of the exact design is already there in your hand. The design has been drawn, and someone has determined how to divide it into the individual pieces and overlays that will create a whole image. You must bring that image to life and make sense of it. You must study the individual parts and determine how they relate to the whole. From there you must determine the correct way to shade to show depth.

This project will expand further on how to use shading and contrast to define form and space. As the artist who gets to make the decision, I have determined that the primary light source is coming from the upper right.

WHAT YOU'LL NEED

- Large Acanthus Leaf Pot stencil from Royal Design Studio
- FolkArt Acrylics: Burnt Umber, Cappucino, Tapioca and Terra Cotta
- FolkArt Extender
- 1" (3cm), ½" (1cm) and ⅜" (1cm) stencil brushes
- blue tape

1 Base-paint the pot

As with the stenciling of the group of leaves, I have gone through with a 1" (3cm) brush and lightly base-painted the design with Cappucino so that I am now able to study it to determine how the various parts should be represented in relationship to each other and to my point of view. At this point, you can differentiate between the various elements of the design, but the lack of contrast in values leaves it looking flat. Once you are familiar and comfortable with a design, this base-painting step may be eliminated and you can shade as you go.

2 Carefully reposition overlays

Theorem stencils are generally not cut so that one overlay contains all of the highlighted elements and another contains all of the shaded elements. Sometimes that works and sometimes it doesn't, depending on the design. In this case I have carefully repositioned the first overlay back where it originally was, using tape to hold it in place. I want it to be secure but have the ability to lift it back to study each element individually. I am now ready to use shading and highlighting to create more dimension by visually pushing back some areas by increasing the shading and contrast and pulling others forward by either leaving them lighter or actually adding a lighter highlighting color to them.

3 Establish middle values

It is always best to start light and build up layers of color slowly. It is very easy to go back and add just a touch more color, and you want to leave yourself someplace to go with your values. With Terra Cotta and a ½" (1cm) brush, use a light touch to begin separating and defining the different elements by adding deeper shading.

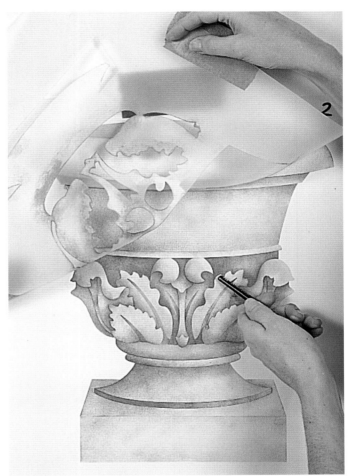

4 *Shade in relation to form and light source*
As you start to add the shading that will sculpt and model the form, you will need to be constantly aware of two things: the light source and the push-pull effect. How you shade an element will be affected by both of those factors. An element may be rounded and protruding forward. If it is in the direct line of the light, you will be shading deeper on the side that is opposite of the light, but also using lighter shading to create the illusion of roundness on the highlight side. Another factor to consider as you work is color value. If an element is in front of or on top of other elements, you will want to leave the value lighter where it comes in front. When the behind element is given a contrasting darker value, it will recede, and the illusion will be successful. In this case I am using my deepest shading color, Burnt Umber, with a smaller ⅜" (1cm) brush. The smaller brush size allows for better control of the color in tighter areas.

5 *Create sharp contrast to make the image "pop"*
Your viewer's eyes will be drawn to the areas of greatest contrast. To create a sharper, crisper contrast, add darker darks and lighter lights using more Burnt Umber and Tapioca respectively with the ⅜" (1cm) brush. These accent colors need to be added selectively and do not simply repeat previous shading. Reserve these colors for the deepest recessed areas for the dark shading and those areas in the most direct line of the light for the highlights.

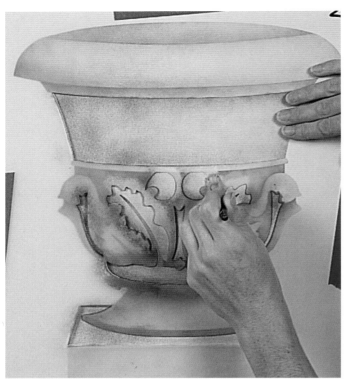

6 *Highlight*
Stipple on a lighter highlight color (Tapioca) on the areas of the object that would receive the most direct light. Use the ⅜" (1cm) brush and concentrate the color just along the edge of the stencil.

SHADING AND HIGHLIGHTING: NOT A BLACK-AND-WHITE ISSUE

Many beginning or untrained artists commonly and mistakenly paint deep shadows as black. While this would certainly provide a lot of contrast and pop, it is incorrect. The colors of shadows and highlights are always affected by the surface they appear on. They do not obliterate it, and they are transparent, not opaque.

For this reason, we will be using transparent, thinned colors for shading and highlighting. The dry brush stenciling technique lends itself very well toward helping to create a transparent effect, since the color is generally applied in thin transparent layers anyway, allowing the background color to reflect through it.

The Completed Pot
The finished project uses strong contrasts and accents, which draw your eye to it, and shading, which makes you believe that it actually has dimension. It jumps out at you. In mural work, you will want to save this type of contrast for those objects that are close to the viewer and seen under artificial light. For a pot that is in soft, filtered light or farther back in the picture plane, you will want to limit your shading and highlighting to the medium values.

Notice how the shading on the base of the pot differs from that on the pot itself. Because the base is made up of flat planes rather than rounded areas, each plane is shaded a uniform value. The front of the base is positioned away from the light source (upper right), so it is a deeper overall value than the top of the base, which is in the direct light. A citrus topiary from Royal Design Studio provides the finishing touch.

Establishing a Dominant Light Source

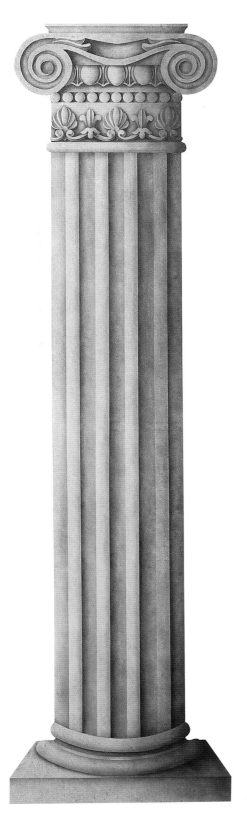

Whether you are painting and stenciling an entire mural or just a single element, you need to first establish the light source. If you look around the room that you are in, you will probably notice that there is light coming from a variety of sources and directions. There may be multiple windows or doors as well as overhead or table lighting. These varied light sources will cause ill-defined shadows and multiple shadows falling in different directions away from and on the surfaces of objects in the room.

As an artist, you will want to simplify your task of creating a convincing illusion for your viewer by choosing a single and believable light source. In the instance of a mural that contains both an interior and exterior view, there will be two light sources: the artificial light that is illuminating objects inside the room and the sunlight that is affecting objects outside, and, in many cases,

inside as well.

The choice of a light source may be very obvious. If your object or mural is in close proximity to a sunlit window, for instance, you may use that as your light source. Using a real-life source of light will only add to the realism of your illusion. If there is not a nearby or obvious source of light for your work, you will have to impose one. My standard choice is generally to have the light coming from the upper right-hand corner, which means that surfaces that are closest to that source and in the most direct line of the light will receive the most illumination. Those surfaces on the opposite side of the light source (in this case the surfaces on the lower left side) will be shielded from the light and therefore cast in shadow. Once you establish a light source, it must remain consistent.

This detail of an Ionic capital and column highlights the use of a strongly defined light source coming in from the upper left-hand side. After the shading detail was completed within the capital and column itself, the whole form was shaded darker on the right-hand side (away from the light source), to create the illusion that the entire architectural structure is cylindrical. The column and fluting detail was created entirely with tape.

Creating Carved Molding With Tape

One of my favorite techniques is creating carved molding with tape because it uses the stenciling technique to such an advantage. Even better, it is simple and doesn't even require you to cut or buy a stencil! All you need is tape, some measuring tools and a molding profile to follow, and you can create the illusion of any type of molding or trim, raised-panel effects or even carved detailing within an object. Oil-based paint cremes, which stay wet and workable for some time, are ideal for this technique because you can easily go back and reblend and smooth out any rough spots. Acrylics will be used later for the Limestone Niche and Lattice Window projects.

As with anything you are trying to copy and simulate with paint, it is very useful to have the real thing to refer to. Here are some examples of different types of molding, next to which I have measured carefully and sketched out exact profiles.

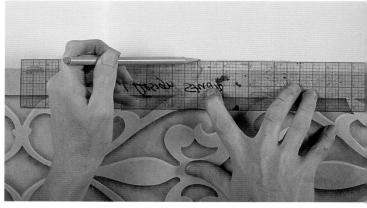

1 After copying and transferring the lines to my project with a grid ruler and light pencil marks, I start working from the bottom up. Start the shading on the bottom line and work your way up to avoid smudging the wet oil paint when you reposition the tape.

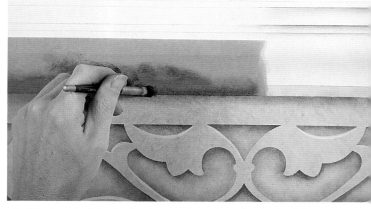

2 The length of the shadow I create depends on the depth of the area of molding I am shadowing. If it is a shallow protrusion, the shadow it casts will be small. If it is deep, the shadow will be longer. This is another device for simulating depth. Once again, I am using a medium-value gray for the shading and reserving the darker value for the deepest recessed areas. Notice how I have hugged the edge of the tape with the stencil brush, allowing only a small portion of it to deposit paint in the exposed area.

3 For the beveled area of the molding, I shade the whole area in an even value of color to represent this portion that is angled away from the light source.

4 Soft curves in the shape of the molding can be represented by running the brush freehand along an imaginary horizontal line down the area that would be curving inward. Use a very dry brush to get a more smooth, softly blended effect.

Any blotchy or uneven areas can be softened and blended by rubbing lightly with a paper towel or cotton swab.

Here is the complete crown molding atop a trompe l'oeil carving created from a Florentine Grille stencil from Royal Design Studio.

Free-Form Stenciling

Free-form stenciling is using separate elements or groups of elements to create one-of-a-kind designs. While stenciled borders have a static quality and repeat at regular intervals, free-form stenciling is more artistic and natural looking—more painterly. This is most useful and effective when stenciling organic designs, such as foliage, flowers and fruit. The stenciled elements give you a quick and easy way to get the paint on the surface, with shading that creates dimension and realism. Simple details painted with a liner brush, such as veins, vines and tendrils, are added at the end to

connect the leaves, flowers, and fruit. The overall look appears hand-painted and spontaneous, artistic and one-of-a-kind.

For trompe l'oeil murals, where you are creating one-of-a-kind artwork, free-form stenciling is especially important and useful. Oftentimes, stencil artists will attempt to create free-form designs out of complicated floral border stencils. This involves isolating various elements and groupings by cutting the design apart or masking off unwanted elements with tape. This can be effective but is also very cumbersome and confusing, since the artist is trying to use the stencil for something it wasn't designed for. On the other hand, there are now many stencils designed specifically for mural

work that depict small trees, bushes, topiaries, floral arrangements, etc. These stencils work wonderfully for duplicating the exact design that the stencil artist envisioned, but they can appear static and have a limited, specific use.

Free-form stencils, however, offer many options and limitless possibilities for artistic interpretation. They allow you, the artist, the freedom to easily create something unique and site-specific. Because each item or group is individually placed, however, you must also be a designer. This can be both liberating and intimidating. There are some simple basic rules for design that you can refer to, as well as tools to help you to visualize and plan your free-form artwork.

NOTE

I first developed the concept of free-form stenciling back in 1988. I was beginning to do a lot of custom stencil work for clients in the San Diego area when I was asked to paint some bougainvillea vines on an outdoor entrance wall of a beautiful Spanish-style home. The client wanted these to be hand-painted and realistic looking as if they were a continuation of the real plants growing on either side of the doors. She definitely did not want them to look stenciled.

While I felt very comfortable and confident with my ability to paint with stencils, hand-painting realistic flowers was a skill I had definitely not mastered, and haven't to this day! So, I was off to the local nursery to find a blooming bougainvillea plant, which I brought home and studied. From it, I sketched a variety of leaf and flower shapes in realistic sizes (I measured!). I designed the flowers to be two-overlay stencils so that I could shade them and give them real depth and dimension. Some of the leaves were cut in two overlays as well, so they looked as though they were curling around themselves, for more realism.

I was then able to take these series of elements to the job, and after charcoal sketching on the wall exactly where and which way the vines would "grow," I began to lay out the design. I began with the flowers first, noticing that they grew away from the leaves. Using stencils allowed me to capture the translucent quality that bougainvillea petals have. They are very thin and papery, like onion skin. I was able to create a clean, defined edge while applying just a thin layer of paint so it looks like light is shining through them. After placing the leaves appropriately, I used a liner brush to paint delicate veins, and a round brush to paint the vine. The client was later disappointed that most people who came through the door said, "What painting?" when the homeowner asked if they had seen the painted bougainvillea as they entered. The illusion was successful!!

Here are several examples of free-form stenciling.

Hand-Painting Details

Individually stenciled elements and groupings in free-form murals need to be connected with hand-painting. For those who haven't had much experience doing freehand brush work, the idea of this may seem a little daunting. It is a skill that is fairly easy and well worth mastering, though, because it frees up a lot of possibilities for designing and contributes to the over-all hand-painted look of the finished work.

Our focus here is primarily on doing work with a script liner brush, which we will use to add veins and create connecting vines to our leaves and flowers. The script liner brush has very long bristles that will hold a lot of paint, so creating long, flowing lines is easy. Depending on how we manipulate the brush, we can get anything from very delicate thin lines to heavier vines and even branches, all with one tool. Delicate lines can also be created with a regular liner brush. For thicker branches, a small pointed no. 4 or no. 8 round brush will work well.

LEARNING TO LOVE LINER WORK

Once you become comfortable using the script liner brush, you will find it very enjoyable and relaxing to use. Like any other new skill, it just takes a certain amount of practice. Here are some additional hints to help you along.

Relax. Shake out your arm before beginning if you are tense. Painting involves your whole arm from the shoulder down, not just your wrist, so you need to be able to move freely and easily.

Practice, practice, practice. The more you do, the more comfortable you will become. Just doodle on some scrap paper. Since you will be working primarily on walls, you will need to be able to pull the brush and paint in different directions. Play with putting different amounts of pressure on the brush, and even try rotating it slightly with your thumb and forefinger as you pull the stroke to see the different effect that you get.

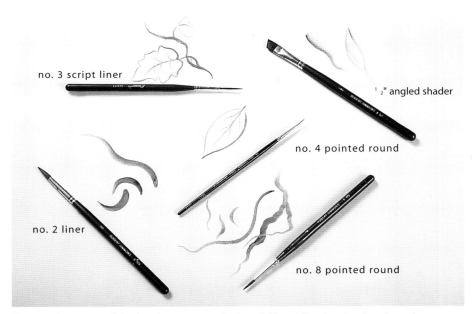

no. 3 script liner

½" angled shader

no. 4 pointed round

no. 2 liner

no. 8 pointed round

Here are just some of the brushes you may find useful in adding hand-painted touches to your stenciled murals, shown with the types of lines and strokes they can make.

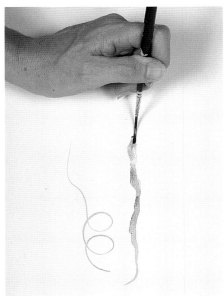

Experiment with different ways of pulling brushstrokes. For veins, begin and end each stroke up on the very tip of the brush, pulling away from the surface as you finish so the end seems to trail away. The more you press and flatten the brush, the thicker your lines will become. Using varied pressure on the brush as you pull the stroke will yield different line widths.

Make sure that you use fresh paint and thin it well. I prefer to use FolkArt Extender, but you can thin with water as well. A good ratio would be one to one. The paint should be very inky and fluid. You can adjust the ratio depending on the situation. Very transparent prints of leaves will not look good with dark stripes of veins going through them, so thin the paint more in that case. If your leaves are very dark to begin with, you might need to have more paint in your ratio, or use a darker color.

I usually use a mixture of the leaf and shading color (usually a shade of brown) for the liner work when doing the veins, and then add more of the darker color to paint the branches or vines.

Wet the brush thoroughly and rinse often in a well of clean water. Remove excess water by dragging gently across paper toweling before loading. Make sure that you load the brush well with paint. Just dabbing it once into the paint isn't going to take you very far. Load the brush by pulling it repeatedly through the thinned paint.

You should hold the brush at least midway up the handle (not down at the bottom like you would a pencil), so as not to restrict your range of motion. You may also find it helpful to rest your pinky against the painting surface to help steady your hand.

One of the nicest things about working with thinned paint is that it is erasable, as long as it's still wet. If you happen to create a less than perfect brushstroke, simply remove it immediately with a piece of dampened paper towel or sponge that you have handy (just in case).

Because the paint does stay wet awhile, you should work left to right if you are right-handed, and vice versa if you are left-handed. This way you can avoid dragging you hand through your nice fresh strokework.

I usually paint in a certain order, painting veins first, then vines, then connecting the leaves to the vines and adding last touches (such as tendrils). Tendrils must be painted very loosely, with the brush held perpendicular to the surface so that just the tip of it is touching.

Pull the brush repeatedly through the paint to load well.

Hold the brush perpendicular to the surface, allowing only the tip of the brush to make contact, for a loose, delicate line.

Liner Work Step by Step

In this demonstration, we will add the finishing touches to the group of leaves that was stenciled at the beginning of the chapter.

It is important to match the look of the liner work to the look of the stenciling. If your stenciled art is dark and heavy, your liner work needs to be darker over it to stand out. If your stenciling is soft and translucent, as in this sample, the liner paint needs to be thinned more to create a more translucent effect.

I always begin by painting the center veins first. Paint in the direction of growth, that is, from the base of the leaf to the tip. I am connecting the leaf to the stem in the process as well. Don't paint the vein out to the end of the lead; rather, pull the brush away from the surface as you near the end so that the line tapers off to nothing.

The side veins will generally conform to the outer shape of the leaf, not run in the opposite direction as shown. Erasing mistakes is as simple as wiping them away immediately with a damp paper towel or sponge!

The side veins should begin on the center vein and arc away gracefully and gently, not at right angles. Two on either side is usually sufficient. Too many veins can become busy looking and distracting.

Side-Loading Technique

Side-loading is an extremely useful brush technique. It creates the same effect as stenciling along the edge of a stencil—color is built up strongly along the edge and fades away to nothing. You can use this in your mural to visually separate elements from each other and their backgrounds where stencils and shields are not available. For demonstration purposes, side-loading is shown here for outlining a line drawing of the outer shape of a brick.

1 Load the brush
Wet the brush in a brush basin and remove excess water by laying the brush on paper towels just until the shine disappears from the brush. Dip just the corner of the short edge of the brush into fresh paint.

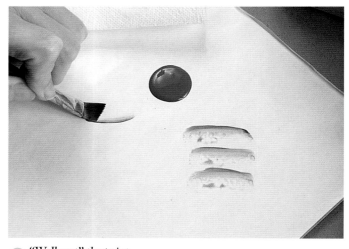

2 "Walk out" the paint
Using short strokes, walk the paint across the brush by repeatedly brushing the brush in the same direction and area on palette paper or a foam plate until you can see that the color fades from dark to light.

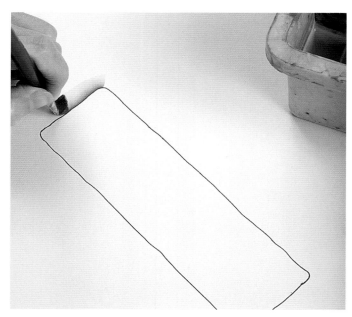

3 Shade and define
Shade around the desired area by pulling brush so the darkest value of color is right along the edge.

4 The finished effect
This brush technique takes some practice. Try drawing or stenciling a variety of shapes on scrap paper first. It is definitely a technique worth mastering!

FREE-FORM RUSTIC FLORAL WINDOW PROJECT

This step-by-step window project begins with a completed window scene and pot. It demonstrates the varied aspects of and applications for free-form floral stenciling: design layout and development, layering, shading and hand-painted embellishment.

WHAT YOU'LL NEED

- Shutter Window and Large Basketweave Pot stencil from Royal Design Studio
- Geranium and Classic Grape Ivy stencil (patterns provided on page 193)
- FolkArt acrylics: Basil Green, Berry Wine, Burnt Umber, Camel, Christmas Red, Cotton Candy, Fresh Foliage, Honeycomb, Medium Gray, Old Ivy, Olive Green, Spring Green, Strawberry Parfait, Sunflower, Wrought Iron
- FolkArt Extender
- assorted stencil brushes
- no. 3 script liner and no. 4 round
- blue tape and soft charcoal

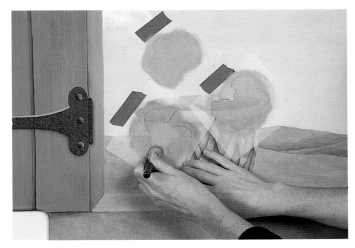

1 When working on a grouping or section of foliage, it is more efficient to lay out several elements at a time. The leaves are basecoated solidly with two to three layers of a pastel Spring Green. The predominance of white in the pastel colors makes them more opaque, providing better coverage. Use a larger 1" (3cm) stencil brush to fill in quickly. Do not add Extender to the paint at this point, as it would only add translucency when you need opacity.

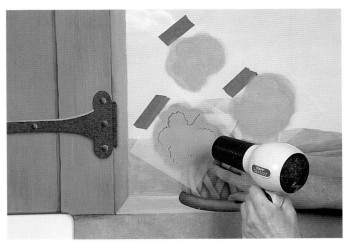

2 It is important to allow each layer of paint to dry thoroughly before adding the next layer. Otherwise the subsequent layers of paint will lift the still-wet layer underneath. A hair dryer will help to speed things along.

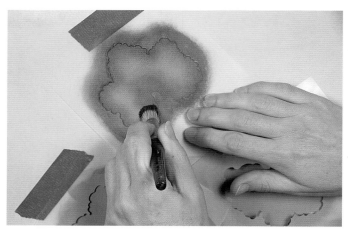

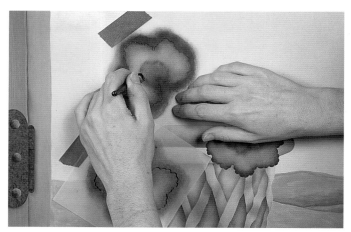

3 The leaves start to come to life with the addition of Olive Green around the edges (I'm using a ¾" [2cm] stencil brush). For geranium leaves, I also create a rounded shaded section at the base of the leaf for added dimension.

4 A blackish-green color, Wrought Iron rims the ruffled edges. For the center ring, add some Berry Wine to the Wrought Iron. Using a ¼" (6mm) brush and a tight circular motion, create a thin ring of color that encircles the center shading and follow the contours of the outer edges of the leaves.

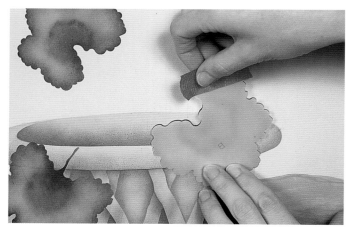

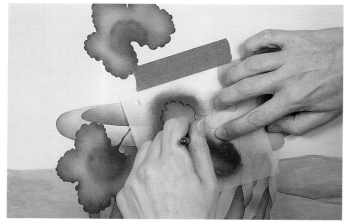

5 One of the unique properties of stenciling is the presence of an edge, a boundary to the design against which you can build up paint and color. In stenciling, we also use shields, sometimes known as friskets or fallouts, as edges. In the case of a shield, we are working with two edges. One edge covers and shields against paint, and one allows us to build up paint against it and create dimension through shading. This picture demonstrates the use of the fallout from the geranium leaf as a shield to protect the art while another leaf is stenciled just behind it.

6 After positioning the leaf fallout securely and directly over the previous stenciling, place another stencil over it, overlapping slightly so that only a portion of the new leaf will be painted. The stencil process is repeated with deeper shading using Wrought Iron. Shade where the newly stenciled leaf will appear to go behind the first leaf and appear to be overlapped by it.

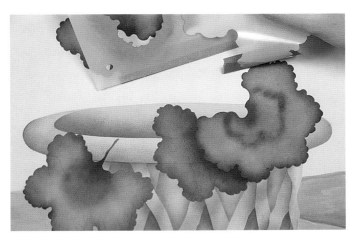

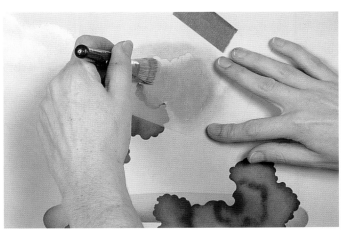

7 Notice the effect that contrast has here and the importance of proper shading. If the top leaf had been painted darker, the viewer would be confused and the illusion ineffective.

8 Many times shields are not available, or perhaps you will decide later that you want to layer something on top of some previous work. It is still possible to create shading and contrast. In this case, I am stenciling over a previously painted leaf but still want to add deeper shading where the leaves overlap for a true trompe l'oeil effect.

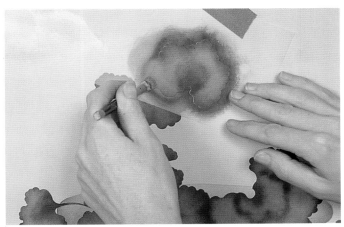

9 After completing the top leaf, replace the stencil of the first leaf and use a ⅜" (1cm) stencil brush to add darker shadow color in the area where it goes behind the forward leaf. If the fallout is available from the forward leaf, you could use that to protect it. If not, or if the forward leaf was painted too dark to begin with, you can go back and highlight it to bring it forward visually.

10 Using first the original base color, Spring Green, followed by light shading with Fresh Foliage, you can effectively bring the color back lighter. It is important to keep in mind that you can always go back and adjust colors darker and lighter as the design develops to establish the proper value and contrast relationships between the elements.

11 Once the leaves are complete, map out a nicely balanced flower placement by using small pieces of 1" (3cm) blue tape.

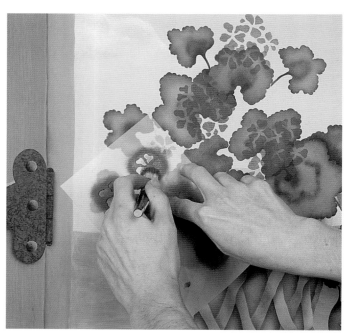

12 The geranium blossoms are also developed by using a layering technique, working from dark to light in value, starting with Christmas Red. The stencil has a variety of petal clusters cut into it, which can be moved around to build the flowers by creating roundish areas of petal clusters. Some of these should overlap to create more density and depth.

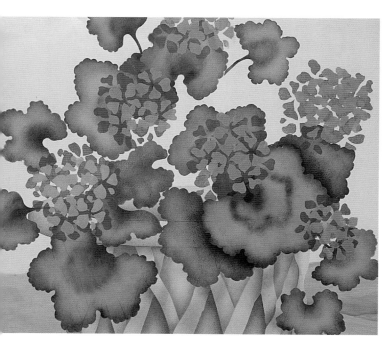

13 The second step is to repeat the process using a lighter shade of the same color, in this case Strawberry Parfait. Concentrate the second and third layers of petals in a smaller area that leans toward the light source, which is coming from the upper right.

14 After completing the third layer of flower petals with Cotton Candy, use a no. 4 pointed round brush to add short little strokes in the centers of the petal clusters. This serves to connect them and also provides more contrast and interest to the flowers.

15 The center portion of the petal clusters has a small painted dollops of both Fresh Foliage and Sunflower. Veins are added using thinned Wrought Iron and a no. 3 script liner. The veins are painted to radiate out from the center of the base, as they do in real life.

16 More contrast can be added to the flowers by hand-painting some shadows where the petals overlap each other. Use a watered-down Medium Gray and a no. 4 pointed round. It is not necessary to paint shadows for each petal. Just a few will create enough contrast to create interest, which should always be your goal!

HINT

When using thinned-down paint, mistakes are easy to fix by simply wiping with a damp cloth. Because the paint does stay wetter longer, though, you need to be careful not to drag your hand through it.

Here's the finished pot of geraniums.

17 After sketching in preliminary lines with soft charcoal to indicate the general direction the vines will grow, lay out individual ivy leaves. For a more natural, random look, place the leaves near to where the vine will be but turn the leaves in different directions for more variety. Because the leaves near the end of the vine would naturally be newer, have the leaves get progressively smaller as the vine grows out.

18 After again basecoating the leaves, this time with Basil Green, use Old Ivy and Honeycomb randomly throughout each leaf to add color and depth. Try to make each leaf a little different, using varying amounts of each color with a ¾" (2cm) or 1" (3cm) stencil brush. Allow the color to float through the leaf, and avoid creating a rounded, dimensional effect that results from concentrating color around the edges. These leaves are flat, not cylindrical.

This picture shows the same layering technique (using a fallout) that was demonstrated for the geranium. At this point, notice how each leaf has roughly the same value. There is no contrast or depth and, hence, no visual separation of the elements.

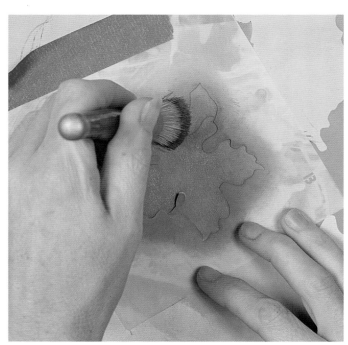

19 Here, the shield and stencil have been put back in place and deeper shading is being added by building up more depth of color.

20 This picture shows the depth and contrast, the push and pull that is necessary in trompe l'oeil painting.

21 When all stenciling is complete, add veins with a no. 3 script liner and a washy mix of the Old Ivy and Honeycomb. Where overlapping occurs, you will need to end the stroke and pick it up on the other side of the leaf.

22 Add Burnt Umber to the paint to create a darker color for the vines. The same no. 3 script liner brush is used, only this time the bristles are pressed parallel and flattened against the surface to create a thicker line. By varying the pressure on the bristles and rotating the handle between the thumb and forefinger as you pull the stroke, a varied natural-looking vine is achieved.

23 Connect leaves to the vine with the same loose stroke. You can have fun by painting the stems off in another direction before snaking them back over the vine to the base of the leaf. Be sure to attach each leaf, unless some are falling off the vine.

24 A few tendrils will add some interest and fill-in here and there. Be careful not to overtendrilize, though, or you will create a very busy and confusing-looking vine.

CREATING SHADOWS

Shadows are areas of darker tone cast by an object. The shadow will be cast onto an adjacent surface on the side opposite the light source. The way a shadow is represented on an object is determined by three things: the source of the light, the shape of the object casting the shadow and the surface on which the shadow is cast.

Sometimes it is both easy and appropriate to use the stencils themselves to create cast shadows. A good example of this would be shadows from leaves and flowers that are cast on a nearby wall that the foliage is growing over. In most cases, though, hand-painting shadows with a translucent glaze will be preferable, as well as more believable.

If the object is sitting or resting on a surface, the shadow will be connected to the object itself and projected onto the surface, and forms that are connected on the object will also be connected on the shadow. If the object is suspended, its cast shadow will be thrown and appear unconnected to it. You can represent distance from the surface by how far you distance the cast shadows from the objects creating them.

One easy way to add shadows is to stencil them using a drop-shadow technique. This involves shifting the stencil down from its original position, away from the light source. The area that is revealed is then stenciled in with a thinned, translucent medium gray, stopping short of the stenciled object with the loaded brush so as not to paint over it. Each leaf that is superimposed over a surface needs to be stenciled in the same manner. The leaves that are on the sky background would not be shadowed because there is nothing for them to throw a shadow on.

An alternative method is to use the same thinned medium gray and a no. 4 round to hand-paint the shadows following the outer contour of the shape of the object. As with the other technique, you need to represent a constant and defined light source, in this case, at the upper right again.

Use the same paint and brush to create cast shadows from the vines and tendrils.

The completed window includes a cast shadow from the pot and leaves onto the windowsill, again in the direction away from the light source.

Use these stencil patterns for geraniums and ivy. Enlarge to suit the space you want to stencil.

chapter three

CREATING YOUR OWN DESIGNS

It wasn't too long ago that precut stencil designs were limited to a few primitive-style borders or traditional Early American designs. Today there are literally thousands of precut stencil designs available that you can purchase! Computer laser cutting has allowed stencil designers to create extremely accurate and detailed multi-overlay stencils, and many stencil manufacturers specialize in designs specifically for trompe l'oeil murals (see resource section for contact information). You can find and purchase a precut stencil for all manner of flora and fauna, pots and vases to place them in, architectural elements to set them on, trellises, fences and gates to entwine them around, and even shuttered windows to view it all through!

If you can't find the right stencil element to fit your design needs, or if financial considerations are a factor (large, intricate stencils are not inexpensive), you may want to create and cut some of your own.

This elaborately designed stenciled mural by L.A. Stencilworks represents the quality and variety of designer precut stencils that are available today.

Stencil Materials

MYLAR

Mylar is a durable plastic that offers many advantages as a stencil material: It is translucent, and, therefore, you can easily see how the image you are creating relates to other images around it. The translucency also aids in placement and registration when using multiple overlays to complete a design.

The durability of Mylar means that, with care, you can use it repeatedly. It comes in a variety of thicknesses. Most precut stencils are cut from 5mm Mylar, but if you are cutting your own, 4mm will also hold up well and is a little easier to cut.

Mylar usually comes with a matte finish on one side, which is easily drawn upon. An ultrafine permanent marker is the preferable choice for transferring designs and registration marks because it will not be removed upon cleaning the stencil.

STENCIL CARD AND POSTERBOARD

Oiled stencil card is used extensively throughout Europe, and you may have seen books written by British authors that feature it. You can find stencil card in art supply stores. It is manila card that has been treated with oil to make it more durable. It is extremely easy to cut, but it has enough stiffness to allow it to hold its shape well, even when there are many elements cut out of it. The disadvantage is that it is not a translucent material, making it undesirable for detailed, multi-overlay stencils. Those same factors make it very useful, however, for cutting larger, simpler architectural elements.

You can create your own oiled card by treating manila file folder material with a mixture of one part linseed oil to one part turpentine. Mix together and apply to both sides with an inexpensive chip brush. Allow to air-dry thoroughly. The turpentine-linseed oil mixture will create a semi-translucent, durable surface that is extremely easy to cut.

POSTERBOARD

Posterboard is inexpensive and can be found in most office supply stores. It can be a good substitute for simple, larger elements if stencil card is unavailable.

FREEZER PAPER

Another method for stencil designing and cutting that works well for larger images and more graphic murals is to use large sheets of freezer paper as your stencil material. Spray the back (non-shiny) side of the freezer paper with repositionable spray adhesive, and apply the sheets to the wall in wallpaper fashion to cover the area to be stenciled. Where one sheet butts against the next, tape the resulting seam with transparent tape. Then project and/or draw the image directly on the paper and cut the separate elements of the design directly off the wall. Remove and replace sections at will while developing and shading the design.

This technique has been developed and perfected by Canadian stencil artists Linda Buckingham and Leslie Bird. A book that features this technique is listed in the resource section on page 302, and you can view some mural examples in the gallery on page 296.

E-Z CUT PLASTIC

E-Z Cut Plastic is another option for stencil cutting. It is good for blade-cut stencils but is especially preferable when using an electric stencil burner for cutting. While Mylar will tend to build up ridges or rough areas along the burned edges, E-Z Cut Plastic edges are smooth and clean. It is completely translucent and accepts and holds lines made with a permanent marker.

Cutting a Multi-Overlay Stencil

This step-by-step project shows you the simplest way to cut an accurate multi-overlay stencil. It begins with a clean line drawing of a classic baluster design. You can take your initial drawings or patterns to a copy center and experiment with sizes by using a copier that will reduce and enlarge. Many copy centers now have self-serve machines that allow you to increase to sizes up to several feet.

In this case, I reduced the size of the original from full-size because I wanted to create a balustrade that was set back into the middle distance of the mural, making it appear smaller to the eye. I've provided you with the pattern I'm using on page 197. Enlarge it to whatever size you require for your mural.

Knives and blades. When I began stenciling back in 1984, computer laser cutting was not yet an option. The first stencils that I purchased were actually just designs printed on Mylar that had to be cut by hand with a craft knife (actually, I used one of those large Stanley knives). I have cut many stencils since then. Long ago, I began using the smaller craft knives with the snap-off blades, and am quite used to the weight of that particular knife and the angle of the blade. Other artists prefer to use X-Acto knives, though, so you should experiment with both to find your own preference.

Cutting with a knife is especially preferable when cutting arching and straight lines. As with any new technique, with practice and experience, you will develop more confidence and accuracy.

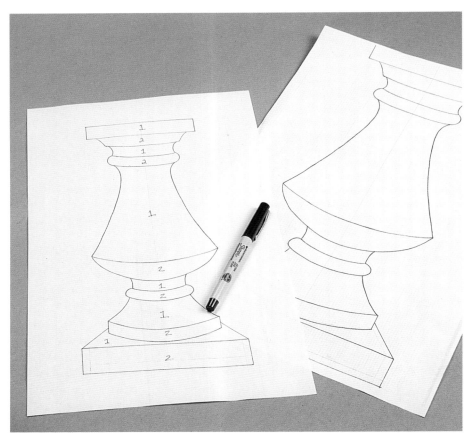

1 Once you have determined the size of the finished design you wish to use, make several copies (it's always good to have extras). Separate the elements of the design into groups that will be included on the same overlay, and identify the overlays with a numbering system. Remember that there has to be a separation of all the elements contained on a particular overlay so that each can be painted and shaded separately. With this particular vertical design, it was easy to break it up into two overlays.

KEYS TO SUCCESSFUL STENCIL CUTTING

When cutting stencils, you will want preserve the strength of the pattern by beginning with the overlays that have the smallest elements in them. For each overlay that you cut, start with smaller elements first and work up to the larger ones to preserve the integrity of the Mylar as you go.

When cutting with a knife, you will be pulling all of your strokes toward you. Try to keep them smooth and to keep the knife moving, especially along long lines. Excessive stopping and starting will translate into jagged, ragged edges.

Try to cut each element completely before lifting the knife. When you come to a corner in the design, keep the knife tip in place as you rotate the Mylar so that you can continue to pull the knife toward you. When cutting curves and circles, pull the knife as you rotate and push the Mylar with your free hand.

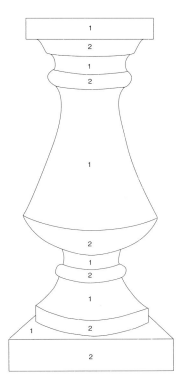

2 Experience has led me to believe that the simplest and most accurate method of cutting is to simply tape one of the copies of the design directly under the Mylar, rather than transferring the design onto the Mylar by tracing. Note: You will need at least a 1" (3cm) margin of uncut Mylar around all edges of your design. If your design is large and requires a lot of Mylar to be cut away, a margin of a few inches (10cm) will be even better, and will make your stencil more secure.

3 While some stencil artists cut stencils on a self-healing mat, my preferred method is to cut on a piece of tempered glass with rounded edges. Glass suppliers usually have scrap pieces that are available at lower prices.

Start in the middle section and work outward. Using a firm, even pressure, cut all of the #2 sections, attempting to split the drawn line as you go.

4 Use a metal ruler to aid in cutting perfectly straight lines. This ruler comes with a rubber backing on it to prevent it from slipping as you cut.

5 As an aid to registration of subsequent overlays, you should transfer other elements of the design with an ultrafine point permanent marker, in addition to labeling each overlay with a number and the name of the design. Note: With a design like this, where the elements lie side by side without overlapping, the overlays can actually be stenciled in any order. The numbering is simply for reference.

6 When finished, carefully remove the #2 overlay and place a new uncut piece of Mylar over the same pattern. Begin cutting the #1 areas. This method of cutting directly on the pattern allows you to see exactly where you have already made cuts. Notice that on this overlay I am cutting slightly inside the edge of the previous cutouts, which will create a very small overlap in the design elements, eliminating gaps.

7 When all overlays are complete, line them up to check for accuracy and to be sure that you haven't missed anything.

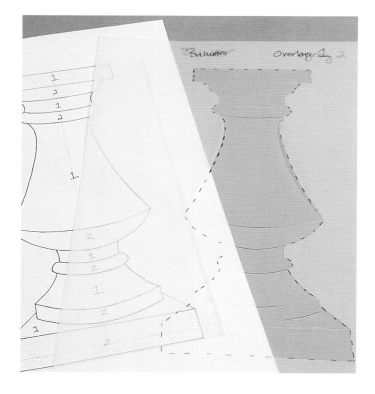

Hot-Knife Stencil Burners

A hot-knife stencil burner is an electric stencil cutter that features a pointed metal tip that actually burns through the plastic. Like a knife, the burner will take some practice and getting used to for you to be able to cut cleanly and accurately. Because you can run the tip of the burner easily in any direction (without having to move the Mylar), it is ideal for cutting things like small circles, berries, leaves and irregular edges.

Important safety tip: Stencil burners are extremely hot and can cause serious burns. Do not leave burners unattended or plugged in when not in use!

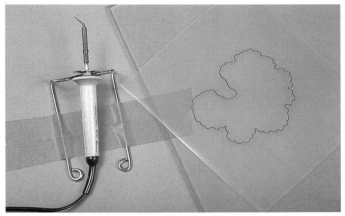

For added safety, stencil burners should be use with a sturdy stand. Tape the stand to your worktable to keep it in place.

Because you move just the tip of the stencil burner and not the Mylar, this tool is ideal for cutting small rounded areas such as these geranium petals.

The jagged, ruffled edges of the geranium leaves are another ideal candidate for a stencil burner. Just as with a knife, it takes a little practice to gain accuracy, but single-overlay elements such as these will not be ill-affected if you get off the line a little.

Quote From a Pro
STENCIL BURNING TIPS
from P.J. Tetreault, P.J.'s Decorative Stencils

Holding the stencil burner like a pencil, work in a continuous stroke, completing the entire cutout of each area (i.e., a whole leaf) before lifting up the burner tip.

Use very little pressure on the tip of the burner as you are cutting. Allow the stencil burner to do the work for you as you guide it.

For a steadier hand and smoother cut, extend the pinky finger and move it along as a balancing point, resting it lightly on the cutting surface.

Hold the stencil material tightly against the cutting surface while cutting to ensure a clean edge.

File the tip of the stencil burner with an emery board or metal nail file whenever it feels like it is dragging, or when residue builds up. This can be done carefully while the tip is hot and will help to keep it clean and sharp.

chapter four

CREATING FAUX FINISHES AND TEXTURES

The cool smoothness of polished marble. The soft nap of a velvet drape. The rough, bumpy feel of natural stone or brick. These are verbal descriptions of what your hands would feel if you touched these objects. When painting in a trompe l'oeil style, you need to provide your viewer with an accurate visual description of the object you are portraying. One way we have already learned to do this effectively is through the use of color and contrast. In this chapter, we will take that lesson one step further and concentrate on creating realistic textures with paint to represent a variety of different types of surfaces. We will also focus more on quality of shading and shading on different types of forms and surfaces. It is careful attention to these types of details that creates truly believable illusions.

Having a wide variety of interesting textures in an environment is crucial to good interior design, and designers acknowledge this aspect by combining luxurious fabrics with woven basketry, smooth polished surfaces with rough texture, etc. You will want to walk into and stay in a room that interests and delights all of your five senses, including the sense of touch. As a mural designer, you, too, can create a more interesting and inviting environment for your viewer to step into by adding the illusion of

appropriate and unique surface textures to the objects in your mural.

To create our surface textures, we will

explore and employ basic faux finish techniques with paint and glaze as well as a variety of manipulative tools.

Materials and Mediums

There is a wide variety of tools available for creating textural-looking finishes and faux surfaces. Most of them are relatively inexpensive and easy to find.

WATERBASED GLAZE MEDIUMS

In order to prevent paint from drying before we have a chance to manipulate it with some sort of tool to create texture, we need to add either water or glazing medium to it.

For mural backgrounds especially, glazes and washes are an effective way to paint in skies, receding landscapes and vistas, and architectural elements incorporating stone, marble and block.

The addition of glazing medium to either latex or acrylic paint will increase its translucency and give it some body, which will allow you to manipulate it with a variety of tools and materials to create textural effects.

Waterbased glazing mediums, such as AquaGlaze, are designed to be mixed with latex paint and should be used when painting in large areas. For increased translucency and extended open time (the time that the medium stays wet enough to be manipulated) you will want a ratio of four to five parts glaze medium to one part paint. For instances where you just want to soften up the paint a bit, use a ratio of one part (or less) glaze to one part paint.

For neutral colors that are used often, premix glazing medium with latex paint and store in squeezable plastic containers. Mark each bottle with the paint chip from the color used. These containers make it easy to squeeze out just a little at a time. Foam brushes provide easy application and cleanup.

When working with glazes in large areas, use a small foam roller and a paint bucket and screen. Just dip the roller into the bucket and remove excess glaze by rolling back and forth across the screen. The excess paint/glaze will return to the bucket.

IMPORTANT NOTE

For mural work, use latex paints with a flat sheen, which will dry to the same matte finish as craft acrylics. Intermixing sheens of paint will cause dull and shiny areas in your work.

For smaller stenciled areas you can use the same craft acrylic paints and FolkArt Extender that are used for the basic stenciling technique.

When working in a smaller, limited area where you want to paint multiple layers quickly, it is oftentimes more desirable to thin paints with water to make a wash rather than use a glazing medium. The addition of water will also increase the paint's translucency and its ability to be manipulated while allowing

for a fairly quick drying time. When painting these various textural techniques through the cutout portion of a stencil, extra care should be taken to work as dry as possible to avoid paint seeping under the edges, and also to be sure that the stencil is affixed securely with repositionable adhesive where necessary.

SEA SPONGE

One of the most useful tools for creating decorative finishes is the natural sea sponge. The prickly types are perfect for creating the textural look of brick or granite, but in many cases, the sponge is used primarily as a blending and softening tool, in which case it is preferable to use the backside of the sponge.

All sponges are not created equal, and each one will give a slightly different print and look, so it is nice to have a variety.

Sponges should always be used wet, but not dripping, so wring out well before using. Also, be sure to rinse and clean sponges immediately after use, as dried paint will render them unusable.

MISCELLANEOUS MATERIALS

Other readily available tools to use for creating interesting surface textures are newsprint, plastic, cheesecloth, terry rags and paper towels. Each of these materials creates a slightly different look, so raid your recycle bin and experiment!

CLOCKWISE FROM THE TOP
Larger sponges are great for blending and softening. Experiment with the looks that you get using different sides of the sponge. Large sponges can be cut or torn into smaller pieces if desired.

Sponges with a prickly surface are ideal for creating the texture of brick, granite and some types of stone.

Smaller artist's sponges work well for creating small, soft, puffy clouds and texturing in tight areas.

Sponges with a fine texture are ideal for creating large, soft clouds and highly blended effects.

BRUSHES

Besides stencil and foam brushes, it is nice to have a variety of bristle brushes on hand for creating wood finishes, dragging effects and rough, linear textures. It is not necessary to purchase any expensive brushes to produce the finishes in this book. In fact, for most finishes, cheap and well-worn brushes are ideal!

Rake brushes, as they are called, are specialty artist's brushes that can be used in small stencil areas to create fine lines for things such as fur, wood and even roughly woven fabric.

An artist's rake brush has bristles cut at different lengths, making it easy to create fine parallel lines. A dry chip brush will offer a similar effect for larger areas.

A variety of softening brushes include (from left to right) a pure China bristle brush, a Chinese hake brush (both inexpensive) and a pure badger-hair brush.

Chip brushes are inexpensive (generally under one dollar each) natural-bristle brushes and can take a lot of abuse.

Lower-quality nylon bristle brushes tend to wear out quickly, and their splayed bristles are ideal for dragging effects.

USED BRICK

FINISH EXAMPLES

The trompe l'oeil textural finishes that follow represent only a very small portion of the many types of visual effects that can be achieved by manipulating paint. I have tried to include a variety of relatively simple techniques that will prove useful for many murals beyond those shown in this book. While each mural project refers back to some of these specific techniques, you should feel free to experiment with alternate colors and finishes for any specific project. In other words, what is represented here are basic techniques that can be mixed and matched, interchanged, expanded on or simplified according to your needs.

This brick finish is easily one of my favorites! It is actually very easy to accomplish, and the addition of a few minor details, such as creating some texture in the grout and adding some flyspecking on the bricks, helps to create a more realistic illusion. It is the final addition of stenciling/shading around the edges of the bricks, however, that separates this brick technique from others I have seen.

This technique uses positive and negative stenciling. The positive stenciling is created by stenciling with highly textured natural sea sponges through the open areas of the stencil that have been cut to the size of standard brick. Upon completion of the positive areas, brick shields are used to protect those positive stenciled areas and build up shading color along the edges to create the effect of shadows created by the bricks that are protruding from the wall. The shields are the actual fallouts of the bricks that are left after the cutting process. The area that is stenciled/shaded around them is the negative area or space.

SUPPLIES NEEDED

Stencils
- Brick Wall stencil from Royal Design Studio

Pants and Glazes
- Benjamin Moore Interior Flat Latex
  Bavarian Creme (brick accent)
  Bouquet Rose (brick accent)
  Earthy Russet (brick base)
  Galveston Gray (grout accent)
  Gullwing Gray (brick accent)
  Revere Pewter (grout base)
  Soft Pumpkin (brick accent)
  Tudor Brown (brick accent)
- DecoArt Easy Blend Stencil Paint
  Ebony
  Neutral Gray
- AquaGlaze

Brushes/Miscellaneous
- two ³⁄₈" (1cm) stencil brushes
- toothbrush
- repositionable spray adhesive
- prickly sea sponges cut into small sizes (about 4" [10 cm] diameter, one for each color used)
- foam plates or paint trays
- bubble level

The finished brick presents a very convincing illusion. Notice the difference between the final effect with the shading details and the stenciled brick shown in step 8.

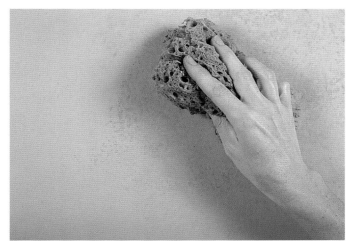

1 Basecoat area to be stenciled with Revere Pewter. When dry, use Galveston Gray (thinned 1:1 with water) to add subtle texture to the grout. Sponge the thinned darker gray on lightly with a damp sea sponge and soften immediately with another clean sponge. Hint: You don't want to create so much texture in your grout that it competes with the texture in you bricks. Keep it subtle.

2 When the background is dry, position the brick stencil that has been misted with repositionable spray adhesive to better secure it to the surface. This will help to hold the larger stencil in place and also help to keep the paint from seeping under the stencil. Check to make sure that the bricks are level. You don't want any faulty construction in your picture.

3 Put all of your paint colors on palettes or foam plates with a separate sponge for each color. I prefer to use smaller pieces of sponge (these can be torn easily), and I also choose sponges that have a lot of prickly texture to them to enhance the texture of the bricks. If you are doing a large area, add one part glazing medium to approximately four parts paint to keep the paint from drying out too quickly on your palettes and on your sponges. It is important to rinse your sponges frequently during the project since they will be ruined if paint dries on them.

4 As always, wet your sponges before use. Be sure to wring them out well so that they are just damp. Dripping water will ruin your effect and cause paint to seep under the stencil. Load the sponge with the brick base color (Earthy Russet) by dabbing into the paint, and remove excess on paper towels or newsprint.

5 Apply the brick base color Earthy Russet to almost completely fill in the stencil. Build up color by tapping up and down with a firm but light pressure to avoid pushing the paint under the stencil. In other words, don't smoosh! Make sure all of the outer edges of the bricks are well defined with paint.

6 Begin layering the brick accent colors randomly and in small, controlled areas. Try to avoid repetition of a pattern by treating each brick differently with paint colors and locations. If you have the pink color on the right side of one brick, put it somewhere else and in a different amount on the bricks around it. Don't feel it is necessary to use each color in each brick, and experiment with layering colors in different orders. As before, don't smoosh. You want to create a lot of texture, and pressing too hard with the sponge will eliminate that and will push the paint under the stencil.

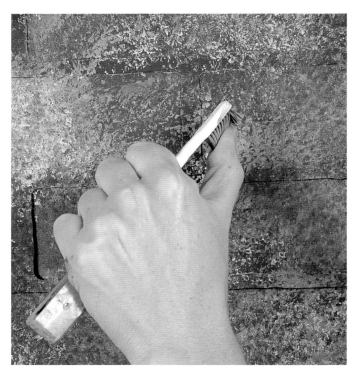

7 You can add a different kind of texture by flyspecking with a toothbrush dipped into the different paint colors that have been thinned 1:1 with water. Release the paint in tiny flecks by dragging your thumb across the toothbrush that is aimed towards the wall. Hint: Be sure you are wearing painting clothes, because those flecks have a way of coming back at you.

8 Here is a completed set of sponge-stenciled bricks. Continue the pattern using these same steps until the entire desired area is filled in. Always check to make sure your bricks are level with each repeat.

9 The precut stencil used for this demonstration comes with fallouts of the brick shapes. These are used to enhance the illusion of the depth of real brick by creating the shadows that visually separate the bricks from the grout. In this case, I have chosen to represent the light source as coming from the upper right. With a ⅜" (1cm) stencil brush, DecoArt's Easy Blend paint in Neutral Gray is used initially to create a shadow along the bottom and left side of the brick (the side opposite the light source). Additional depth and contrast is then added with Ebony along just the bottom edges of the bricks, where the deepest and darkest shading would naturally occur.

This window mural features the same brick technique used in an arched courtyard window stencil to frame a tropical scene.

STONE BLOCKS

Paper or plastic? You can create a formal block wall using ¼" (6mm) masking tape and a frottage technique. With frottage, subtle, random, stonelike patterns are created by laying paper or plastic over a wet glaze and rubbing into it.

The stone blocks can be made to any size or scale you desire, and the level of shading detail is up to you. For this example I have added quite a bit of hand-painting to create additional shadows and highlight on the blocks, as well as some cracks and pitting, but I could have just as easily stopped after the glazing/texture process and been left with an acceptable effect.

As with all of the techniques in this book, this one has many applications and can be used in combination with others for a wide variety of architectural applications. You can also use this effect and curved lines of tape to create stone archways and niches, or create thinner grout lines by using a smaller, ⅛" (3mm) wide tape.

SUPPLIES NEEDED

Paints and Glazes

- Benjamin Moore Interior Flat Latex
  Copley Gray (block color)
  Galveston Gray (grout accent)
  Mesa Verde Tan (block color)
  Revere Pewter (grout base)
  Valley Forge Tan (block color)

- Folk Art Acrylics
  Medium Gray
  Vanilla Cream

- AquaGlaze

Brushes

- no. 4 round
- three 2" (5cm) foam brushes

Miscellaneous

- ¼" (6mm) masking tape
- clear grid ruler
- bubble level
- putty knife
- newsprint
- 1mm plastic sheeting or grocery bags

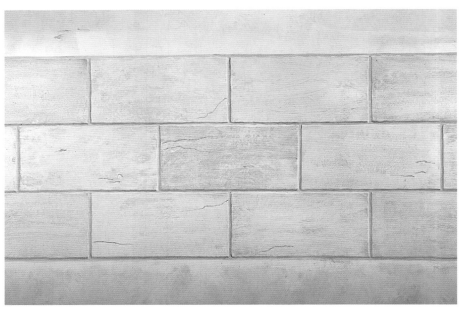

In the finished block wall, each block has slightly different textures and coloration.

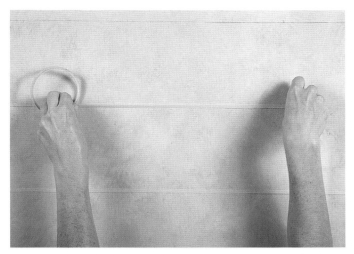

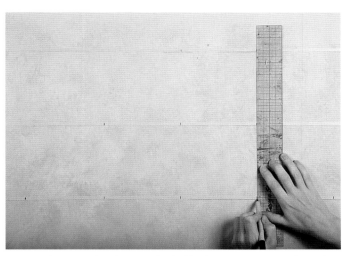

1 Over a textured grout background (previously described under the Used Brick technique) carefully measure and mark level horizontal lines for your blocks. Keep your pencil lines light, and pull the tape taught to keep it straight. The areas that are taped off will become the grout lines between the blocks when the tape is removed and all painting is complete.

2 For this example, I have made the block measurements 6" (15cm) high by 12" (30cm) wide, so after laying out my horizontal lines 6" (15cm) apart, I used a ruler to mark the tape at 6" (15cm) intervals. I then went back and ran tape vertically between two marks in a staggered pattern to create stacked blocks.

3 Leave a little tail of tape extending beyond the top and bottom of the block, which can be removed by holding a putty knife (or similar tool) firmly against the wall and pulling the tape against it. This is an easy way to tear the tape with a clean edge so that you will have clean and well-defined grout lines.

4 For the block colors, mix the latex paint with AquaGlaze at a ratio of one part paint to four parts glaze. Using one color of paint/glaze at a time, use a 2" (5cm) foam brush to paint in individual blocks, spacing the colors so that like colors are not set right against each other. Hint: Don't paint in too many blocks ahead of time before applying texturing, or you may run the risk of your glaze drying before you get to it. Paint in just a few blocks at a time.

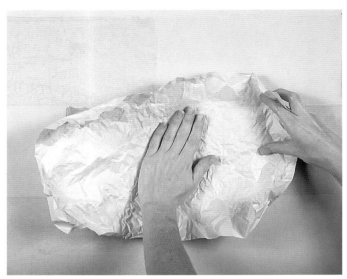

5 Crumple sheets of clean newsprint and open up flat again. You can use either packaging newsprint or the type found in pad form in arts and crafts stores.

6 Lay newsprint in wet glaze, and rub the flat part of your hand firmly across the surface. Keep your fingers together to avoid leaving your handprint in your glazed block. Alternatively, use a folded towel or rag to rub with. To add more variety of color and texture to your block, immediately rub the now-wet newsprint into an adjoining block, depositing some of the wet color onto it.

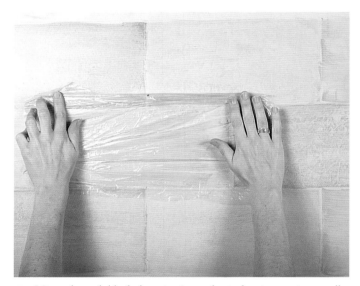

7 Mix and match blocks by using 1mm plastic sheeting cut into small pieces for a different effect. Lay the plastic in while pulling the edges taught to create horizontal lines in your print.

8 After all blocks are glazed and textured, remove tape immediately. Create further definition and dimension by painting in shadow lines on the two sides of the blocks away from the light source (upper right) with Medium Gray (thinned 1:1 with water) using a no. 4 round brush. Rather than painting a straight line, allow the brush to wiggle slightly to create the look of rough-hewn stone.

9 Paint the highlight sides in the same manner using Vanilla Cream thinned 2:1 with water.

10 Create cracks, pits and crevices by painting unthinned Medium Gray and Vanilla Cream side by side with the highlight on the bottom and the shadow on the top, using a no. 4 round brush.

REFINED LIMESTONE

There are many variations of actual limestone as well as various of ways to represent it. I developed this technique on a job where I was required to paint large columns to match an installed limestone tile floor. The technique shown here is quite simple and forgiving, fun to execute, and could be used for creating a subtle background for a wide variety of architectural elements. And by the way, it matches that tile floor exactly.

SUPPLIES NEEDED

Paints and Glazes

- Benjamin Moore Interior Flat Latex
  Stone
  Valley Forge Tan
- FolkArt acrylics
  Charcoal Gray
- AquaGlaze

Brushes/Miscellaneous

- two 3" (8cm) foam brushes
- old toothbrush
- paint trays or plastic containers
- terry towel or washcloth
- fine mist bottle (from drugstore)
- rubbing alcohol

This mural detail of an outdoor wall shows the limestone used with the carved molding technique from page 176. The Trompe L'oeil Fruit Festoon stencil from Royal Design Studio was used with detailed, controlled shading to create the look of a bas-relief carving from the limestone itself.

1 Mix one part paint to five parts AquaGlaze for each color of paint (Stone and Valley Forge Tan). Apply the mixtures simultaneously in diagonal drifts of color using a 3" foam brush. Be careful not to paint these as stripes of color. Each section should be slightly different in direction, size and shape from the others, with irregular jagged edges. Work in small areas, about 3' x 4' (9.1m x 12.2m), so that you will have time to manipulate the glaze easily and effectively. The irregular diagonal edges will blend in with the effect if you keep them light.

2 Fold a damp terry towel (wrung out well to avoid drips of water) in half and then half again. Fold back corners to create a loose but smooth pounce pad. Blend areas of color slightly by walking the pounce pad across the surface quickly in a sliding, skipping motion to break up the edges of the colors. Then pounce up and down lightly over the area. The texture of the terry towel will pull up the glaze and create little pinpricks of color that resemble the pores of the stone.

3 While the glaze is still wet, and before moving on to the next area to be painted, spritz with rubbing alcohol that has been tinted with a small amount of a Charcoal Gray. The alcohol will cause small holes and pits to open in the glaze while the mister bottle will deposit the color in small, irregular flecks.

4 Dip an old toothbrush into the gray glaze color and flyspeck by dragging your thumb across the bristles. Try not to make this too uniform. It will look more natural if some of the flecks are grouped into areas and if the specks are not all of the same size. Soften some of the flecks, especially the larger ones, by padding softly with the terry pounce. Don't press too hard or you will lift the glaze. Move on to the next area, picking up along the irregular edges of paint/glaze from the previous area.

DISTRESSED PAINTED WOOD

Don't throw away those ratty old paint-brushes! They are the perfect tool for this layered dry-brush technique that creates the look of weathered painted wood. Use this effect on trompe l'oeil fencing, paneling, outdoor furniture and tools, doors and shutters. By allowing the base color to peek through the layers, you can easily simulate the effect that time and weather have worn through a previous paint job (or two!).

For smaller areas, you may substitute an artist's rake brush or well-worn flat or round brush for the large paint brushes.

SUPPLIES NEEDED

Paints and Glazes

- Benjamin Moore Interior Flat Latex
    Decorator's White (dry brush)
    Earthy Russet (basecoat)
    Jamestown Blue (dry brush)
    Waterbury Green (dry brush)
- DecoArt Easy Blend Stencil Paint
    Neutral Gray
    Ebony
- AquaGlaze

Brushes

- two ⅜" (1cm) stencil brushes
- three well-worn 2" (5cm) or 3" (8cm) nylon brushes

Miscellaneous

- Easy Mask paper tape
- light-colored watercolor pencil
- newspaper
- bubble level
- 4" (10cm) foam roller and tray

Use old paintbrushes to achieve the look of distressed painted wood.

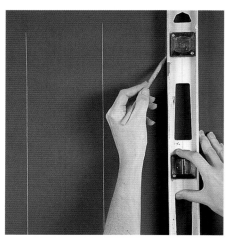

1 Using a 4"(10cm) foam roller, apply a solid basecoat of deep red or brown, which will simulate the color of the raw wood that shows though when finished. After your basecoat has dried, you can use a bubble level to lightly draw in plumb lines at intervals throughout your working area with a watercolor pencil or chalk. These will provide you with a visual reference when you are dragging your paint. Note: For photographic purposes, I have made these lines darker than I normally would.

2 Mix latex paints with AquaGlaze at a ratio of 1:1. Beginning with the blue mix, load just the tips of the bristles of a used paintbrush. Remove excess paint by dragging the brush repeatedly across newsprint so that you are working with a dry brush.

4 Repeat the process with both the green and white colors, overlapping the blue and filling in about 10 percent more of the surface area.

3 Begin applying to the surface using long, light vertical strokes. Hold the brush at an angle that is almost parallel to the surface, and use a light pressure so that just the tips of the edge of the brush are coming in contact with the surface. Begin and end each brushstroke in the air, using a "takeoff and landing" motion so that there are not any visible start and stop lines. Cover about 80 percent of the surface, leaving streaks of the background (wood) color showing through.

5 Use your bubble level and a soft pencil to remark plumb lines 6" to 8" apart (15cm to 20cm). Use two strips of Easy Mask paper tape running parallel ⅜" (1cm) apart to create an opening that will be shaded to simulate a deep groove or space in the wood. Use the Easy Blend Stencil Paint to add shading down the inner edges of the tape with a ⅜" (1cm) stencil brush: Neutral Gray along one edge and Ebony along the other.

VERDIGRIS

A verdigris finish simulates oxidation, or the effects of air and the elements on metal surfaces such as copper and bronze. There are many products on the market that actually create this chemical action, or you can use well-chosen paint colors to create the effect without the use of chemicals.

Stenciled verdigris finishes are appropriate on large planters and urns, accessory items such as lamp bases and candlesticks, and even metal fencing, grillwork and fountains.

SUPPLIES NEEDED

Stencils

• Planting Bucket stencil from Deesigns

Paints and Glazes

• Aqua Finishing Solutions Copper Dutch Metal

• FolkArt acrylics
  Basil Green
  Dark Gray
  Green Forest
  Plantation Green
  Teal Green
  Wrought Iron

Brushes

• ½" (1cm) flat angle shader brush

• 1" (3cm) and ½" (1cm) stencil brushes

Miscellaneous

• three small sea sponges

• blue tape

The completed verdigris bucket shows the stenciled finish.

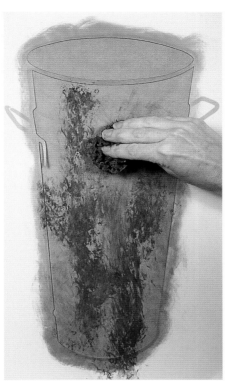

1 Using a 1" (3cm) stencil brush, completely basecoat all overlays of the stencil design with Copper Dutch Metal or a similar opaque waterbased metallic paint.

2 For the darkest green color, mix a 1:1 combination of Green Forest and Plantation Green and thin slightly with water. Apply with a small, damp sponge through the main overlay of the design. Leave some areas textured and soften others by dragging the sponge across to create some vertical movement.

3 Repeat with the Teal Green, both overlapping the dark green areas and filling in previously unpainted ones.

4 Thin the final color, Basil Green, 1:1 with water and use a sponge to drag it vertically through the design, covering and softening the previously painted texture. Hint: Off-load the sponge well on paper towels before applying to design to avoid paint run-unders.

5 Replace overlays that include details of the design and repaint with the copper to separate them visually from the body of the object.

6 Repeat the process but with a lighter touch so that the elements don't just blend in with the background again.

7 This picture shows the beginnings of the shading detail using a mixture of Dark Gray with a little Wrought Iron applied with a ½" (1cm) stencil brush. Note that the inside of the pot is shaded much darker along the bottom, which helps to pull the outside top of the pot forward.

8 This is an excellent example of how you can use the side-loading technique on page 184 to enhance your stenciling. This particular stencil is not cut to allow shading underneath the ridged areas, so I have used side-loading to easily create that added detail and dimension.

TERRA COTTA

Here is a great effect for creating aged terra cotta pottery, statuary, tile floors or even a distressed wall that has been ravaged by time and the environment, à la Pompeii! This technique works best when using a large silhouette stencil as the first overlay or for designs developed and defined with tape, rather than something with small multiple overlays that get pieced together. You will want to be able to create this overall texture in one shot!

For large areas, you will probably want to use latex paint and regular paintbrushes. For filling in smaller stencil designs, use craft acrylics and artist's brushes.

Great hint: You can easily create your own silhouette for many designs. Stencil out the entire design on Mylar or oiled stencil card and cut carefully around the whole perimeter, leaving yourself with one stencil (the silhouette of the design) and one fallout. Use the silhouette to lay in the entire background texture at once, follow with the individual overlays for shading and details and use the fallout for additional shading around the edges of the design where needed.

SUPPLIES NEEDED

Stencils
- Large Courtyard Pot and Bamboo stencils from Royal Design Studio

Paints and glazes
- Benjamin Moore Interior Flat Latex (for Courtyard Pot)
  - Audubon Russet
  - Delightful Golden
  - Mystic Beige
  - Passion Fruit
- FolkArt acrylics (for Bamboo)
  - Burnt Umber   Nutmeg
  - Buttercrunch   Old Ivy
  - Dapple Gray   Olive Green
  - Honeycomb   Spring Green
- AquaGlaze

Brushes
- three 2" (5cm) chip brushes
- assorted stencil brushes
- 2" (5cm) foam brush

Miscellaneous
- blue tape and masking tape
- oiled stencil card or posterboard
- small foam roller and tray
- repositionable spray adhesive
- ultrafine point permanent marker
- craft knife
- terry towel or washcloth

The completed design would be a great element to add height to a tropical or Mediterranean mural, or even to stand on its own as a colorful accent on a blank wall.

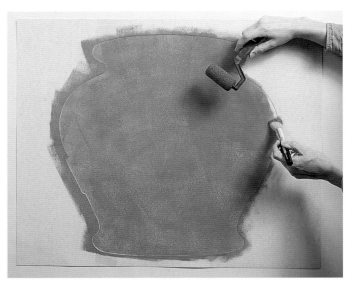

1 For this technique I first created a silhouette of a large multi-overlay pot. To create a large, stable stencil, I butted two large pieces of oiled stencil card together and ran masking tape along the seam on both front and back to secure it. I then traced the perimeter of the design onto the card through the stencil overlays with an ultrafine point permanent marker and cut it carefully with an craft knife. The silhouette stencil is secured with spray adhesive and the entire area basecoated with Audobon Russet.I like to use a foam roller for quickly painting in the interior and a stencil brush at the edges for a clean, crisp line. Allow paint to dry.

2 Use a chip brush to scrub in the peach color, Passion Fruit, in a random criss-cross fashion. Concentrate on creating a random pattern with varying thicknesses of paint, rather than a repetition of spots of color. Repeat the same technique using the yellow-toned Delightful Golden, both overlapping and filling in previously painted areas.

3 Immediately go back over approximately 80 percent of the entire design surface with the off-white, Mystic Beige, using the same criss-cross strokes. In some areas the underlying paint will still be wet and will blend with the top color. Some of the background colors should still show through, but they will be softened and knocked back by the off-white. Note: Be sure and carry the random colors out to the edge of the stencil design using a dry brush to prevent paint from seeping under the stencil.

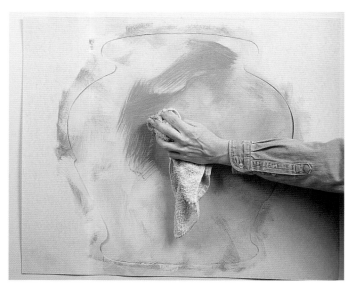

4 Make a glaze using your original base color, Audobon Russet, by mixing one part paint to one part glazing medium. Apply in small areas with a foam brush, and immediately blend and rub out and around with a damp terry towel.

Here's the completed pot without shading.

5 Stencil and shade as usual using the design's overlays.

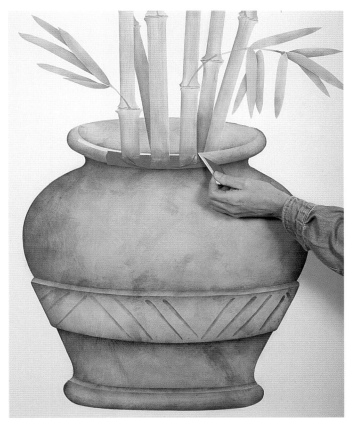

6 After completing the pot, I decided it would be the perfect size to hold a grouping of bamboo (see the bamboo finish on pages 231–235). Use tape to shield the top edge of the pot from the painted bamboo. Be sure to run some thin tape following the curve of the pot right along the edge to ensure a clean, smooth line.

7 In order to properly shade the inside of the pot, place tape on the bamboo stalks to act as a shield and to protect them from being painted over.

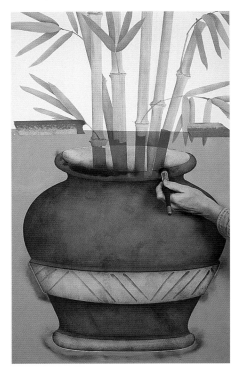

8 Replace the overlay of the pot stencil that contains the element that represents the inside of the pot, and shade it deeply along the edge and around the bamboo stalks.

9 Remove the tape from the bamboo, but keep the stencil in place to add slightly lighter shading on the stalks themselves.

10 As a final touch, dry brush in some of the Olive Green on the pot to give it more of an aged mossy look.

MARBLE

Marble finishes create a sense of cool formality, refinement and luxury. They will most commonly be used in murals in classical settings for columns, capitals, floors, panel insets, plinths and bases.

I call this finish "marbleous" because it is not meant to represent any specific type of marble, but the use of closely related, neutral colors applied in diagonal drifts and accented by the inference of veining patterns, creates an easy and effective marble finish.

Like the previous terra cotta finish, this marble finish also works best with larger silhouette-type stencils or taped-off designs.

SUPPLIES NEEDED

Stencils and Patterns

- Corinthian Capital stencil from Royal Design Studio
- pedestal pattern on page 300

Paints and Glazes

- FolkArt Acrylics
  Barnwood (marble color)
  Dark Gray (stencil color)
  Medium Gray (marble and stencil color)
  Potpourri Rose (marble color)
  Vanilla Cream (stencil color)
- FolkArt Extender
- AquaGlaze

Brushes

- three 2" (5cm) chip brushes
- no. 4 round brush
- softening brush
- assorted stencil brushes

Miscellaneous

- terry towel, cheesecloth or rag
- natural sea sponge
- blue tape
- gray watercolor pencil
- clear grid ruler and bubble level
- oiled stencil card or posterboard
- craft knife
- repositionable spray adhesive

This picture shows the completed capital, column and base. You can use this kind of creative construction to create many large but simple architectural elements for your murals.

1 Create glazes by mixing the marble colors separately with Aquaglaze at a ratio of 1:1. Apply glazes in the center of the exposed area in diagonal drifts, using either a chip brush or foam brush. Try to avoid creating a uniform striped effect; instead, lay in drifts that have a similar direction but create areas of differing shapes and volumes. Note: It is easier to create varied shapes if you lay the brush in sideways (as shown) instead of holding it perpendicular to the surface. Leave about 20 percent of the surface uncovered in the same directional, uneven shapes. These will become your negative space.

2 Use your blending tool (terry towel, cheesecloth or painter's rag) to break up the edges of the glaze, blending the colors slightly. Walk the glaze out toward the edges of the stencil with a side-to-side pushing and padding motion.

3 Hit randomly with a dampened sea sponge to blend further and create stonelike textured areas.

4 Use the pointed wooden end of the chip brush to remove the glaze and create a negative veining pattern. Vary your pressure and the angle of the brush to create a more natural appearance to the veins. Place these sparingly and allow them to follow obvious patterns that have already been created with the application of the various glaze colors.

5 With marble, especially, it is very important to soften the glazes well and often to promote the appearance that the color and texture are embedded in the surface. You will want to blend out all traces of your method of application. Any large, soft, natural bristle brush will do the trick for this technique.

6 Use an artist's no. 4 round brush and the Medium Gray glaze to add positive veins. Use a light touch and a rather jerky turning and twisting motion with the brush so that there are thinner and thicker areas, and even some spots that the brush skips. Avoid creating any straight lines.

7 Don't forget to soften!

8 This picture shows the capital after the stenciling/shading details have been completed. The column area below was originally created by measuring and taping off the desired area with a bubble level and ruler and creating the marble effect inside. Now the tape has been replaced to complete the shading, using Medium Gray.

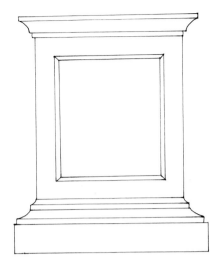

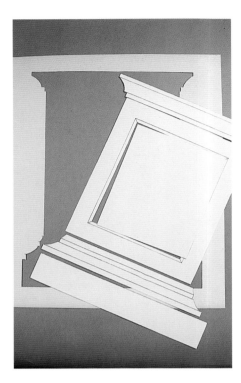

10 Cut the entire silhouette of the design. You can cut it down further into pieces to use for stenciling the edges. Most importantly, cut out the center panel for use in shading.

9 Use the stencil pattern on page 300 for the pedestal. An easy way to transfer and cut a simple pattern is to make a photocopy of it and affix it to the stencil material with spray adhesive. This eliminates the need for tracing and, in the end, is more accurate as well.

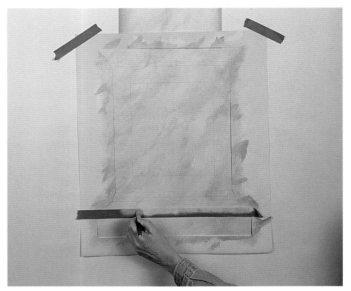

11 After base-painting the marbleous finish, transfer the lines using the stencils, ruler and a gray watercolor pencil.

12 The bottom portion of the base is shaded differently than the top. Some of these edges will be highlights painted with Vanilla Cream rather than shadows, because they will be in direct line of the light source. Rather than running the tape and shading below, highlight just above using that same stenciling/shading technique.

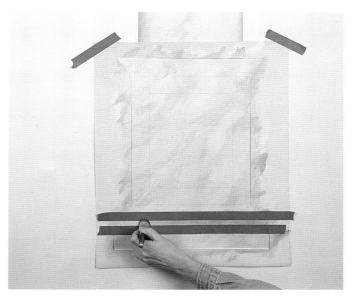

13 To differentiate the separate planes of the molding, tape off both tops and bottoms of those sections and stencil in a solid block of translucent color.

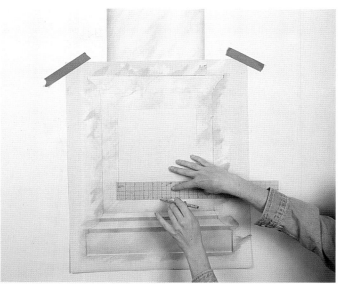

14 Measure and mark a line ¼" (6mm) out from the inner panel of the base. Here, I have simply used the spray adhesive to secure the fallout of that section.

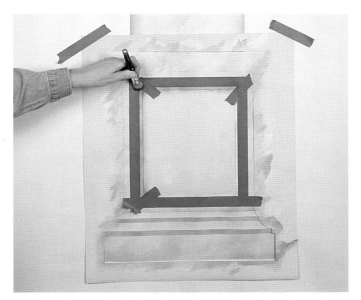

15 Add a stenciled shadow along the top and left side edge, and a highlight on the bottom and right. Note how I have defined the corners by shielding with tape and creating more contrast.

16 Run tape or replace that cutout portion of the stencil to shade around the edges of the panel, furthering the illusion that it is recessed from the light source.

VELVET BROCADE DRAPERY

Evoke a sense of luxury and refinement by adding draped velvet around a doorway or window. Drapery treatments are easily basecoated with stencil rollers, and the painting/shading technique used with the stenciled edge makes this a simple way to create the illusion of folds of fabric.

Many stencil design companies offer elegant drapery treatments, or you can create your own by enlarging or projecting a photograph of a drapery treatment that you like from a home magazine or catalog. Most designs will involve only a two- or three-overlay stencil.

The key to this velvet technique is the use of sumptuous, rich color and even, blended, gradual shading that contours to the large, soft folds of the heavy velvet fabric. Using an allover brocade or damask pattern stencil is an easy way to add pattern and texture, and to customize the look.

SUPPLIES NEEDED

Stencils

- Large Drape stencil from The Mad Stencilist
- Small Allover Brocade stencil from Royal Design Studio

Paints and Glazes

- FolkArt acrylics
  Burnt Umber
  Huckleberry
  Licorice
  Metallic Inca Gold
  Metallic Rich Gold
  Vanilla Cream
  Yellow Ochre
- FolkArt Extender

Brushes/Miscellaneous

- assorted stencil brushes
- 4" foam roller and tray
- blue tape
- repositionable spray adhesive

Note the difference that some simple shading techniques created in the finished swag compared to the picture on page 229, lower left.

1 Using a 4" (10cm) foam roller, basecoat all overlays of the design with Huckleberry. Apply two coats for opaque coverage; dry thoroughly between coats. Use repositionable spray adhesive for more stability with larger stencils. I also like to go back with a large stencil brush and stencil/paint along the edges of the design to ensure a clean, crisp print.

2 After all overlays are basecoated, reposition each overlay one at a time for the stenciled pattern treatment. This can be done with a stencil brush or a roller.

3 For the stenciled brocade, mix two parts Huckleberry with one part Yellow Ochre and one part Metallic Inca Gold for a tone-on-tone effect. A little gold in the paint mix will create a little more subtle luminosity for the stenciled pattern without becoming garish or overwhelming.

This picture shows the completed brocade pattern with some of the shading and highlighting underway. The arrow in the upper left indicates the direction of the light source.

 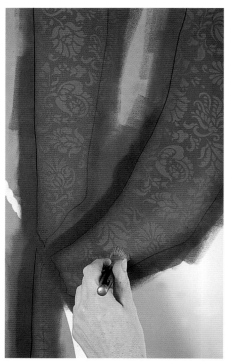 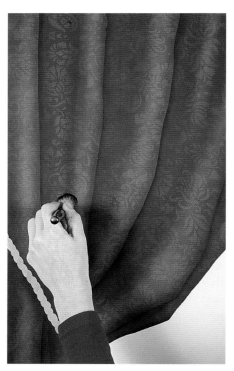

4 This detail focuses on different depths of shading used on the opposite sides of the folds. On the left side, the fold is disappearing under another fold of fabric and is opposite the light source. This fold should receive the deepest shading with a combination of Burnt Umber and Licorice. On the right side of the fold, the fabric is rolling back under itself. Since that area will not be as shielded from the light as the other, you will still want to shade it (lighter with Burnt Umber only) to simulate a soft rounded area that is receding from view.

5 Highlights are added on the tops of the folds by using one part Huckleberry to four parts Yellow Ochre. The same tight, smooth, circular stenciling motion is used, but rather than building color along the edge, you are freehanding it, so to speak, in the body of the cutaway portion of the stencil.

6 The same technique is used with Burnt Umber to create a soft shadow next to the highlight to create contrast and some soft forward and backward movement within the folds of the fabric.

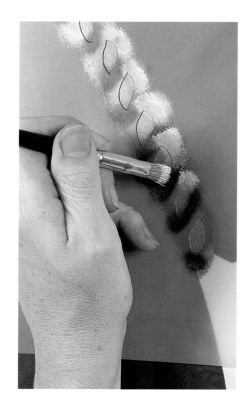

7 After a solid base-coating with Metallic Rich Gold, shadows are added on the underneath edges of the twisted cord with Licorice, with Vanilla Cream highlights painted opposite them on the top edge of the cord.

BAMBOO AND BASKETRY

Add an exotic touch to your murals with this easy technique for simulating bamboo. There are precut stencils available for a variety of styles of bamboo furniture and accessories, as well as live free-form bamboo to place in tropical mural settings. As with all of the techniques in this book, it is attention to the small, sometimes very simple, details that creates a believable texture and illusion.

Baskets are a very popular theme with stencil designers and many different shapes and sizes are available as precut stencils. One of the keys to creating interesting and successful murals is using varied textures. Many stencil artists mistakenly rely on the use of colors to represent different objects and elements within a mural. This project really demonstrates how effectively the addition of a few quick swipes with a ratty, old brush can bring an object to life.

SUPPLIES NEEDED

Stencils

- Bamboo Table and Orchid stencils from L.A. Stencilworks

Paints and Glazes

- FolkArt acrylics (bamboo table)
  Burnt Umber
  Buttercream
  Buttercrunch
  Caramel
  Coffee Bean
  Honeycomb
  Yellow Ochre
- FolkArt Extender

Brushes/Miscellaneous

- assorted stencil brushes
- rake brush
- no. 4 round (cut the bristles of an inexpensive brush at uneven lengths with scissors)
- 2" (5cm) chip brush
- blue tape
- palette or foam plate

Here's an overall view of both the bamboo table and basket of orchids.

A NOTE ON COLORS

Although they are not specifically part of this project, these are the colors I used to make the orchid and basket.

- FolkArt acrylics (orchid): Ballet Pink, Burnt Umber, Lemonade, Olive Green, Raspberry Sherbet, Rose Pink, Spring Green, Wrought Iron
- FolkArt acrylics (basket): Brown Sugar, Burnt Umber, Licorice, Teddy Bear Brown, Warm White

1 Basecoat entire table design solidly with Buttercrunch. While this demonstration focuses on one overlay only, each overlay will be replaced, one at a time, and the texture detail added before any shading begins.

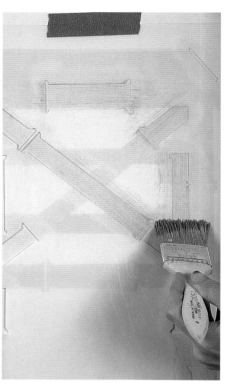

2 Put some Yellow Ochre out on a palette or foam tray. Dip chip brush in water and pull some paint out, dragging across the tray and through the brush to load it slightly with the thinned color. Drag the brush lightly through all of the cane openings, following the long direction of the canes. A light touch will keep the paint from going under the stencil and will produce thin scratchy, irregular lines.

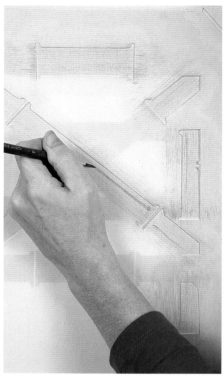

3 Use Honeycomb (thinned 2:1 with water) and a no. 4 round brush to create some long slashed lines in some of the canes. These indicate the areas where the bamboo fronds were stripped from the canes after harvesting.

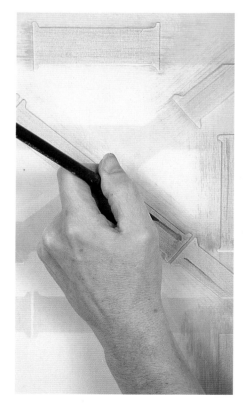

4 Use Caramel and a no. 4 round brush to create a thin shadow line on the edges of the slashed lines away from the light source.

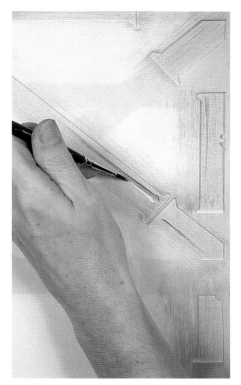

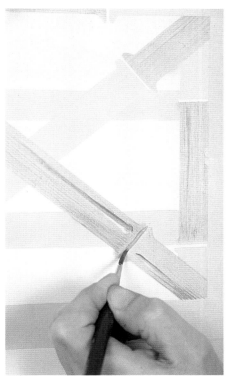

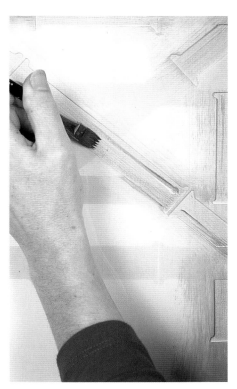

5 Using the no. 4 round brush again, apply highlights on the opposite sides with Buttercream.

6 Because this stencil design leaves unpainted gaps between the canes, I have painted this in with Honeycomb and a no. 4 round brush to add to the overall handpainted look.

7 Additional texture can be added over the lines created with the chip brush by using a smaller rake brush and thinned Honeycomb (2:1 with water) to create more depth and interest.

8 This picture shows the texturing completed on each overlay. Because the shading and highlighting that follows is done with thinned, transparent paint, the texture will show through. You will always want to complete your texturing steps completely before shading. The texture is on the surface and will be affected by light and shadow in the same way as the object as a whole.

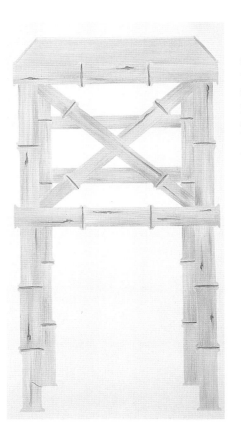

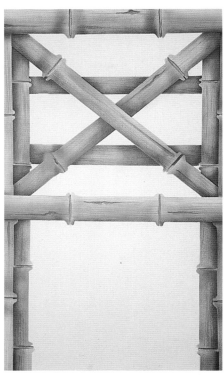

9 The shading is completed with Caramel to create the rounded effect of the canes, and a mixture of Coffee Bean and Burnt Umber to create the contrast shadows that separate the elements and add depth to the painting. Use a ¾" (2cm) stencil brush for all shading.

10 This detail emphasizes the importance of properly applied shading where there are so many overlapping elements. Each element that is overlapped by something in the foreground must be shaded darker at the overlapping point to place it behind visually.

11 In this second detail, notice how I have used the freehand stencil shading to create a soft shadow under the areas where the canes bump out at their ends.

This project is near completion. I have left the basket portion of the design for this demonstration with only the basecoat of Brown Sugar completed and ready for its texture treatment.

12 Use your uneven no. 4 round brush to add some texture detail here and there along the woven wicker, following the direction of the weave, of course.

13 Repeat.

14 For more control over where the texture is applied, replace the stencil overlays. This will allow you to texture the top and bottom edges of the wicker without the chance of applying paint in the wrong places.

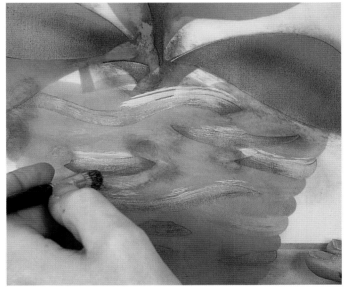

15 Once the texturing is complete, apply shading details. As usual, you will want to shade darker on the sides of the elements that are blocked from the light source and where overlapping occurs.

HEAVY METAL

Ironwork is used extensively in Mediter-ranean and Mexican types of architecture and design and you will find stencils avail-able for iron sconces, shelves, fencing, grillwork and decorative items such as this candlestick.

This technique creates a heavy, dra-matic look and is best suited to use with bold, dramatic colors in murals such as deep warm golds, reds and rusts.

SUPPLIES NEEDED

Stencils

• Italian Candlestick stencil from L.A. Stencilworks

Paints

• FolkArt Acrylics
Gray Mist
Licorice
Light Gray
Maple Syrup
Persimmon
Wrought Iron

Brushes/Miscellaneous

• assorted stencil brushes

• four small natural sponges

• blue tape

Stencils are available for decorative iron-work, such as this completed candlestick.

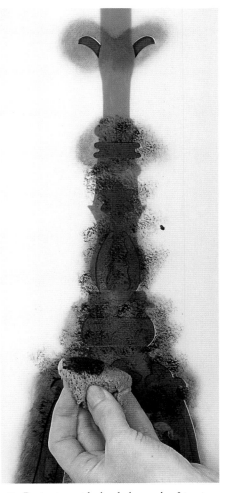

1 With a 1" (3cm) stencil brush, apply a solid basecoat to the entire design with Wrought Iron.

2 For fine texturing on metal, use smaller natural sponges to apply the following unthinned paint colors randomly. These sponges have a more delicate texture than the larger sea sponges, with fine holes throughout and are easier to control and manipulate. Use one for each color.

3 Beginning with the darkest color, Licorice, apply random texture throughout the design, leaving a lot of open space. Be sure to off-load excess paint from the sponge onto paper toweling before applying to your stencil!

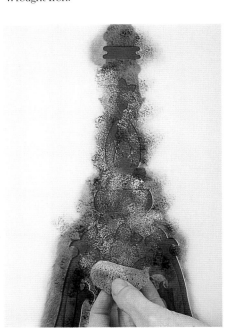

4 Now apply the Light Gray in the same manner. Try to vary the amounts of all of the colors in the separate portions of the design so as not to create the look of a pattern.

5 Continue with the Maple Syrup. Notice that each sponge creates a slightly different type of print. Don't forget to keep changing the direction of your hand to avoid repetition of prints.

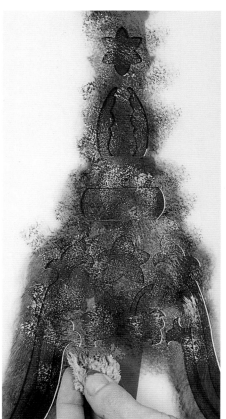

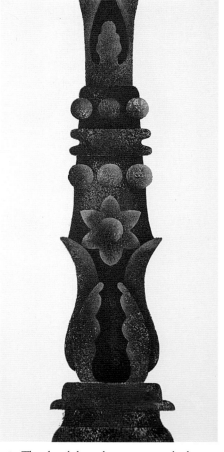

6 Apply the Persimmon last, selectively. This is a very strong color, and you will want to keep it to a minimum.

7 Once the texturing is complete on all overlays, replace the stencils and define the form with a careful studied use of highlights and shadows. Use a ⅜" (1cm) stencil brush to stencil Licorice for the shadows and Gray Mist for the highlights. Add extender to the shading colors for easier blending.

8 This detail shows how creating a highlighted contrast effectively catches the eye and pulls those areas toward the viewer. Keep your highlights and shadows just along the edges of small cutout areas of the stencil.

FAUX BOIS

The centuries-old art of reproducing various types of fine woods with paint is known as *faux bois*, which is French for "fake wood." Traditionally executed using multiple layers of rich oil glazes and expensive tools and softening brushes, it is truly an art form in the hands of master artisans.

For the purposes of providing the look of wood graining in a quick and easy fashion, I have included a technique I like to call *faux faux bois*, or *faux bois* light. You can use this technique for painting wooden beams, doors and furniture in your murals.

SUPPLIES NEEDED

Paints and Glazes
- FolkArt acrylics
    Yellow Ochre (basecoat)
- FolkArt Pure Pigment Colors (glazing)
    Asphaltum
    Raw Sienna
    Raw Umber
- AquaCreme

Brushes
- two 3" (8cm) chip brushes
- 2" (5cm) chip brush
- 3" (8cm) foam roller
- no. 10 round
- softening brush

This faux bois section was completed in only a matter of minutes and is a very believable representation of wood graining.

1 Basecoat the entire area to be painted with a solid application of Yellow Ochre using a 3" (8cm) foam roller. Mix two separate glaze colors. The lighter color will be a 1:1 mix of Asphaltum and Raw Umber and the other will be Raw Sienna. To one part pigment, add three parts AquaCreme glazing medium. Using a 3" (8cm) chip brush, apply the lighter glaze color to the surface first using long, vertical strokes, creating a random stripe effect.

2 Using another chipbrush, fill in and overlap the unpainted areas with the darker glaze, blending and softening the edges where the two colors meet by continually dragging the brush through them. It is preferable to have some unevenness of color depth, as visible in the top portion of the picture.

3 After the surface has been coated and blended, begin adding some detail and interest to the woodgrain in the form of knots. Use a clean 2" (5cm) chip brush to pull through the glaze. Begin by pulling a thinner line by holding the brush so that just the edge of the brush is being dragged vertically through the glaze.

4 Using a continuous motion, turn the brush as you are pulling so that the bristles flatten out more on the surface as you pull the brush around an imaginary knot in the wood.

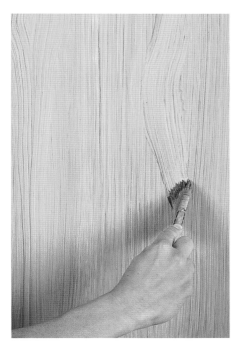 

5 Revert to the original position of the brush as you complete the stroke. Repeat the same procedure as a mirror image (identical, but reversed) on the other side of the knot.

6 To further establish the knot, bring the brush back down the middle, executing a U-turn around the knot.

7 A more detailed option is to then pull the brush through the glaze using a skipping, side-to-side motion, which will create subtly wavy lines in the grain. Soften everything lightly with a softening brush.

8 Use a no. 10 round brush and the darker glaze mixture to create more contrast and definition around the knots and here and there throughout the grain. Soften.

chapter five

COMPOSITION, COLOR AND PERSPECTIVE

We have already focused on creating depth and dimension in single stenciled forms and objects in chapter two, and studied the creation of textural illusions in depth in chapter four.

Much of the remainder of this book shows various stenciled mural projects to further illustrate a variety of techniques and applications that can be used as building blocks for creating trompe l'oeil stenciled murals. Each one is an important lesson unto itself, and although each one is presented with a different and singular project, it is the appropriate application of any or all of these techniques and principles to each mural that you paint that will result in a higher level of artistic success.

Besides presenting a variety of easy step-by-step murals you can re-create for yourself, my goal with this book is to provide you with the inspiration, confidence and techniques to create unique, one-of-a-kind pieces of mural art of your own design, from your own imagination, for your own specific purposes. In order to do that successfully, you need to be aware of some general rules for good design and composition. While planning your composition and executing your mural, there some basic principles of organization that you should keep in mind: balance, harmony and variety, movement, dominance and, of course, contrast.

There is space in this book only for a brief overview of these important principles. For more in-depth study I highly recommend taking drawing and design classes through a local resource such as adult education, community college or studio classes. There are also some listings in the resource section on page 302 that you may find valuable.

This Stone Cottage mural illustrates how various aspects discussed in this chapter work together to create a pleasing composition. Every aspect is deliberate, even the placement of the daisy on the shelf, since it leads the eye back down to the flower bed along the bottom of the picture.

Composition

As a mural designer and painter you have no real limitations on the variety of subject matter and the type of composition that you choose to paint, other than that of size and scale, which will be determined by your site. You may be creating a composition for an entire room, a single wall or a small shelf. Once your working area is determined, you may choose your subjects and arrange and manipulate them at will.

The key to success is in organizing your composition and subject matter to the best advantage. You will want to create a pleasing, harmonious and believable arrangement and illusion that will interest your viewers, draw them in and lead their eyes through your mural.

SYMMETRICAL BALANCE

The simplest way to achieve balance in a composition is through symmetry. If you imagine a vertical line running through the middle of your mural with identical objects (or sizes of objects) equally distributed on either side, you will have achieved symmetry, and balance along with it.

ASYMMETRICAL BALANCE

Asymmetrical balance involves creating a felt equilibrium between all parts of the composition. Balance can be achieved not only by an even distribution of the weight and size of objects but also by balancing such things as a small area of strong color with a large area of empty space. Because there are no set rules to dictate asymmetrical balance, the artist must feel, judge and estimate the ways that the various elements and their arrangements will balance each other in the total composition.

HARMONY AND VARIETY

You can create harmony in a composition by introducing repetition and rhythm. Repetition and rhythm are inseparable because rhythm is actually the end result of repetition. Repetition of forms is an easy way to unify a mural. Some classic examples of this in mural work are the repetition of architectural elements, such as columns and balustrades, and the repetition of landscape elements, such as similar types of trees and flowers, or even repetition of shapes and colors.

Variety is the counterweight of harmony and provides the other side of organization that is essential to unity. While repetition of forms helps to bind the picture together as a whole, variety adds essential interest to the total work. For instance, a balustrade or the repetition of fence posts creates rhythm and unity in a mural. It is the introduction of an element with a contrasting line, shape or color against that pattern that grabs and holds the attention of the viewer.

MOVEMENT

Movement in a composition is what visually binds the various elements of a mural together and helps to draw the viewer's eye through the picture. You can achieve this by directing lines and shapes toward each other in a way that keeps the viewer's eyes moving in a self-renewing way. In other words, you want to keep bringing the focus back into the mural, not out of it. Foliage and trailing vines are an easy and obvious tool for this. Rather than creating a vine that shoots off and out of the picture frame and takes your viewer along with it, you can plan the direction of growth so that it visually leads one's eyes to another element in the mural.

DOMINANCE

In mural work, a sense of dominance is generally created by making an object or group of objects into a focal point. This is usually the foreground object that the viewer's eye is initially drawn to and represents the most important element in the mural. If each object is given similar or equal importance in the composition, the lack of contrast that is created will provide a confusing image that gives no direction to the viewer.

CONTRAST

Our eyes are naturally drawn to contrast, and contrast should be used as an aid to creating dominant focal points. Contrast comes in many forms in the composition of a mural: Contrasts of sizes, shapes, values, colors, textures and directions of lines are all key to creating interesting and exciting visual images.

Symmetry — Limestone Niche

This is a good example of symmetry, even though there is some difference between the left and right side of the bromeliad (just enough to add interest). Symmetry makes for a very pleasing and balanced arrangement that is easy to design and execute.

Asymmetry — Lattice Window

This is an asymmetrical arrangement set against a unifying backdrop element, the lattice. The strength of the orchid in the basket is well-balanced by the more delicate bougainvillaea, primarily because of the intensity of their color. The ferns along the bottom, like the lattice, provide a unifying element.

Movement — Romantic Window

The dynamics and movement created by the direction of the trailing foliage in this mural ensures the viewer's eye will keep moving throughout the composition in a circular, self-renewing way.

Dominance — By-the-Sea

Even though there is not a lot to look at in this composition, the shells sitting on the ledge are made to be the most important element because of their dominance in the mural. The fact that they are placed in the foreground in a still-life arrangement and are painted with the greatest amount of value contrast makes them the first thing to catch the eye.

Contrast — Round Brick Window

The contrast that is created by the dark bars against the distant landscape and the red bricks brings your eye directly to the foreground of the picture, which is exactly where the artist wants it to be. Likewise, the contrast of the purple/blue flowers on the red brick holds our attention there as you follow the graceful curves of the twining vine with your eyes.

Color Basics

USING COLOR

Color is the one element of composition and painting to which we are most sensitive, the one that touches our emotions and arouses our senses. A pleasing use of color is essential. You may be trying to create a serene, elegant mood through the use of cool neutrals, or an exciting and dynamic composition full of vibrant color. Whatever the case, some basic understanding of the general principles of color theory will prove helpful.

HUE

Hue is the property or characteristic of a color that refers to its position on the color wheel. It refers to the color name, such as yellow or green.

VALUE (OR TONE)

Value refers to the lightness or darkness of colors, or the quantity of light that a color reflects. To change the value of a color, you must mix it with another pigment that is darker or lighter in character. Note: The only pigments that will change the value of a color without altering the hue are black and white.

INTENSITY

While value refers to the quantity of light that a color reflects, intensity refers to the quality of light in a color. The intensity of a color, or hue, can be bright and saturated or dull, grayed and neutralized.

TEMPERATURE

Color temperatures fall into one of two groups: warm colors and cool colors. Red, orange and yellow, the colors of fire and the sun, are considered warm colors, while blue, green and violet, the colors of the sky and water, are cool. The temperature of a specific color can be made warmer with the addition of a warm color or cooler with the addition of a cool color.

Quote From a Pro
from Susie Wolfe, CDA
Color Theory Expert and Educator

Adding a small amount of the same color to all of the colors in your palette is called adding a "mother color." This will harmonize all the colors in your mural. This "mother color" could be gray, an earthtone or any neutral color.

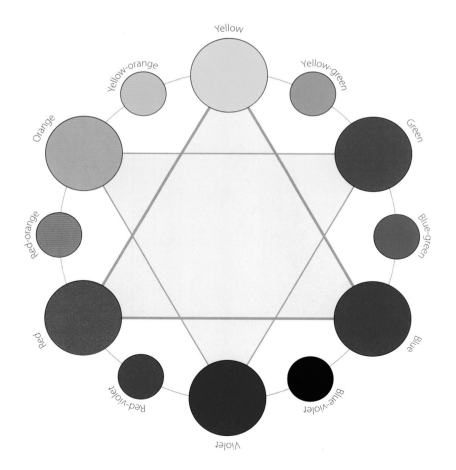

Creating More Depth in Your Murals

SIZE

Size is simple to depict. The farther away an object in the mural is from the viewer (i.e. the closer to the horizon line), the smaller it appears. To effectively represent great depth and distance in a stenciled mural, it is important to include objects of different scales and to have them positioned correctly in the picture plane according to their sizes.

COLOR

As a general rule, objects in the distance are duller and those that are closer to the viewer appear more vivid in color and intensity. This is due to atmospheric conditions. When painting areas and objects that are near the horizon line, and therefore more distant, use more toned-down or grayed colors. As you move forward in the composition, objects should be more colorful, so choose brighter, warmer greens for shrubbery, more vivid colors for flowers, and brighter blues for water in the foreground.

CLARITY

The same atmospheric conditions that affect color also affect clarity. Objects in your mural that are placed in the foreground, close to the viewer, should be painted in greater detail and more intense colors. Objects that are placed farther away, in the middle and background, will be less distinct. Their colors will be closer in value and painted with less contrast.

CONTRAST

Areas of lower contrast will recede into space. High contrast between values creates crisp, well-defined edges that appear to come forward in space. Painting areas in your murals with a variety of different values is a sure way to add depth to your work. Closely related values naturally recede, so they should be used for distant objects and landscapes. Also note that painting with closely related values makes edges, even stenciled edges, appear softer. Using a heavy contrast in values attracts the eye and brings an object or area to the front, so use the most intense contrast in values in the foreground of your painting.

TEMPERATURE

In general, cool colors seem to recede while warm colors seem to advance. In the case of trees and shrubbery, for instance, using duller and cooler shades of green for the background foliage will help to keep it in the distance. Adding more warmth to your foliage, that is, adding yellow to the green, will help bring greenery forward.

A NOTE ON DEPTH

Imagine the difference between a sharp focus in the foreground and soft, blurry focus in the background. As images become more distant from us, we notice less intensity of color, less value contrast, softer edges and the smaller scale.

Perspective

The dictionary defines perspective as "a technique of depicting volumes and spatial relationships on a flat surface," and also "the manner in which objects appear to the eye in respect to their relative positions and distance." A detailed study of perspective and its wide range of mechanical rules would be impossible and impractical in this book. We will limit our investigation and use to simple one-point linear perspective, two-point perspective and aerial perspective. For more in-depth study, there are several good books listed in the resource section.

LINEAR PERSPECTIVE
Linear perspective involves a system for representing depth by means of converging lines at a point, or points, on the horizon. It is a system of representation that was developed at the time of the European Renaissance as an aid toward representing the appearance of reality.

AERIAL PERSPECTIVE
Aerial perspective relies on the fact that as objects recede into the distance, there is a reduction in color intensity and clarity. Consequently, you can use both color and clarity as tools to easily create a sense of depth in your stenciled murals, to push objects back and to help reduce the flat look that is all too common.

TWO-POINT PERSPECTIVE
Two-point perspective is used for creating open windows, gates and doors. While there are a variety of precut stencils available that feature these elements, they may not fit your particular design needs and measurements. With some simple measuring and planning and the use of tape as your edge, you can easily create an open window or door to represent any angle or point of view.

POINT OF VIEW
While stencils are very useful for easily painting and shading elements, they do have one drawback for use in mural work: They are designed and cut to represent only one view, one perspective. It is not a matter of simply redrawing a line, as in freehand painting, so you must be careful to correctly position the stenciled object in the mural according to the point of view that it represents.

A good example is a stencil of a clay pot. If a clay pot is placed below our eye level, we will be able to see inside it, and to see that it is, in essence, a cylinder. It will be represented to us as rounded on the top and bottom. The closer we are to the pot, the more we will be able to see the inside surface. If the clay pot is placed at our eye level, the roundness at the top and bottom will be represented as straight horizontal lines, and we will see only the outer surface of the pot. If it is placed at a point above our eye level, the top edge will be represented as a curved surface, only the curve will arch up. We will not be able to view any of the interior surface of the pot. In fact, if it were not resting on something, we would actually be able to see the bottom of it.

SCALE
As objects recede from our view they appear to become smaller. Therefore objects that are placed near the horizon line (the greatest distance from the viewer) need to be proportionally scaled down from the objects that are placed in the foreground. To help understand this concept better, it is helpful to look at a perspective floor grid. Richard Tober of A Matter of Perception has created a step-by-step model on the opposite page. You can follow the steps to create a grid for any mural project to assist you in determining the scale and placement of design elements in your mural, and/or you can use this grid technique to plot out tile and floor designs for your murals.

The perspective floor grid is also the beginning step for creating perspectively correct open doors, windows and gates and will be used later in the By-the-Sea mural.

HOW TO CREATE A PERSPECTIVE FLOOR GRID

1. Select a horizon line, usually located at eye level. We selected 40" from the floor.
2. Select a vanishing point on the horizon line (the point at which all parallel lines converge). Attach a string to the VP.
3. Measure and mark the floor tile widths at the bottom of the grid; these tiles should be equal.
4. Stretch the string from the VP to the tile points, mark dashes with a watercolor pencil and use a straightedge to draw in the converging lines.
5. The floor grid consists of square units. Select a tile depth that is about half of the tile width; this creates a three-dimensional effect.
6. Using a straightedge, intersect the first floor tile on the diagonal and mark where the straightedge intersects with each parallel line. This tells you how small the tiles become as they recede into the background.
7. Use a level to draw in each of the tile depth lines.

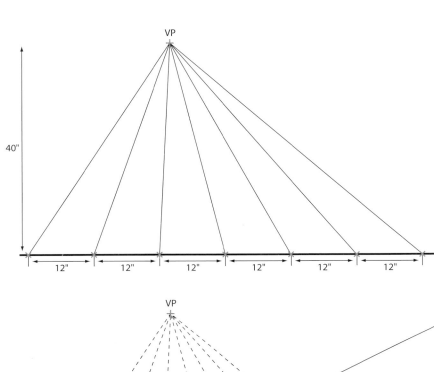

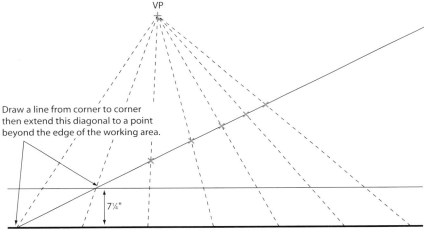

Draw a line from corner to corner then extend this diagonal to a point beyond the edge of the working area.

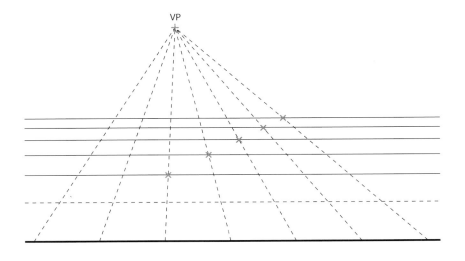

Tips From a Pro
from Andrea Tober,
A Matter of Perception

• Placement of the vanishing point (VP) is the single most important step in mural design. The VP determines the proper angles of your oblique lines and helps you determine sizes of objects placed within the mural. Improper placement can cause a mural to look askew.

• The perspective floor grid is the second most important step in design because it is used to place mural elements with correct perspective sizes and orientations.

• Once you select the horizon line, don't change it. Likewise, once the VP has been established, don't move it.

SKYSCAPE

Any mural that incorporates an outdoor scene will also naturally include a sky, and there are many variations on techniques for creating interesting skies with paint and glazes. Sunrise, sunset and moody or stormy skies can be very dramatic and colorful and create quite a focal point. In landscape painting, for instance, oftentimes the sky is the most important element in the picture and can be painted with great detail.

In most stenciled murals, however, the sky is merely a part of the background, a backdrop for the more detailed elements that make up the mural. In most instances, you will want to keep your sky fairly simple and unassuming, but a very interesting and believable effect can be achieved simply by fading color with softened glazes, and using small sponges to create layers of soft clouds.

As always, it is easier to paint something believable if you have a visual reference to go by, so gather a collection of pictures of skies that you can use as a starting point. Differing atmospheric conditions produce a wide variety of possible cloud formations. The skyscapes in this book feature what I consider to be classic clouds. They are the soft, puffy, cumulus variety that come to most people's minds when they think of idyllic summer days, and so they create a very recognizable and acceptable backdrop.

All of the skies that are featured in the murals in this book are painted with the same easy and effective technique.

SUPPLIES NEEDED

Paints and Glazes

- Benjamin Moore Flat Interior Latex
  Harbor Fog
- FolkArt acrylics
  Barnwood
  Ultramarine Blue
  Wicker White
  (optional colors: Bayberry, Potpourri Rose
  and Purple Lilac)
- AquaGlaze

Brushes/Miscellaneous

- higher-quality 3" (8cm) nylon paintbrush
- softening brush
- small natural artist's sea wool sponge
- large natural sea sponge
- spray bottle (optional)

This completed skyscape shows the finished clouds. Note the variety of depth and shape and also that the clouds become smaller and less distinct as they near the horizon line, simulating a greater distance from the viewer on Earth.

1 Basecoat the sky area with a solid, even coat of Harbor Fog. For this technique, you will need to work fairly quickly in the next step. The idea is to get a uniform, blended effect while pulling soft cloud shapes out of the wet glaze with a dampened sea sponge. For small, limited areas, such as in window murals, this should not be a problem. If you are working on a large mural with a large expanse of sky, you may want to ensure some more working time by wetting the wall with a 1:1 mixture of water and glazing medium. This can be applied easily with a spray bottle. Because you are now working wet-on-wet, you will have more time to manipulate, blend and soften the glaze over a large surface.

Note: Because of the additional layer of glaze, it will take longer for your sky area to dry and cure. Wait until it is completely dry before attempting any additional painting work over the area.

2 Blend Ultramarine Blue with Harbor Fog to deepen the color. Mix a washy latex glaze with one part Harbor Fog–Ultramarine Blue blend to four parts glazing medium. To that mixture, add 10 percent water. Beginning at the top of the surface, apply the wash with a foam roller or higher-quality paintbrush using long horizontal strokes.

3 In nature, the color of the sky will appear to lighten and become less intense as it nears the horizon line. This is caused by the fact that we are viewing it through the layer of heavier, hazy atmosphere that is closest to the Earth. To replicate that effect, feather your glaze out more thinly with the brush as it nears the horizon line. You may even go back to the top, while it's still wet, and add an additional layer of blue to deepen it there.

4 Working quickly while the glaze is still very wet, use a dampened sea sponge to push out soft cloud shapes. Basically, you are opening up the darker blue glaze back to the lighter blue background. The soft contrast between the colors creates the diffused, subtle look of the background clouds. Pushing more forcefully with the sponge here and there will create a variety of depth in the cloud colors even at this early stage in the process.

Note: The bottom edges of the clouds should appear to run horizontally, parallel to the surface of the Earth. The billowing occurs on the top edges of the clouds, extending into the atmosphere.

5 As you work over the surface with the sponge, immediately soften the edges of the clouds by brushing very lightly with a softening brush. You are really just tickling the surface with this brush so that you are just softening the top layer of the glaze, not moving it around. Vary the direction of your brushstrokes. Also soften the areas that have been just brushed in with glaze to remove the lines left by the brush. In this case, if the brush lines are running horizontally, soften by brushing vertically. I call this softening against the grain.

6 Once your background of negative clouds is dry, you can begin creating more distinct layers of positive clouds. Negative refers to the fact that you are creating an effect or shape by removing the paint/glaze. Positive refers to the fact that you are applying paint to create a shape. Use a smaller artist's sponge to apply white acrylic paint. To create a less harsh effect, I first press my sponge into some glaze medium before loading it with the acrylic. Notice that I am holding the sponge so that it rounds up at the top. Just the top portion of the rounded area has been loaded with paint so that the effect is one of a distinct print at the top of the cloud that fades into the blue at the bottom.

7 Work back to front, layering your clouds forward as you go. If your more distinct positive clouds are layered over the softer negative ones, a realistic sense of depth is achieved. You do need to be constantly aware, though, of designing your cloud shapes. They should appear flatter, with a more horizontal line on the bottom. You want a lot of variety. Do not allow your clouds to be of all the same shape and size, or to be spaced evenly apart. It is also important to not end all of your clouds at the edge of your picture frame. Create a sense that life is going on outside of your window by showing just small portions of much larger clouds at some of your edges.

8 Optionally, you can add some subtle color into your clouds by sponging in washes of thinned colors, such as Bayberry (green), Potpourri Rose (mauve) and Purple Lilac. Keep these very light and soft. Create even more dimension and realism by lightly sponging the bottoms of your clouds with a very soft warm gray, such as Barnwood. Be sure to soften any additional colors or washes that you place in your clouds with either a damp sponge or softening brush.

ROUND BRICK WINDOW

A trip to the lumber aisle in the local hardware store was the inspiration for this mural in the round. I was looking for alternative surfaces for the murals in this book, things that were readily available and easily movable. My idea was to provide mural options other than those painted directly on the wall surface, so that murals could move with their owners to different houses and apartments or from room to room. After spying these perfect circles precut from pressed particleboard, I set to work trying to figure out a suitable design for them.

A round brick opening seemed an easy and obvious choice. The bars were brought in to add another texture and element to the mural, and to provide a structural support for the morning glory vine. The addition of the decorative detail in the middle keeps it from looking like a jail window! I had a lot of fun painting it and ended up being very pleased with the uniqueness of the final result.

You could substitute stone blocks or marble for the brick for a more Mediterranean or formal look. Or, for a nautically themed room, you could use the cut round board to create a port hole!

SUPPLIES NEEDED

Stencils and Patterns

- Morning Glories, Victorian Grille and Foliage stencils from Royal Design Studio

Paints and Glazes

- Benjamin Moore Flat Interior Latex Harbor Fog

- white waterbased primer (suitable for wood)

- FolkArt acrylics
  Aspen Green (background, trees)
  Basil Green (foreground, trees)
  Bayberry (foreground, trees)
  Bluegrass (background)
  Buttercup (trees)
  Cinnamon (grille)
  Clover (morning glories)
  Coffee Bean (trees)
  Dark Brown (grille)
  Dark Gray (bricks)
  French Vanilla (bricks)
  Dove Gray (grille)
  Gray Plum (distant trees)
  Lavender Sachet (morning glories)
  Licorice (grille)
  Light Periwinkle (morning glories)
  Limelight (morning glories)
  Mushroom (trees)
  Plum Chiffon (morning glories)
  Raw Umber (bricks)
  Spring Green (landscape foreground)
  Wrought Iron (grille)

- FolkArt Extender

Brushes

- assorted stencil brushes
- no. 8 filbert and no. 8 round
- 1" (3cm) flat
- no. 3 script liner
- 2" (5cm) foam brush

Miscellaneous

- blue tape and ¼" (6mm) masking tape
- repositionable spray adhesive
- 4" (10cm) foam roller and tray
- small natural sea sponge
- Mylar, acetate or posterboard
- 36" (91cm) diameter circle cut from ¾" (2cm) pressed hardboard
- clear grid ruler, string, pushpins and pencil

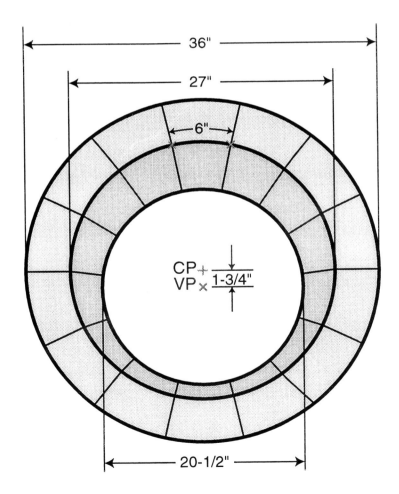

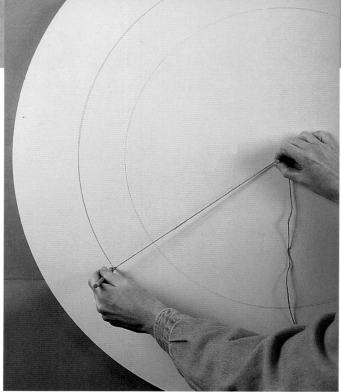

1 Basecoat front and sides of board with two to three coats of white waterbased primer. Use a 4" (10cm) foam roller for the smoothest effect. Tie a length of string around a pencil, pull it taught along a ruler or yardstick and make a mark on the string with a permanent marker at 11½" (29.2cm) and 13½" (34.3cm). Use a pushpin at the 11½" mark on the string to secure the string at the eye level mark near the center of the circle (see "VP" on pattern). Holding the pencil perpendicular to the surface, trace a complete circle. Reposition the string so that the pin intersects the 13½" mark and place the pin in the center point. Trace another line. The outer circle indicates the face of the brick, which is flush with and on the same plane as the inside wall.

2 Now that you have a reference as to where the scene will be placed in the circle, using a 2" (5cm) foam brush, base in the center area of the circle and a little beyond with Harbor Fog and paint a skyscape down to the horizon line according to the instructions on pages 250–253.

With a 1" (3cm) flat artist's brush, basecoat the foreground with a wash of Bayberry thinned with water. With a no. 8 filbert, paint a stand of distant trees using Gray Plum. Applying paint with a jerky, scrubbing motion will create diffused color and soft edges.

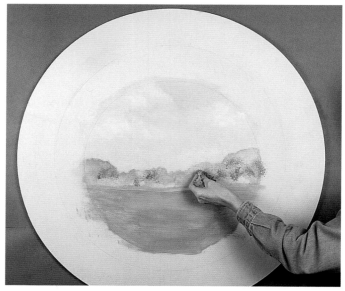

3 Repeat the same painting technique using Basil Green to create a closer group of trees. Use a small natural sponge and Aspen Green to create some subtle treetops with a varied texture.

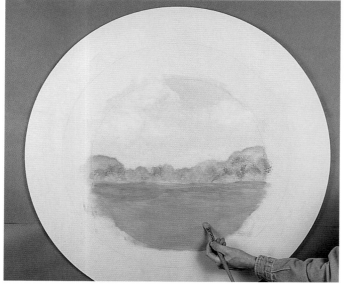

4 Create more depth in your landscape by painting in additional washes of color. Use cooler, grayer greens such as Bayberry and Bluegrass in your background, and warmer, yellow-greens such as Spring Green in the foreground. Because cool colors seem to recede and warm colors advance, this will aid in your illusion of depth.

5 Beginning with the darker Aspen Green, stencil the various shapes that will become the more distinct foliage of trees seen in the near distance. Overlap the darker areas of foliage with the lighter Bayberry and Basil Green. Using a variety of different shapes placed randomly and at different heights will ensure that each tree appears unique and natural.

6 Sketch in the basic lines of a tree in the foreground with soft charcoal. Use a different foliage pattern with the same stenciling technique to create layered groupings of leaves that extend primarily from the ends of the branches.

7 Use a no. 8 round to paint in the trunks of the trees using Mushroom. Notice that the color has been thinned to more of a wash for the distant trees, so that the lack of contrast allows them to fade more into the haze of the background. The foreground trunk is painted in a sharper focus with a deeper concentration of color and the addition of Coffee Bean for contrast.

8 More contrast, warmth and light can be brought into the foreground tree with the addition of a yellow color, Buttercup, to the top layer of foliage.

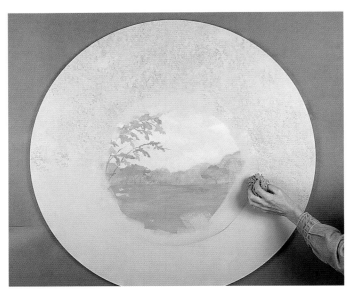

9 When the landscape is complete, shield it by cutting a circle from Mylar or posterboard to the diameter of the inner circle, 21" (53cm). Use your pencil, string and pushpin again to create a perfect circle, and secure in place with spray adhesive. This will remain in place until the entire brick texturing and shading has been completed. Basecoat the entire brick area with a light gray and sponge with a darker gray wash according to the brick instructions on pages 204–207.

10 Use your string again, from the center point, to redraw the outer circle.

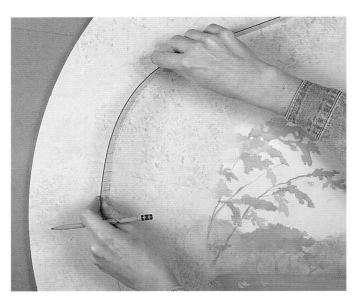

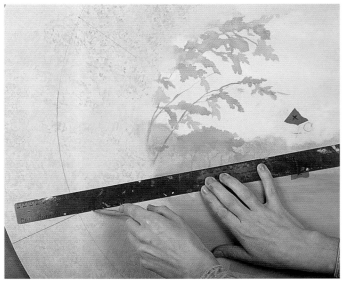

11 A flexible, clear grid ruler makes it easy to mark off 6" (15cm) increments along the circle.

12 Use a ruler to draw grout lines on the outer face of the brick that extend from the edge of the brick directly to the center point of the circle. Draw lines from the outer edge of the inside face of the brick to the eye level point, which is lower than the center point of the circle.

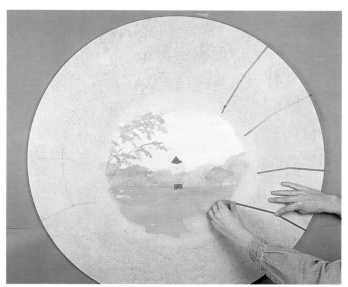

13 Use ¼" (6mm) tape to mask off the grout lines, either bending it around or cutting it and changing directions at the corner where the face of the brick changes direction. The inner circle represents the portion of the brick or block that extends through the wall space to the outside. Because of our point of view, we can see most of it, although we can see more of the top inside area because our eye level (on the horizon line) is dropped below the center. If eye level had been placed dead center, we would see an equal portion of the inside of the brick all the way around. The grout lines of the outer face of the bricks would seem to extend in straight lines through the inside face to the center point. The slight change in direction of the grout lines, which occurs by the slight adjustment of the eye level, adds a great deal to the illusion.

14 After completing the brick painting and shading techniques outlined on pages 204–207, remove the protective shield to complete the painting. Because the primary light source is coming from the outdoors and the upper left, paint a definite highlight in the inside face of the bricks using a highly thinned wash of French Vanilla.

15 Paint a translucent shadow on the remaining area of the inner face of the bricks using a mixture of Raw Umber and Dark Gray.

16 Create more contrast between the highlight and the outer face of the bricks by defining that edge with some of the shading color. Allow it to fade out to nothing from a sharp edge.

17 Use a bubble level and pencil to make plumb lines that will become the iron bars. The bars themselves are ⅜" (1cm) thick and are spaced 3¼" (8.26cm) apart, beginning in the middle of the circle. Use 1" (3cm) tape to define the straight edges, and ¼" (6mm) tape to create a curved end. The bars should be placed in the approximate center of the inside face of the bricks.

18 Basecoat the iron bars with Wrought Iron. Create additional texture according to the steps outlined in the Heavy Metal technique on pages 236–238, using a small sponge to apply random patches of Dark Brown and Cinnamon. With a ⅜" (1cm) stencil brush, shade the bars on the side opposite the light source (right) with Licorice. Highlight on the side closest to the light source (left) with Dove Gray.

19 To add some decorative detailing to the iron bars, I adapted a section of the Victorian Grille from Royal Design Studio. I created the design by using only a portion of the original and flipping it to create a mirror image. Alterations of stencils are best worked out on paper first. You can stencil out a proof, make multiple copies and cut and paste until you find an arrangement of elements that works best for your purpose. Refer to your paper proof as you stencil to easily determine which elements you want to paint and those you need to tape or shield off.

20 Sketch in a free-form vine arrangement, in this case Morning Glories from Royal Design Studio. Use a ¾" (2cm) stencil brush to basecoat the leaves with Limelight and the flowers with Lavender Sachet. Create some dimension and interest in the leaves by shading darker with Clover.

21 Notice here that the green of the leaves has been highlighted and set off from the green background with the addition of Lavender Sachet, the flower color. The flowers themselves are shaded with Plum Chiffon.

22 Use a combination of Limelight with a painted shadow of Clover to add definition to the delicate veins and vines that connect the morning glory vine using a no. 3 script liner. Define and shade the morning glory flowers with Light Periwinkle and Plum Chiffon using a ⅜" (1cm) stencil brush.

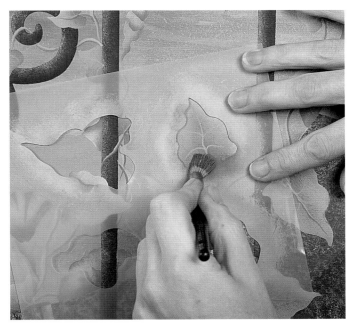

23 It is always desirable, and creates a more interesting and unified composition, if you allow your colors to travel through and reflect off each other. In this case, use the deep floral color, Plum Chiffon, in a selective way to add more realism and depth to the leaves. The addition of Clover to certain areas of the flowers will have the same positive effect on them.

24 The final touch is to handpaint cast shadows using your thinned shadow glaze of Dark Gray. As always, these shadows mimic the shapes of the objects that are casting them, and will fall in the direction that is opposite the light source.

LATTICE WINDOW

A lattice background provides a great backdrop filler that unifies the mural area while providing a means of support for a multitude of twining and vining plant options. These can grow in from the outside, providing a visual connection between the interior and exterior of the mural. The shallow shelf/ledge can be used to display a pretty plant, such as this tropical orchid and basket, providing even more color and interest to the mural.

WORKING WITH TRELLISES AND LATTICEWORK

You can use trellises and latticework to create simple but formal support structures and architectural elements that visually connect different areas of your mural. A trellis with some sort of colorful vine and flowers growing through it is a great vertical element that takes your viewer's eye up and through your mural.

Latticework, fencing and trellises can be easily executed by using tape and careful measuring, or using the large variety of precut stencils that are now available. They can be created by using either a positive method or a negative method, meaning that you will either be taping off or using a stencil to define the lattice background (positive), or taping off and shielding the lattice itself (negative).

POSITIVE LATTICEWORK

In the case of positive lattice, you will be painting your structure, usually in white or off-white, after the entire background has been completed. You can follow the measurements of real lattice and framing to plot out and tape off a multitude of lattice configurations. Tip: Getting the white paint to cover the previously painted background may require two to three coats of paint. It is always important when painting multiple coats to allow each layer of paint to dry thoroughly before repainting. If the previous layer is still slightly wet, you will run the risk of lifting the paint in those areas. Use a good-quality acrylic paint that has good coverage. White latex paint has less pigment and will take more coats, with a longer drying time between coats.

NEGATIVE LATTICEWORK

The term negative implies that we are painting the space around the actual element. That means if your latticework is white, you will need to start with a white background.

Our project involves an arched lattice opening with a negative stencil, through which we see a sky background, so the painting will be done in blue, leaving the unpainted areas to become the effect of the white lattice. The working surface is actually a shape that has been cut from ¾" (2cm) MDF (medium density fiberboard) with a router and hung like a large picture or mirror. The advantages of this are that you can move your mural around at will after it's finished, and the real dimension of the wood adds to the illusion of depth. You could paint directly on your wall surface, of course, or paint the design on PolyMural Canvas (see resource section), cut it out and mount it with wallpaper paste. If the wall surface is properly sized, you will be able to remove your mural at a later date and hang it elsewhere.

Stencils and Patterns
- Classic Garden Lattice, Bougainvillaea and Sword Ferns stencils from Royal Design Studio
- Orchid stencil from L.A. Stencilworks
- full-size blueprint of pattern available from Royal Design Studio

Paints and Glazes
- Benjamin Moore Flat Interior Latex Harbor Fog
- FolkArt acrylics (for sky and lattice) Barnwood Medium Gray Ultramarine Blue
- white waterbased primer (suitable for wood)
- AquaGlaze
- FolkArt Extender

Brushes
- assorted stencil brushes
- no. 3 script liner
- no. 8 round

Miscellaneous
- clear grid ruler and soft charcoal
- 1" (3cm), 1½" (4cm) and ¼" (6mm) blue tape
- large natural sea sponge
- terry towel or washcloth
- ¾" (2cm) medium density fiberboard cut to shape

A NOTE ON COLORS

Although they are not specifically part of this step by step project, these are the FolkArt acrylic colors I used for the orchid, basket, bougainvillaea and sword ferns.

- Orchid and basket: Ballet Pink, Brown Sugar, Burnt Umber, Lemonade, Licorice, Raspberry Sherbet, Olive, Rose Pink, Spring Green, Teddy Bear Brown, Warm White, Wrought Iron
- Bougainvillaea: Clover, Dusty Peach, Olive Green, Red Orange
- Sword ferns: Clover, Dapple Gray, Italian Sage, Thicket

1 Basecoat the MDF in a waterbased white primer. Use 1½" (4cm) tape to define the bottom and side edges of the window. This will create a frame for the lattice.

2 To accurately mark in a 1½" (3.8cm) thick arc for the top of the window, use a clear grid ruler to make little tick marks about 2" (5cm) apart and 1½" (3.8cm) from the edge. (My edge was made round by the router, so I am measuring in from the top point of the curve.)

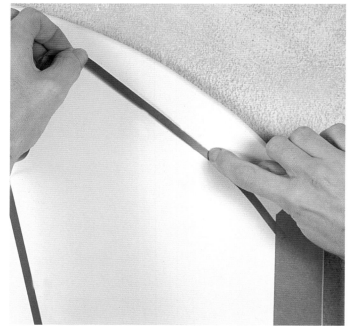

3 Stretch ¼" (6mm) tape (which curves easily because of its thinness) to connect the tick marks in a graceful arc. Add wider tape on the outer edge to further protect the surface from unwanted paint.

4 Position the lattice stencil so that it is centered in the arc and so that you will end with some crossed lattice at the point where it crosses the frame. Begin stenciling using a 1" (3cm) brush with blue glaze (Harbor Fog deepened with Ultramarine Blue acrylic, mixed 1:1 with latex glazing medium). Be sure to off-load the brush well. See the Skyscape project on page 250 for specific instructions.

5 To add some subtle depth and variation, you may want to immediately pull out some soft cloud shapes with a dampened sea sponge. Continue stenciling the lattice in all directions from the starting point, right into the edges of the taped frame.

6 Use a combination of Barnwood and Medium Gray to create a soft shadow line on the lattice with the stencil (use a ½" [1cm] or ¾" [2cm] stencil brush). This particular stencil includes an overlay for the short dashed shadow line running in one direction, and a long continuous line (like a stripe), running in the opposite direction. The "stripe" is created by moving the stencil overlay along as you go. In order not to have a hard-edged stopping and starting point, allow your color to fade out to nothing before reaching the end.

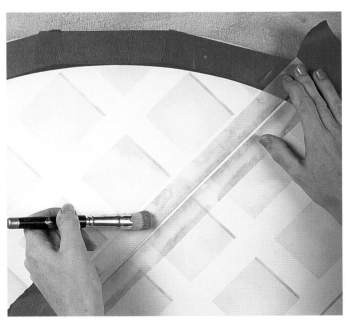

7 Move the stencil forward and pick up the stenciling where you allowed it to previously fade out to nothing. These shaded lines, or planes, indicate the narrow side edges of the lattice.

8 Use the first overlay with the cut squares positioned strategically where the lattice strips appear to cross, to shade right up into the edge with the stencil brush and Barnwood, creating a cast shadow on the underneath lattice strips.

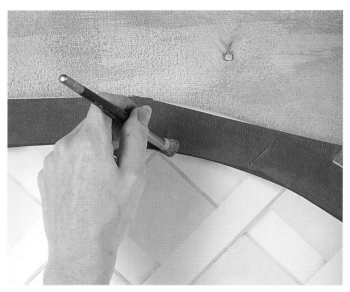

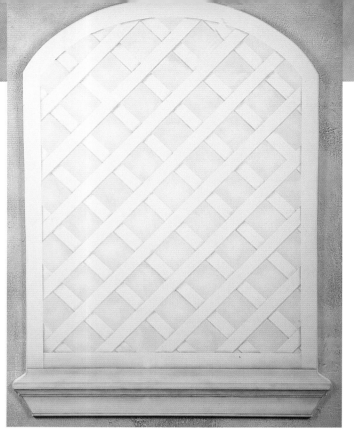

9 Shade similarly on the lattice strips where they meet up with the outer frame. Note: Don't shade the blue areas of the sky. The shadows will only occur on actual surfaces, not in the atmosphere!

10 Here is a detail of the completely shaded lattice and window ledge. The molding underneath the ledge was shaded according to the instructions outlined in chapter two for creating carved molding with tape. Weave your way through your mural. One of the really fun and easy things to do with free-form floral stencils is to manipulate them in and out and around architectural elements in a mural. It also adds more to the overall sense of depth and realism in your work as well.

11 I have used two different types of free-form stencils for this project, Sword Ferns and Bougainvillaea. Where I want my foliage to go behind the lattice I can simply protect it with pieces of tape or replace the stencil. With the stencil in place, I can use various shades of green to create layers of ferns growing outside the window.

12 To allow the ferns to come inside, remove the protective stencil or tape and paint over the lattice. In this case I am using another piece of Mylar taped in place to shield the bottom edge of the fern where it goes behind the lattice.

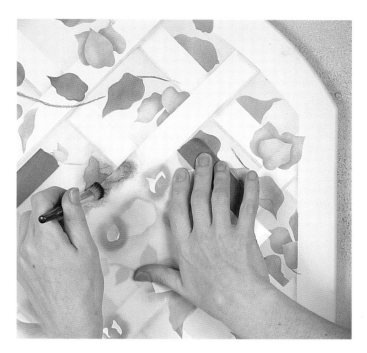

13 The free-form Bougainvillaea is painted and woven through the lattice in the same manner. The charcoal lines were sketched in first to establish the direction and form of the vines.

Where the floral design of bougainvillaea grows in front of the lattice, I have simply painted as usual. Where I want it to go behind, I have shielded the lattice portion with tape. The tape protects the areas of the lattice I want to avoid painting over, and also provides an edge against which I can build up shading contrast.

The orchid in a basket stencil from L.A. Stencilworks was the perfect element to complete the composition. See the page 263 for specific colors used.

14 Cast shadows are added with the same Barnwood–Medium Gray mix that was used to shade the lattice. Thin the color with additional extender or water to make it more translucent. Mimic the shapes of the elements onto the lattice only (not the sky).

15 When I was finished I decided that the white lattice was too clean and boring looking. I simply took the thinned shading paint and dragged it across the lattice with a terry towel, in the direction of the grain of the wood. Sometimes these subtle little extra details can make all the difference!

LIMESTONE NICHE

Creating a classical, curved niche is an effective way to create an interesting architectural feature on an otherwise blank and boring wall space. A niche is an excellent way to extend the illusion of space in tight quarters, such as a hallway or small bathroom. The fairly deep shelf offers a multitude of options for bringing in additional color and/or interest. I have chosen to include an elegant and classical pot and simple plant, but you may choose a colorful vase of flowers, a stack of books or an urn of abundant fruit, to name a few options.

This mural project is suitable for beginners because you are only concerned with portraying shallow depth and can focus on developing the strong contrasts of values that are inherent in architectural trompe l'oeil. This particular project was painted on ¾" (2cm) MDF (medium density fiberboard) that was cut from a paper pattern with a router. The dimension and thickness of the material helps to aid in the illusion, and also creates a movable mural that can be hung where you wish. You may notice that this is the exact same shape and pattern that was used to create the previous Lattice Window Mural. A few changes in tape placement and shading patterns, and voilà, you have a completely different mural!

An additional lesson to be learned from this project is how to create the illusion of an architectural carving from a simple theorem-style stencil design. You can use this technique to create a bas-relief-style carved ornament from any multi-overlay stencil that features classical lines and large, connected design elements.

SUPPLIES NEEDED

Stencils and Patterns

- Large Shell Onlay, Large Acanthus Leaf Pot and Bromeliad stencils from Royal Design Studio
- blueprint of niche dimensions available from Royal Design Studio

Paints and Glazes

- FolkArt acrylics
  Barnwood (shell onlay and niche)
  Barnyard Red (bromeliad)
  Charcoal Gray (shell onlay and niche)
  Country Twill (pot)
  Dapple Gray (bromeliad)
  Dark Gray (pot)
  French Vanilla (shell onlay and niche)
  Glazed Carrots (pot and bromeliad)
  Italian Sage (bromeliad)
  Licorice (pot)
  Medium Gray (shell onlay and niche)
  Metallic Antique Copper (pot)
  Olive Green (bromeliad)
  Wrought Iron (bromeliad)
- FolkArt Extender
- AquaGlaze

Brushes

- no. 4 and no. 8 round brushes
- assorted stencil brushes

Miscellaneous

- blue tape
- repositionable spray adhesive
- Mylar or E-Z Cut Plastic
- craft knife
- tracing paper
- clear grid ruler
- hair dryer
- small artist's sponge
- ¾" medium density fiberboard cut to shape

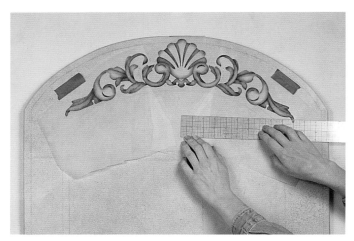

1 After creating an allover limestone finish (pages 212–213) on your working area, transfer the working lines of the pattern using a ruler and pencil. These will be defined later with tape and stenciling/shading, as well as some simple hand-painting.

Here, on tracing paper, I have stenciled a proof of the stencil design I intend to use to create my bas-relief carving, which helps to determine a pleasing and properly centered placement of the element.

2 Stencil all overlays of the design using a sharp contrast of values to define each element using a ⅜" (1cm) stencil brush. Because the desired effect is to have the stencil design appear as if it is carved from the same limestone as the niche, concentrate the stenciling just around the edges of the design elements while allowing the background finish to remain intact and visible. Each shape is defined with Barnwood, and a mixture of Medium and Charcoal Gray are used in the most deeply recessed areas of the design, which would naturally receive the least amount of light.

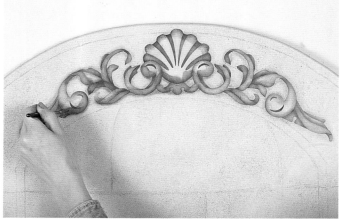

3 In order to visually lift the design from the background and complete the illusion, a shield needs to be created and cut. Stencil the complete design accurately onto Mylar or E-Z Cut Plastic or paper. With a craft knife, cut carefully around the whole perimeter of the design to create a shield against which you can shade and define the outer edge of the stencil design.

4 After spraying lightly with repositionable spray adhesive for a secure hold, affix the shield carefully in place so that is lines up accurately with the design. Use a ⅜" (1cm) stencil brush and Medium Gray paint to shade around the entire perimeter of the design. Use the darker Charcoal Gray to then shade a deeper value and a sharper contrast on all of the underneath edges of the design, which would be opposite the light source (above).

5 Thin French Vanilla slightly with either water or extender. Use an artist's brush to hand-paint highlights on the top edges of the design. Pick out those edges that would most naturally be in direct line with the light source, which is coming from above.

6 Because the shell onlay is positioned on top of the molding detail, replace the shield before proceeding to your stenciling/shading with tape. Use flexible ¼" (6mm) tape to define the curve and burnish well. Add 1" (3cm) tape on the outer edge to protect the surface you don't want to paint. Stencil/shade a dark shadow below the edge with Charcoal Gray.

7 After removing the tape, soften that edge and create some roundness to the opposite side by stenciling/shading along the line. Use the lighter Medium Gray color and a firm, even pressure with a very dry brush.

8 Continue the same process for both sides (inside and outside) of the outer carving that runs across the top and down each side of the niche.

9 Position tape so that it defines the inner niche, using both the ¼" (6mm) and 1" (3cm) tape again to define the top arch. Use a large stencil brush loaded with Medium Gray and a sweeping motion to bring the shading down into the curve. Define the edges further with Charcoal Gray.

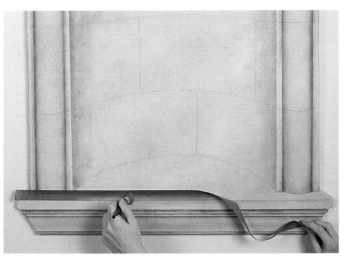

10 The molding under the ledge is shaded in the same way as the previous Lattice Window. To define the edge of the ledge, use tape and a light pressure to create just a subtle contrast where the plane of the top edge of the shelf meets the plane of the front edge. Both would naturally receive a lot of light, but with it coming from above, the top edge of the shelf would be slightly more illuminated. As always, you need to create contrast between different elements to visually define them, even if it's just a little!

11 Use your tape to define the curved back edge of the shelf and shade the wall behind with Medium Gray, then the deeper Charcoal Gray.

12 Remove the tape and add some depth and color with Medium Gray.

13 The grout lines are painted by hand with a no. 4 round. Thin Medium Gray about 1:1 with extender and follow pattern lines. Some slight variation of line width is okay. Notice how the horizontal lines curve in relation to the eye level, which falls midpoint on the third block from the bottom. The closer the lines are to eye level, the more they seem to straighten out. Above eye level, they appear to curve upward. Below, they curve downward, with the arc becoming more pronounced as the lines get farther away.

14 You can add further detail to the grout lines by painting a thin highlight with thinned French Vanilla along the top edge of the blocks using a no. 4 pointed round brush.

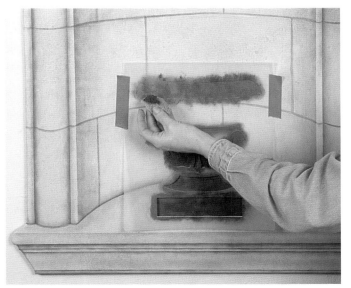

15 Use a paper proof of the stencil design you plan to place in your niche to determine the best placement. The visual depth of this pot must appear to be accommodated by the visual depth of the niche shelf. If it is placed too far back it will appear to be squished in; too far forward, and it may look like it is ready to fall out. It is also very important to your illusion that the object you place in the niche appears to be viewed from the same perspective as the shelf itself, and the perspective of the base of this particular pot works nicely.

16 Each overlay of the pot is first basecoated with Country Twill to completely cover the previously painted grout lines. Dark Gray then covers that, but in a way that is not completely smooth and even, to add to the rustic look of the pot. Use a small artist's sponge to add texture with slightly thinned Metallic Antique Copper. As always, change the direction and pressure of your hand to create a random, nonrepetitive look. Complete all overlays of the design in this same manner.

17 Soften the texture on each overlay now by stenciling over the entire surface lightly with Dark Gray.

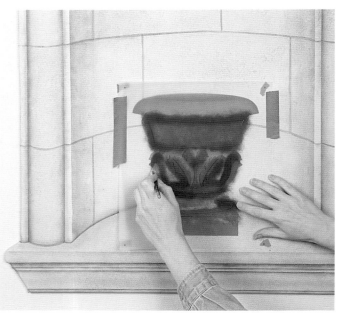

18 Use Licorice and a ⅜" (1cm) stencil brush to add shading and Glazed Carrots to create highlights, creating contrast and definition between the various elements of the design. Note: The detailed stenciling of this same pot is demonstrated in chapter two.

19 Again, I have used a stenciled proof on tracing paper to help me predetermine design placement. I wanted to use this bromeliad design, but its size is slightly too large for the niche, so the proof allows me to see where I need to make some adjustments and alterations, and that I need to push the design down farther into the pot. Some leaves will also need to be eliminated or shortened.

20 Carefully placed pieces of tape are used to easily redefine the shapes of the leaves. Basecoat all leaves with Italian Sage. It may take two to three thin layers of paint to completely cover the darker grout lines that are behind. Use a hair dryer to speed things along.

21 Shade with a mixture of Olive Green–Dapple Gray. Use Wrought Iron for the deepest shading on the leaves and flower head, which is painted with Glazed Carrots and Barnyard Red.

22 Mix a very thin wash of Medium Gray, and add hand-painted shadows with the no. 8 round brush, mimicking the shape of the leaves and flower on the limestone surface behind. Note: The farther away from the surface object is, the more the shadow will be thrown from it. Consequently, the shadows of the back leaves are painted much closer to them than the shadows of the leaves that are positioned more forward in the design.

23 Add a dark painted shadow extending from the pot along the shelf and up the back wall of the niche. Notice how the shadow itself changes direction where the two planes of the surface meet. Add some more weight to the pot by also shading slightly just along the underneath edge.

ROMANTIC WINDOW

Windows give us a sense of connection to the outside world while expanding our living spaces and our view. Maybe you have a wall or room that is lacking in architectural interest or seems to be closing in on you.

Create this idyllic sunny scene to turn any room into a room with a view. The best part is that you can change your view easily, because this mural is painted on stretched artist's canvas, which can be easily moved from wall to wall, room to room, and house to house.

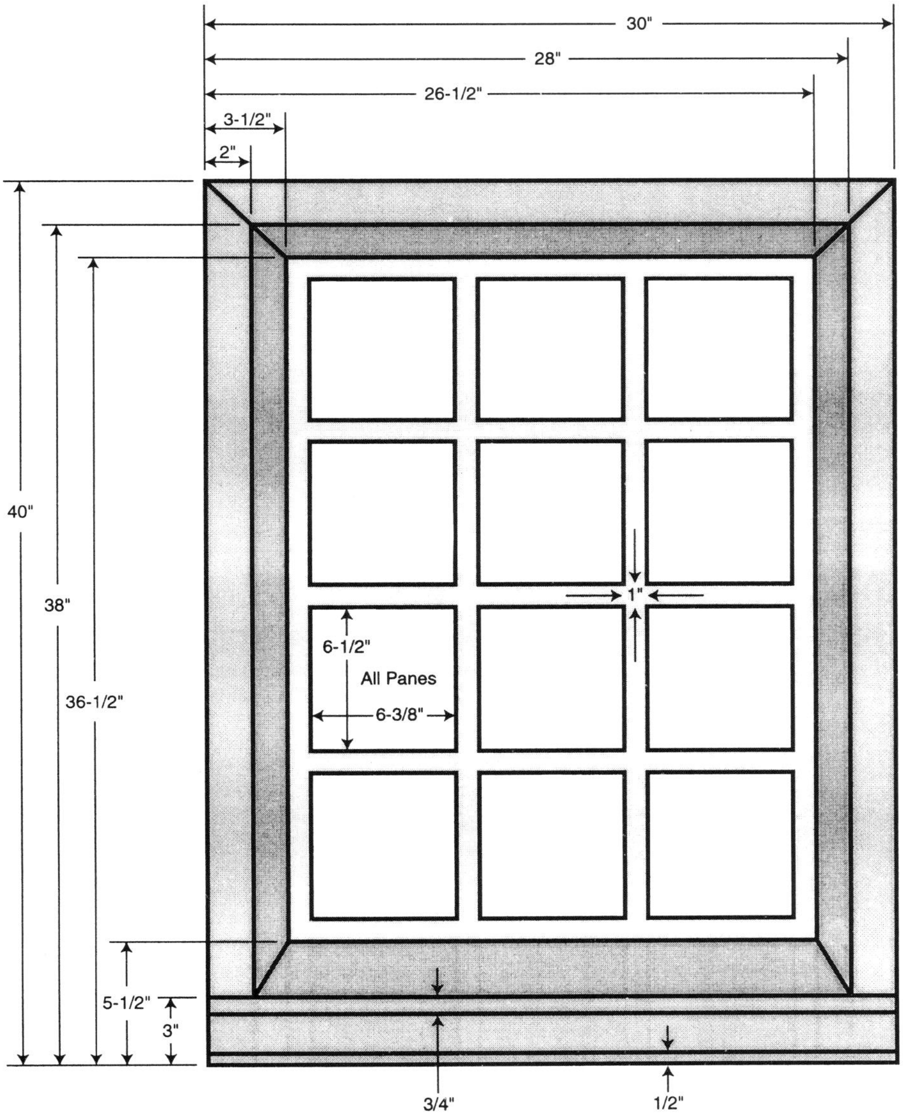

SUPPLIES NEEDED

Stencils and Patterns

- Lovely Little Lace and Sweetheart Ivy Topiary stencils from Royal Design Studio
- Twisted Fabric Border and Fabric Drop stencils from The Mad Stencilist
- patterns for cypress and foliage on page 301

Paints and Glazes

- Benjamin Moore Flat Interior Latex
    Decorator's White
    Harbor Fog
- FolkArt acrylics
    Berry Wine (topiary)
    Buttercrunch (landscape and topiary)
    Butter Pecan (landscape)
    Dapple Gray (landscape)
    Dark Gray (landscape)
    French Vanilla (curtains)
    Gray Green (landscape)
    Gray Plum (landscape)
    Honeycomb (landscape)
    Italian Sage (landscape)
    Light Gray (window frame)
    Medium Gray (window frame and curtains)
    Olive Green (topiary)
    Pink (topiary)
    Spring Green (landscape and topiary)
    Teddy Bear Tan (topiary)
    Thicket (landscape)
    Whipped Berry (curtains)
    Wicker White (curtains and topiary)
    Wintergreen (topiary)
- FolkArt Extender
- AquaGlaze

Brushes

- assorted stencil brushes
- no. 8 round
- no. 6 filbert
- no. 3 script liner

Miscellaneous

- prestretched artist's canvas: 30" x 40" (76cm x 102cm), ¾" (1cm) thick
- natural sea wool sponge
- clear grid ruler and blue tape
- 4" (10cm) foam roller and tray
- gray watercolor pencil and soft charcoal
- Mylar or E-Z Cut Plastic

Diagram labels:
30" · 28" · 26-1/2" · 3-1/2" · 2" · 40" · 38" · 36-1/2" · 1" · 6-1/2" · All Panes · 6-3/8" · 5-1/2" · 3" · 3/4" · 1/2"

(See Skyscape instructions beginning on page 250 for specific colors and painting techniques used for the sky and clouds.)

1 Using a 4" (10cm) foam roller, basecoat canvas with two coats of flat white latex. Following the measurements on the pattern, use 1" (3cm) tape to divide and define the windowpanes. Tape around the outer edges of the window frame. Burnish well. In order to preserve a clean tape edge for the painting to come, seal the edges of the tape by rolling on an additional layer of white latex, the same color as the basecoat. If there is any seepage under the tape, it will blend completely.

2 Basecoat entire window area with Harbor Fog. Reference the Skyscape instructions and materials on pages 250–252 to create a soft cloud scene down to the horizon line. Use soft charcoal to sketch in the basic shapes of the landscape.

3 Painting from the background to the foreground, use thinned acrylic paints to slowly build up layers of washed color. Using a stiff filbert brush allows you to scrub in the color, and painting in a horizontal motion will add movement to your landscape. Begin with the Gray Plum in the farthest background, blending into Gray Green, Italian Sage, and Dapple Gray. Use the brighter Spring Green as you come into the foreground.

4 The path is painted with the same filbert brush using washes of Butter Pecan and Honeycomb. Using a lot of variety in the depth of color will aid in creating a soft impressionistic effect. Avoid painting flatly, with solid blocks of color. Add some of the green colors into the path and vice versa to create unity, flow and interest in the landscape.

5 Small cypress tree stencils provide an easy way to paint in distant trees quickly (you may cut your own from the provided pattern on page 301). Use a variety of gray/greens to stencil in a stand of trees along the horizon line, overlapping them slightly.

6 You can create some filler foliage in the landscape by stippling in some scrubby bushes with a ¾" (2cm) stencil brush. To create depth, work from dark to light. I first stippled in a combination of Thicket–Dapple Gray and highlighted the top edges of the bushes with Spring Green to create some simple but effective shapes.

7 Thin Dark Gray and lightly paint in the branch shapes using a no. 4 artist's round brush.

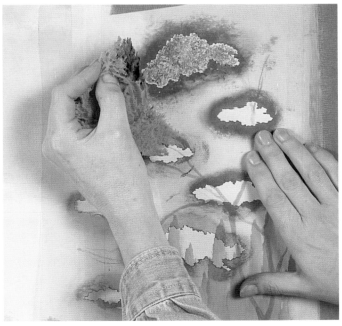

8 In order to create a lacy leaf effect, use a sea wool sponge loaded with paint to sponge through tree foliage stencils. Vary the sizes and shapes of the foliage stencils, and again, work from dark to light colors (Dapple Gray, Thicket and then Spring Green) to create depth. Be sure to overlay some of the foliage stencils to create a nice dense effect. Lastly, sponge some Buttercrunch on the top edges of the foliage to create highlights.

9 After all of the scene painting has been completed, remove the blue tape. The areas that have been protected by the tape are now ready to be transformed into dimensional frames for the windowpanes with some well-placed shadows and highlights.

10 Use your grid ruler to mark a ¼" (6mm) line around the edges of all the squares. Draw miter lines connecting the corners of the inner and outer squares. Also transfer all of the lines from the pattern for the outer detailing of the frame, shelf and molding. Use a gray watercolor pencil to create the lines. When painting, the color will dissolve and blend slightly with the shading and overpainting.

11 Thin Light Gray with water, and lightly paint all the inside areas of the window frames.

12 Use tape to shield the outer corner, and a piece of paper, acetate or Mylar (you will need something with a perfect 90° angle) to protect the inside corner before stenciling the top and left side of the frame with Medium Gray. Notice the angled tape in the upper right and lower left, which protects and defines the mitered corners.

13 The dominant light source chosen for this mural is coming from outside, at upper left. This would create shadows angled away from it that fall inside the room onto the window casing. The lower right areas of the molding that surrounds each small pane were left the original white, which now creates a highlight. Use tape and Mylar to define the cast shadow from the window onto the inner casing of the window. Stencil with Medium Gray. Keep this light and uniform.

14 Use tape again to define the cast shadows (using Medium Gray) from the inner frames of the window onto the ledge and casing. Make sure that these shadows end at the edge of the ledge

15 The window scene is shown with completed shading, all done with tape and the stenciling/shading techniques outlined in previous projects. You could easily stop at this point and have a very believable window illusion. The depth of the canvas casts a real shadow on the wall, emphasizing the illusion. If desired, though, you can continue to decorate your window to match the room it will hang in.

16 I decided to further dress my window using the Twisted Fabric Border stencil from the Mad Stencilist. The first step is to define the folds of the fabric by stenciling with Wicker White that has been thinned with extender or glaze medium. You want this to be sheer, not opaque! Concentrate more color around the edges, though, to give them some depth and dimension. This stencil design was just slightly too large for this window, so I have adjusted it to fit by taping off on the left side.

17 To create a delicate lace pattern, stencil a small-scale, overall design (such as Lovely Little Lace), using Wicker White again. The pattern is stenciled with the swag stencil still in place. For each section of the swag, angle the pattern of the lace in a slightly different direction for a more realistic, natural look. Shade and define the folds of the fabric with Whipped Berry. Add Medium Gray to the deepest parts of the folds for more depth.

Here is the completed window with the addition of a lace drape on the side. At this point you could stop and have a sweet and lovely view. The windowsill provides ample room, however, for additional painting possibilities. A stack of books with some reading glasses, a vase of fresh-picked flowers and a sleeping feline are a few ideas that come to mind. I chose to stencil a sweetheart rose topiary, in keeping with the romantic theme.

18 This topiary is a free-form design. Because the leaves and rose buds are individual and hand-placed, you can easily create a topiary of any configuration, size or shape. It is just a matter of deciding then defining the shape and building it. In this case, the pot was based in first with French Vanilla for positioning, and the basic form of the topiary was sketched in lightly with soft charcoal. I chose to create a ball shape, but you can choose open circles or hearts, cones, double balls or spirals. The background leaves are placed first using Olive Green. This goes quickly. Just use the various leaves, turned in all different directions, to block in the form.

19 To fill in further and create more mass, go back with a dry brush and the same color and fill in between the open spaces of the leaves.

20 Use a lighter color, in this case Spring Green, to solidly layer some more forward leaves on top and in between the first layer of leaves.

21 Position the roses, spreading them throughout the topiary so that they are balanced and facing different directions. Paint the rosebuds solidly with Pink and shade with Berry Wine using a ⅜" (1cm) stencil brush.

22 Finish off the pot by building up a solid layer of Buttercrunch, deepened in tone with Yellow Ochre and shaded with Teddy Bear Tan. Add some of the yellow, Buttercrunch, to the top layer of leaves and the roses to highlight them and bring them visually forward.

23 To carry the yellow color throughout the composition and to add more contrast, sponge some of the Buttercrunch into the foliage of the tree in the foreground.

24 Free-form ivy leaves are used as some filler at the bottom of the pot. These also help to soften the harsh lines of the pot and to bring in some more green toward the bottom of the composition. Different colors of green are used to further define these different types of leaves. With a ¾" (2cm) stencil brush, basecoat the leaves with Spring Green. Use a small ⅜" (1cm) stencil brush to add the darker Wintergreen in the centers of the leaves.

25 In order to make the leaves pop out, trim the edges with Wicker White, using a ⅜" (1cm) brush and "hugging" the edge of the stencil so that just a small portion of the brush is allowed into the stencil "window."

26 The shadow from the window frame is no longer applicable with the placement of the pot, so it is painted out with the background color, Decorator's White. Stipple the color over the area to be covered with a 1" (3cm) stencil brush.

27 An alternative to hand-painting cast shadows is to stencil them. With free-form stencils such as these, the most difficult part is to go back and match up the individual stencils with the leaf shapes. You will be rewarded with a nice clean stencil print of a shadow that is easily executed. For those of you anxious about hand-painting, this is a good substitution. Remember that shadows are only cast on *objects*, so don't have shadows falling on thin air. Use thinned Medium Gray and stencil just to the edge where the previously stenciled leaf begins, not around the whole perimeter of the cutout.

28 In the case of free-form, you will of course still have to hand-paint in the vines using a no. 3 script liner. Make these vine shadows relate to the leaf in the same way as the original stenciling.

29 Lastly, with a no. 8 round brush, paint in the shadow from the pot onto the windowsill, falling away from the light source in the same direction as the shadows from the window frames.

BY-THE-SEA

Wouldn't it be great to have a getaway vacation home to go to? A place where you could spend the morning leisurely wandering the beach and searching for shells and then come home and put your feet up while you listen to the sounds of seagulls and pounding waves, with the smell of salt air drifting through an open window on the summer breeze. Oh well, you can dream about it!

Or you can paint it. Here is another movable mural on pre-stretched artist's canvas, a relaxing coastal scene in muted colors. I have tried to incorporate a variety of painting techniques, that, as always, can be copied and/or adapted in any number of ways. An important addition and lesson here, though, is how to create open windows using simple two-point perspective.

While some of the stencil companies who provided designs for use in this book offer precut stencils for open windows and doors, none of them was exactly the right size and configuration for this project on 36" x 48" (90cm 1.2m) canvas, so I decided to design my own. I have always had an irrational fear of perspective, thinking it must be very complicated (and besides, dealing with numbers generally gives me an artist's headache). I called on Andrea and Richard Tober of A Matter of Perception to help me plot out the steps involved in creating my own windows with tape. Well, anything is easy when you know how! All that is really required to create these perspectively correct windows is some patience and some accurate measuring. Even better, you can follow these same simple steps to create windows and French doors of any size and dimension.

SUPPLIES NEEDED

Stencils and Patterns

- Three Shells and Large Shell stencils from The Mad Stencilist
- Hinges stencil from L.A. Stencilworks
- The Nubble stencil from Red Lion Stencils
- Seagulls stencil from Deesigns
- pattern on page 300

Paints and Glazes

- Benjamin Moore Flat Interior Latex
    Autumn Bronze
    Harbor Fog
    Valley Forge Brown

(See Skyscape instructions beginning on page 250 for specific colors and painting techniques used for the sky and clouds.)

- FolkArt acrylics
    Barnwood (window)
    Blueberry Pie (water)
    Bluegrass (landscape and lighthouse)
    Buttercrunch (shells, seagulls)
    Clay Bisque (window)
    Country Twill (landscape, lighthouse, shells)
    Dapple Gray (landscape and lighthouse)
    Dark Gray (window and seagulls)
    Honeycomb (landscape)
    Icy White (window)
    Medium Gray (lighthouse, shells, seagulls)
    Metallic Antique Gold (window)
    Mushroom (shells)
    Robin's Egg (landscape)
    Slate Blue (water, shells, seagulls)
    Spring Green (landscape)
    Sweetheart Pink (shells)
    Ultramarine Blue (water)
    Valley Forge Brown (window)
    Wicker White (shells and seagulls)
- FolkArt Extender
- Golden's Matte Gel Medium

Brushes

- assorted stencil brushes
- no. 8 filbert
- no. 1 liner
- 2" (5cm) chip brush
- higher-quality 2" (5cm) or 3" (8cm) nylon brush

Miscellaneous

- prestretched artist's canvas: 36" x 48" (90cm x 1.2m), ³⁄₄" (2cm) thick
- blue tape
- soft charcoal
- cotton swabs
- string
- clear grid ruler
- palette or foam plates
- terry towel or washcloth

1 To begin, measure in and mark 3" (8cm) from the top and sides, and 5" (13cm) from the bottom of the canvas. Run tape on the outside of the lines to define the window scene area. Basecoat the entire area with a flat sheen of Harbor Fog. Sketch in the basic shapes of the landscape and paint the sky according to the technique outlined on pages 250–253, ending at the horizon line. Note how the cloud formations become smaller and closer together at the horizon line, indicating their greater distance from the viewer. Place the water paint colors out on a palette and thin with water.

2 Using a lot of water in a no. 8 filbert, apply the colors in long horizontal strokes. Begin with the deepest color, Ultramarine Blue, at the horizon line. When you get to the middle ground area of water, switch to Blueberry Pie, and then Slate Blue for the shallowest portion of the water. Be sure to blend the transition areas well with a wet brush.

3 While the washes of color are still wet, go back and create some whitecaps by pulling a damp cotton swab through paint here and there in horizontal lines. Roll the cotton swab between your fingers as you drag it and vary your pressure to create a realistic, irregular shape.

4 After sketching some lines with soft charcoal, basecoat the masses of land using thinned washes of the landscape colors (Spring Green, Bluegrass, Robin's Egg and Dapple Gray), again using long, horizontal strokes. Add variety and interest to the terrain by layering various washes of color over each other. The layering of colors adds more richness and depth. Predetermine where the stenciled lighthouse scene will fall on the peninsula in the background and leave that area unpainted.

5 Stencil the lighthouse scene using the recommended colors on the supply list or the colors of your choice. Because it is in the background, it is important to use colors and values that are closely related. Using sharp contrasts of values and intense colors would visually bring the painting to the forefront.

6 Note from this detail of the completed stenciling that the rocks and rolling landscape that the building sit on are part of the stencil, but additional hand-painting has been added to the cliff area that goes down to meet the water.

7 In the foreground, a meandering path that recedes into space (a common element in murals), was painted in to help create more movement and depth. It is always nice to break up the masses of land with some foliage. In this case, some clumps of sea grass are painted using the edge of the same no. 8 filbert brush used to paint in the background, but you could easily use a pointed round brush as well. Vary the size and shape of the clumps, the colors used and the length of your brushstrokes for a more natural look.

8 Use a small round brush to paint the flower heads as shown with Honeycomb. Again, variety in the height and size will aid in a more natural look. It is very easy to fall into patterns of repetition, so try to be aware of that and consciously avoid it.

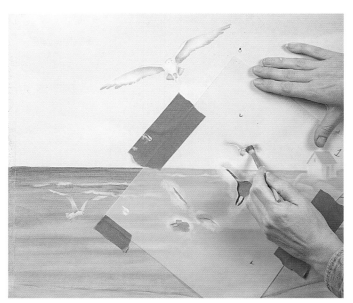

9 Stencil a group of flying seagulls, using the colors listed in the supplies, paying careful attention to placement. Notice that the medium bird is placed with a focus in toward the center of the scene. The reverse would have led the viewer's eye out of the picture. Notice also that one of the smaller gulls is placed near the horizon line, aiding in the sense of distance.

10 Once the distant scene is complete, remove the tape and reposition to shield the edge of the scene and expose the frame of the window. Burnish the edges, and basecoat with two coats of Valley Forge Brown. Allow to dry.

11 For this step, use chip brushes and the layered-dry brush technique outlined under Distressed Painted Wood on pages 214–215. Thin the acrylic paint 1:1 with water and apply in layers using Barnwood first, then Dark Gray, finishing with Clay Bisque. The next picture shows how the grain follows the direction of the wood. Miter the corners by taping off the adjoining areas as you come to the corners.

12 Create a perspective grid following the steps outlined on page 249, and by referring to the illustration on page 300. Use a light-colored watercolor pencil, which is easily removed with a damp cloth when finished. Mark an X on your drawn arc to indicate the open position of the doors.

13 Run a string from the starting point (bottom left corner of window) straight across the X and extending to vanishing point right, which is the point where the string eventually crosses the horizon line (not shown in picture). Be sure to mark that point (VPR). Determine the angle of the top of the window frame by running the string from the beginning edge (indicated on the pattern) to the same vanishing point.

14 Use a level to draw a plumb line from the bottom right edge of the open window straight up to where it connects with the top right edge. Note how the revealed edge of the open window is drawn in on the bottom left. This indicates the thickness of the window frame, which is exposed because the window is opening away from the viewer. Repeat the same process for the window on the right side, referring to both the pattern and perspective illustrations.

15 Run blue tape around the perimeter of all the drawn edges of the window frames and burnish well. As an added precaution against having any paint seep under the edges of the tape and spoiling both the clean edge and the previously painted landscape, you may seal the edges of the tape. Use gel medium and apply two thin coats (allowing to dry thoroughly between coats) with a no. 8 filbert along the edge of the tape that will be painted.

16 Use a foam brush or roller to base-paint in the window frame color Valley Forge Brown. Two to three coats may be needed to cover the painted landscape. Apply the painted texture to the window frame in the same manner as the outer frame, taping off to define where the strips of wood abut in the corners.

17 Use a grid ruler to mark a ¼" (6mm) line at the top, bottom and inside edges of the inner frame of the windows. This will indicate the depth of the inside of the window frame that holds the glass. You will not see this area on the outer edges of the frames because of the position of the open windows.

18 Tape off on both sides and use Dark Gray to solidly stencil a shadow in the areas that are along the top and sides. Use Clay Bisque to stencil a highlight along the bottom of the inside edge. Also refer to step 21, which shows the mitering of this inner corner and the addition of a lighter shadow (optional) on the bottom right window. This is done while the tape is still in place and is a lighter application of the Dark Gray. It is the shadow created by the left edge of the window frame when the light source is coming from the upper left of the picture.

19 To shade and define the inner edge of the window frame, tape off on either edge. Use tape to also shield the corners of the windows that overlap the frame. Shade with a solid application of Dark Gray on the underneath portion of the window frame, using a piece of tape or shield held in place at the mitered corner to define the edge.

20 Stencil/shade down the sides using the same Dark Gray but with a lighter pressure to create a lighter value. Note: If you have trouble controlling the value with an adjustment of pressure, you can thin the color with extender to make it more translucent.

21 This picture shows the completed shading pattern. Notice that the inside edge of the bottom ledge of the window has been defined with a slight change in values. A piece of tape was run across the line horizontally and shading added below.

To set the hinges, measure down 6" (15cm) from the top and bottom edges of the corners of the window frame to indicate the position of the hinges. Paint these by stenciling with Metallic Antique Gold and shading with Dark Gray. Notice how the angle of the hinges changes from the top hinges to the bottom. This is accomplished by simply turning the hinge upside down, so that the angles of the hinges are perspectively correct.

22 Add details to the hinges with a liner brush and Dark Gray. Line the outer edges of the screws to add definition. Add a straight line across to indicate a groove for the screwdriver. Place the grooves at different angles for variety. Circular lines were added on the hinge pins.

23 To create the frosted look of the windowpanes, tape off around the outer edges and apply Icy White that has been thinned with two parts water using a good-quality nylon bristle brush. Soften immediately with a towel, but allow some areas to show streaks.

24 Complete the scene by adding some pretty stenciled seashells in the foreground on the windowsill. There may be ridges of built-up paint along the edges of the window frame where it was taped. Sand these down lightly so that the ridges don't show through on your stenciled shells.

25 Base in the solid shapes of the shells with Wicker White. It will require several coats to cover completely. Be patient! Use thin layers to avoid run-unders. The shells are colored with varying combinations of Buttercrunch, Sweetheart Pink and Country Twill. Darker accents are Mushroom and Slate Blue. Deepest shading is Medium Gray.

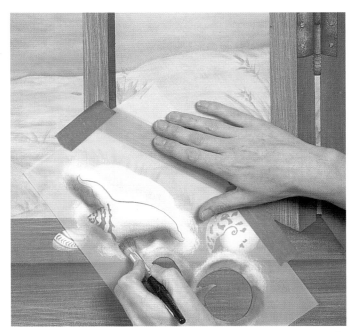

26 Notice that the colors and shading used on the foreground shells is much more intense and shows greater contrast that the colors and shading used in the background scene. This sharper focus of the foreground elements versus the soft focus of the background helps to create a believable sense of distance and depth.

27 Add cast shadows from the shells onto the top surface of the ledge using thinned Dark Gray. Notice that the shadows fall away from the outside light source and echo the shapes of the objects that are creating them.

GALLERY

Following is a selection of stenciled trompe l'oeil murals by various artists and stencil designers that is sure to inspire your imagination. The variety of different artistic and painting styles highlights the many creative possibilities that can be brought into play when designing and planning a stenciled mural.

These murals were created by decorative artist Peggy Eisenberg for a California Showcase House in a mud room, which was the back entrance to the house. The stencils she used are from Deesigns.

GOLF SCENE

A golf scene, complete with trompe l'oeil clubs, painted in a closed area provides a backdrop for the real thing. To the right, a perspectively correct shelf mural on canvas that contains items that relate to the potting area was affixed to an old freezer door.

Artist: Peggy Eisenberg
Photographer: John Cannon

POTTING AREA

The "potting area" skillfully combines both illusionary and real objects (note the stack of painted pots "resting" on the table behind the real ones and the trompe l'oeil seed packets "tacked" to the wall).

Artist: Peggy Eisenberg
Photographer: John Cannon

These two large murals were completed using a "projection stenciling" method that was developed and perfected by the artists. Large sheets of freezer paper are affixed to the wall surface and the mural scene is then "projected" onto it. The stencil is created on site by cutting away those portions of the design that are to be painted. This technique is excellent for large, simple graphic elements, where a precut stencil would be awkward and expensive, and is outlined in the book Projection Stenciling by Linda Buckingham and Leslie Bird.

ARBOR

Notice how effectively the use of some simple perspective and a subdued background expand the feeling of space in this room. Projection stenciling was used to create the large architectural features and background trees. Foreground details were added with a variety of free-form stencils from Buckingham Stencils, and they serve to create movement and soften the architecture while bringing focus and color to the foreground.

Artist: Linda Buckingham
Photographer: Lionel Trudell

GREEK ISLE SCENE

This simple and serene mural creates impact through the use of interesting shapes and angles and the dramatic red tile roofs which punctuate the otherwise cool and soothing color scheme. The look is uncluttered and sophisticated.

The large, angular shapes of the buildings here are easily created and cut using the projection stenciling method. You can employ this technique for creating architectural elements of any size, shape or style. Save postcards, travel photos, calendar scenes and the like for your own resource for future mural scene possibilities.

Artist: Linda Buckingham and Leslie Bird
Photographer: Lionel Trudell

These two whimsical murals were created by talented airbrush artist and stencil designer Sheri Hoeger, "the Mad Stencilist."

"BUNNY" THE DONKEY
The subject of this mural was first photographed by the artist at a State Fair, after she was drawn to his charm and personality. Working front to back, the artist used templates and shields to paint the donkey first, and then stenciled the background "behind" him.

Artist: Sheri Hoeger
Photographer: Dave Adams

GARDEN MURAL Below
This sweet scene was created to be the focal point on a nursery wall. The soft colors and shading create a serene feeling while adding color and interest to an otherwise blank wall.

Artist: Sheri Hoeger
Photographer: Dave Adams

FREE-FLOWING GARDEN MURAL

Not all murals need to be contained to one area, or even one wall! In addition to being the entryway to a home, this area also leads to a home office for a financial consultant. A fun, uplifting atmosphere was created with this garden in the hallway to relieve the tension/anxiety that often occurs when making decisions about money.

To create an even more personal statement, each family member took part in choosing elements for the mural and stenciling small portions of it. The rest was up to artist P.J. Tetreault who used custom designs from her collection of precut stencils. The result is whimsical, but the attention to color and shading as well as shadowing makes these elements come to life with the illusion of dimension and depth.

Artist: P.J. Tetreault
Photographer: Skip Dickstein

COUNTRY SCENE DINING ROOM

Stencil designer and artist P.J. Tetreault created this custom mural, which covers all four walls and envelops this dining room in nostalgic comfort. The scene depicts life in the 1700s around the time that the home that is featured in this view was built. Working from photographs, the artist designed stencils depicting both the former and current homes of the family, a hunt scene, flying Canadian geese, and even the family dog to create a very personal and significant work of art that can be enjoyed and appreciated as a family heirloom.

Artist: P.J. Tetreault
Photographer: Skip Dickstein

PATTERNS

pedestal pattern for marble finish

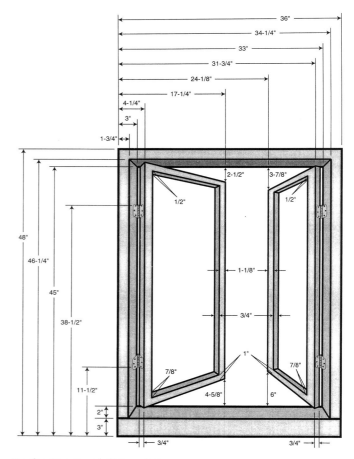

By-the-Sea mural dimensions

PATTERNS

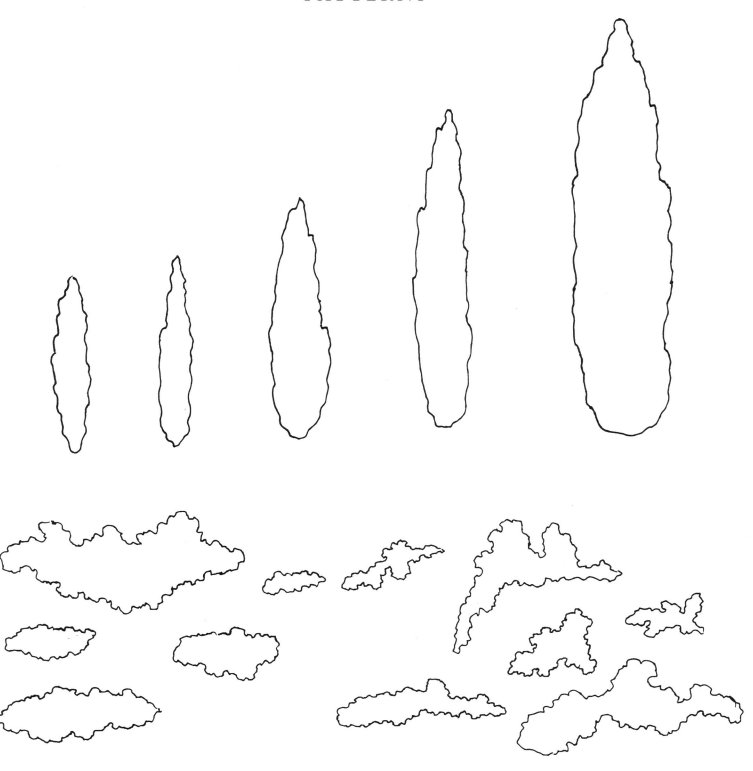

cypress and foliage stencil patterns for
Romantic Window mural

RESOURCES

SUGGESTED BOOKS

The Art of Faux by Pierre Finkelstein. Watson-Guptill, 1997.

Basic Perspective Drawing, a Visual Approach by J. Montague. John Wiley and Sons, 1998.

Basic Perspective for Artists by Keith West. Watson-Guptill, 1995.

Grand Illusions: Contemporary Interior Murals by Caroline Cass. Phaidon Press Ltd., 1988.

The Handbook of Painted Decoration by Yannick Guegan with Roger LePuil. W.W. Norton and Company, 1996.

Marvelous Murals You Can Paint by Gary Lord and David Schmidt. North Light Books, 2001.

Painting Murals by Patricia Seligman. North Light Books, 1988.

Projection Stenciling by L. Buckingham and L. Bird. Hartley and Marks Publishers, Inc., 1999.

Stenciling Techniques by Jane Gauss. Watson-Guptill Publications, 1995.

Stencilling on a Grand Scale by Sandra Buckingham. Firefly Books, 1997.

Trompe L'oeil: Creating Decorative Illusions with Paint by Roberta Gordon-Smith. North Light Books 1997.

Trompe L'oeil: Murals and Decorative Wall Painting by Lynette Wrigley. Rizzoli, 1997.

PERSPECTIVE

A Matter of Perception
6748 Hunter Rd.
Elkridge, MD 21075
(410) 379-5112
www.aperception.com
specializing in practical "perspectives" education for artists and designers; offers trompe l'oeil studio classes, travel teaching, multimedia CD-ROMs, and instructional videos.

STENCIL SOURCES

Many of the products and tools used in this book are available at your local home or hardware store. Additionally, many of the stencils, glazing mediums and supplies are available through:

Royal Design Studio
2504 Transportation Ave., Suite H
National City, CA 91950
(800) 747-9767
www.royaldesignstudio.com

Instruction in the art of stenciling is available from Royal Design Studio in the form of a complete video series, as well as workshops held at the San Diego School of Decorative Arts.

Additional stencil designs, artwork and materials were graciously provided by:

Decorative Accents by Peggy Eisenberg
111 Comstock Rd.
Woodside, CA 94062
(650) 851-7110

Deesigns Decorative Stencils
107 Jefferson St.
Newnan, GA 30263
(800) 783-6245
www.deesigns.com

Jeff Raum Stencils
4950 Moorpark Rd.
Moorpark, CA 93021-2211
(805) 523-0052
www.jeffraumstencils.com

L.A. Stencilworks
16115 Vanowen St.
Van Nuys, CA 91406
(877) 989-0262
www.lastencil.com

LakeArts
361 Quail Hollow Dr., Ste. A
Lawrenceville, GA 30043
(888) 464-2787
www.lakearts.com
source for PolyMural canvas, artist's canvas, floorcloth and other art supplies

The Mad Stencilist
P.O. Box 219, Dept. N
Diamond Springs, CA 95619
(888) 882-6232
www.madstencilist.com

Natures Vignettes, Inc.
205 West Meeker Street
Kent, WA 98032
(877) 813-2593
www.naturesvignettes.com

P.J.'s Decorative Stencils!
Box 1555
Newburyport, MA 01950
(978) 463-5444
www.PJstencils.com
source for E-Z Cut Plastic and stencil burners

Red Lion Stencils
1232 First NH Turnpike
Northwood, NH 03261
(603) 942-8949
www.redlionstencils.com

Web site links to additional stencil companies offering precut stencils, as well as further stenciling and painting resources can be found at www.stenciling.com

The Stencil Artisans League, Inc.
An international non-profit organization dedicated to the promotion and preservation of the art of stenciling and related decorative painting.

Stencil Artisans League, Inc.
P.O. Box 3109
Los Lunas, NM 87031
(505) 865-9119
www.sali.org

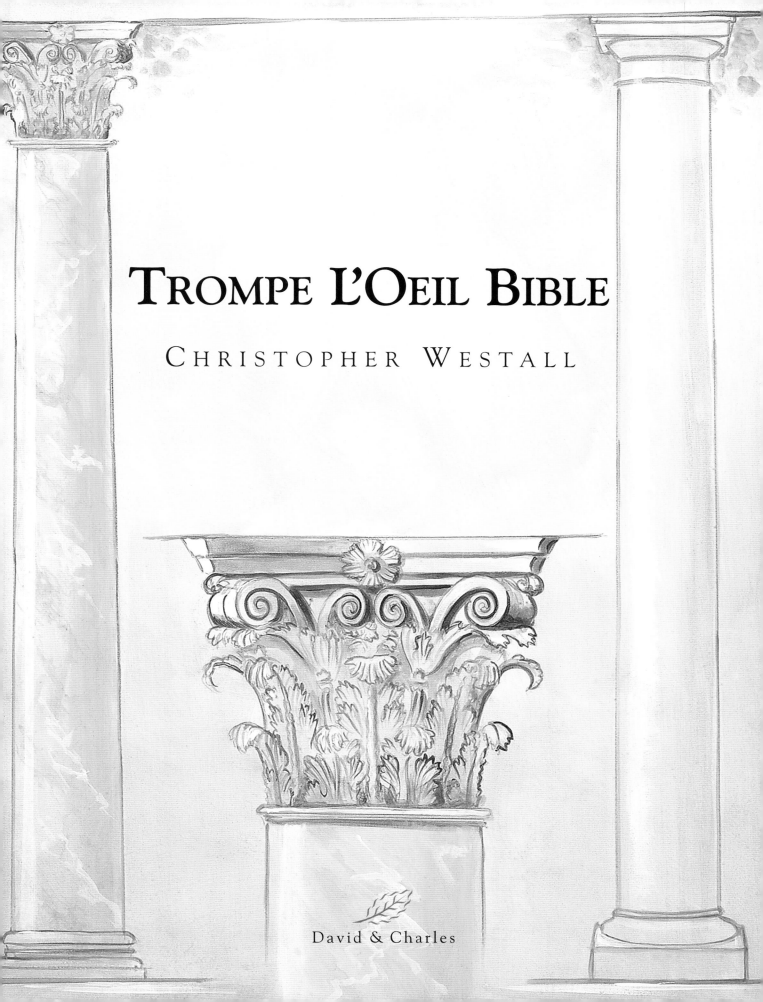

TROMPE L'OEIL BIBLE

CHRISTOPHER WESTALL

David & Charles

Contents

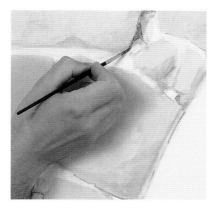

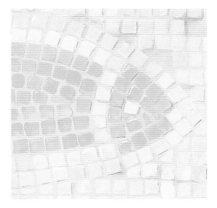

Introduction

Trompe l'oeil is a French expression meaning simply 'trick the eye', and it describes a visual joke: a painted illusion, specifically designed to fool viewers into believing that what they are looking at is real. Only when they come closer to inspect the work in more detail – perhaps even as they reach over to pick up a realistically painted wine glass – do they realize to their delight that they have been duped.

The expression 'less is more' is relevant here. It is often the simple, small-scale trompe l'oeil pieces that fool more often and for longer. A small painting of a plant pot tucked away on a shelf will fool many people, as it will look perfectly natural in its situation and will not draw too much attention to itself. On the other hand, while a grandiose Arcadian landscape viewed through classical columns can be awe-inspiring to behold, we immediately realize that it is a painted illusion. However, even after the trick is discovered, the painting continues to have the desired effect of visually opening up the space in the room. And in the end we all secretly want to be found out, and receive a pat on the back for painting such a convincing illusion.

People often say to me that they wish they could paint, but feel they cannot even draw matchstick men. But with this self-defeating attitude many potential artists write themselves off before they have even dipped a brush into paint. I was a very reluctant painter myself, but I'm glad I took that first step.

You may find that your initial attempts do not come up to your expectations, but do not be discouraged, as you will learn more and more each time you paint – much more, in fact, than I could hope to teach you through this book. You may also find yourself looking in awe at other muralists' work, and envying their skill. I have been painting for over eighteen years, and I still do the same. Do look at murals by other artists for ideas and inspiration, but always be conscious that you are an individual with your own personal style, interests and aspirations – the world would be a boring, uniform place if we all painted the same way. My wish is that this book will help to spark your own artistic journey – you will be amazed at what you can achieve.

Before you begin

Before you even consider picking up a paint brush or preparing a wall for a mural, establish a clear idea of what it is you want to paint. Are you aiming to add the illusion of period architectural details to a plain room, or to create a feeling of greater space by painting a distant view? Will your mural occupy part of one wall, or transform the whole room? The function of the room may suggest themes and ideas.

The kitchen is often the hub of the home, and a place where the family regularly gathers. Because of the space taken up by kitchen cupboards, there may be little wall space on which to paint a mural. One idea would be to paint a decorative frieze along the top of a wall, such as a trailing grapevine. If a blank wall is available, a vibrant summer landscape seen through an open window would bring sunshine into the kitchen, and growing crops would give it a suitable culinary theme.

In a dining room, most of the furniture is in the center, so there may be a lot of wall space available. This is an ideal opportunity to paint something dramatic to impress your dinner party guests. A classical theme would be popular, such as a colonnade with a view over an Arcadian landscape or a formal garden. Link the view to the room by painting a bottle of fruity red wine on a window ledge, with a half-emptied glass perched beside it.

A mural in a sitting room needs to enhance its relaxed ambience and be easy to live with. As in the kitchen, it is likely that you will usually have the top half of the wall as your canvas, because of the furniture in the room. A fireplace makes a good focal point, maybe with a painted firescreen or a decorative design on the chimney breast. Even if you have no fireplace, you could paint your own trompe l'oeil one.

If your hall is long and narrow you may have a lot of wall space, but the effect of a grand painted vista will be lost if you cannot stand back from the wall to view it. A formal and subtle stone-blocking effect could be a better solution, perhaps with a niche containing an urn on the end wall, where you and your visitors can enjoy the illusion to the full.

In the bedroom, relaxation is the key element – colors should be harmonious and restful. Here you can indulge in a touch of fantasy, such as a softly painted cloudy ceiling, with gentle drapery and fluttering cherubs. A child's bedroom is a great opportunity to kickstart your mural skills. There is a lot of satisfaction in making children's favorite characters and stories come alive on their walls. It's a good idea to involve the children in the design process, and maybe even let them help with the painting. An advantage (or disadvantage) of painting a mural for children is that they have not yet grasped the concept of diplomacy, and they will tell you straight away whether they like it or not. So if you can please them, you can please anybody!

If your bathroom is tiled, there will be little, if
any, wall to paint. An alternative would be to
paint a mural on a moisture-resistant board and
hang it on the wall. Water themes, such as fish,
leaping dolphins or the sea, are the obvious
choice, but twining greenery can also create a
relaxing setting. If you have the space you could
surround the bath with a harmonious Roman
vista, seen through columns and twisting ivy, to
transport you to a classical spa as you soak.

How to use this book

The first section gives an overview of the techniques of trompe l'oeil painting, with practical
advice that will enable you to
follow the detailed instructions given for the
projects in the other
sections. Based on
four themes –
Country Views, Classical
Details, the Water's Edge
and Children's Worlds –
each section includes two
step-by-step projects, as
well as numerous design library pages – additional ideas for mural subjects and decorative
details. Although many of the images in the
design libraries form a complete picture in
themselves, such as a shelf full of toys, or a view
from a window, don't be afraid to mix and
match different elements to create your own
unique trompe l'oeil. Why not take a vase of
flowers from one page, and sit them on a shelf
from another? Alternatively, choose your favorite
outdoor scene, and paint it as seen through any
of the beautiful windows or doorways featured
throughout the book. Every idea in the design
libraries has practical hints and tips to help you
create them, plus inspirational ideas for how and
where to use them. With this book, your painting
equipment and your imagination, you can create
a world of illusion in every room of your home.

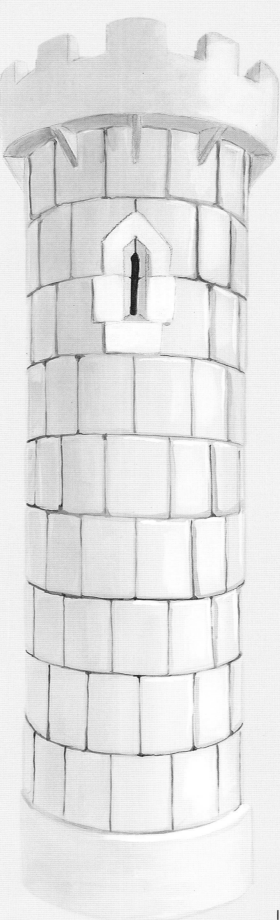

Techniques

Planning and Sketching

The best starting point for inspiration is yourself: your interests, your favorite flowers, where you like to go on holiday, and so on. Artists through the centuries have included personal elements in their paintings: Van Gogh's love of sunflowers inspired a series of paintings, and the painting known as *Vincent's Chair* includes his pipe, tobacco and handkerchief. When I paint a mural for clients, it is fun to add a little element that links the scene to them – maybe a bottle of their favorite wine.

Once you have some ideas for a mural, start collecting reference material. Cuttings from travel brochures could help you plan a landscape if you have a particular country in mind. Leaf through magazines for examples of elements such as windows or trees. Architectural references

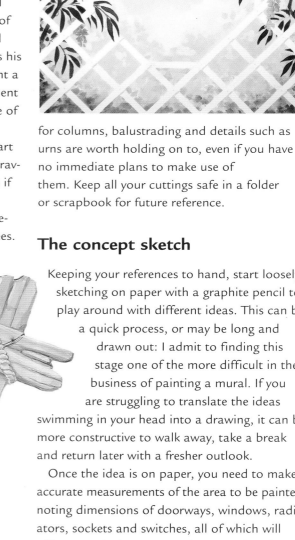

for columns, balustrading and details such as urns are worth holding on to, even if you have no immediate plans to make use of them. Keep all your cuttings safe in a folder or scrapbook for future reference.

The concept sketch

Keeping your references to hand, start loosely sketching on paper with a graphite pencil to play around with different ideas. This can be a quick process, or may be long and drawn out: I admit to finding this stage one of the more difficult in the business of painting a mural. If you are struggling to translate the ideas swimming in your head into a drawing, it can be more constructive to walk away, take a break and return later with a fresher outlook.

Once the idea is on paper, you need to make accurate measurements of the area to be painted, noting dimensions of doorways, windows, radiators, sockets and switches, all of which will affect your design to some degree. Using these measurements, draw an elevation of the wall using a suitable scale (such as 10cm:1m or 1in:1ft). Use a ruler to check the scale and keep the lines

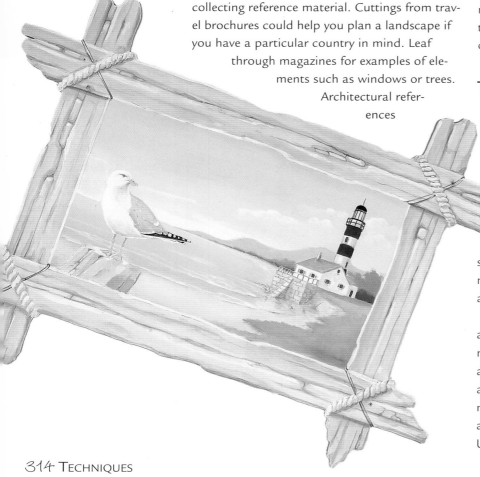

When you come to work your design on the wall, you may find you need to make slight adjustments. For example, in the concept sketch for the seagull and lighthouse design, the bird was standing on the edge of the frame. At full size this made the seagull too big for the composition, so I decided to make him smaller by placing him further back in the scene (see opposite).

straight. A calculator can also be a useful tool. It's wise to make a few copies of your accurate elevation on a photocopier or scanner before you begin to sketch your mural, so that you can try out different variations.

Sketch the main elements of the design, then use colored pencils to build up the coloring. The level of detail is up to you – I generally keep the designs quite free and loose, as I am looking at the overall composition and colors, and how they will relate to the wall and room. Include any colored fixtures, such as a red door, in the design so you can see how the colors will relate to one another. Finally, pick out the outlines and detailing using a black fine liner pen.

Equipment

- **Sketching paper**
- **Graphite pencils:** for sketching
- **Colored pencils:** for trying out initial ideas for color schemes
- **Tape measure:** to measure wall
- **Ruler:** to check scale measurements and keep lines straight
- **Calculator:** to calculate measurements to scale
- **Black fine liner pen:** to outline the final design

Surface Preparation

Surface preparation is generally regarded as a nuisance, as we would all prefer to be painting a beautiful landscape to filling cracks and sanding down the wall. However, this is arguably the most important step, as the preparation work will affect the quality of your finished painting. The amount of work needed will depend on the current state of the wall.

Wall painted with matt emulsion (latex)

This is the ideal surface for mural painting, and if the room has not been wallpapered, it is very likely to be the surface you will be dealing with. If the wall is painted white or off-white and in good repair, just wash it down with a sugar soap solution. You should then be able to proceed with the planning of the mural.

Newly plastered wall

When dry, new plaster needs to be lightly sanded and primed, either with new plaster sealer or an acrylic satin varnish, before painting it with at least two base coats of light emulsion (latex) paint.

Wallpaper

If the wallpaper is sound, matt and smooth-textured, you should be able to paint over it. Otherwise, carefully remove the paper and then make good any damage to the plaster before applying the base coats.

Oil-painted surface

If possible, strip this back using a hot air gun and scraper. You can rub down the surface and prime, but the oil-based paint will prevent air passing through the wall and will extend the drying time of the mural paints.

Cracked and chipped wall

Use an old brush to clean dust and loose plaster out of cracks, and fill with a good quality decorator's filler (spackling paste). Use the powder variety that you have to mix yourself in preference to the ready-mixed version, as it will be easier to sand down. Smooth the filler into the cracks using a filling knife, and when dry sand down with fine to medium-grade sandpaper. You may need to fill deeper cracks in two stages.

Sometimes you may not wish to repair too much damage on the wall, as it can be utilized in the design. If you are painting a rustic Italian scene with a crumbling wall, for example, blemishes and imperfections in the surface may enhance the effect.

Salt deposits

These may be evidence of damp problems, which will need to be rectified. Remove the deposits with a hard brush and then prime the wall with an alkali-resistant stabilizing solution before painting.

Mold

This could also point to damp problems, so you may need to seek professional help. A common cause is condensation, so you should consider improving ventilation or installing a dehumidifier. The mold itself can be cleaned off using a specialist mold cleaner.

Panels

If the wall is damp or in very bad repair, it is worth considering painting a trompe l'oeil mural on a panel and fixing it to the wall. This has the advantage of portability: if you move home, you can take your masterpiece with you rather than leaving it to the mercy of somebody else's decorating preferences.

Panels can be made from MDF (medium density fiberboard), chipboard, hardboard, plywood, or canvas stretched on a frame. MDF is the most versatile board as it has the smoothest surface, comes in various thicknesses and is easy to cut to shape using a jigsaw. A version for exterior use is available, which is ideal for murals in bathrooms where humidity is high. Wear a mask when cutting or sanding MDF, as inhaling the dust can be harmful.

Before priming the panel, lightly rub down the surface with fine sandpaper to provide a key for the paint. The board can then be primed with an acrylic primer or a good quality emulsion (latex). This will need at least two coats – the first should be slightly watered down. Prime both sides of the panel as a precaution against warping, particularly if you are using hardboard.

Equipment

- **Stepladder:** a small aluminum stepladder will usually suffice, but if you need to hire a scaffold tower, try to get the supplying company to assemble it and instruct you on how to use and move it safely.
- **Sugar soap:** for use in solution to remove dirt and grease from surfaces before painting.
- **Sandpaper:** in a range of grades from fine to coarse, for removing flaking paint, rubbing down filler, and rubbing down panels to provide a key.
- **Plaster sealer:** for priming newly plastered walls (**acrylic satin varnish** is an alternative).
- **Hot air gun and scraper:** for removing oil-based paint.
- **Decorator's filler** (spackling paste) and **filling knife:** for repairing cracks or chips in the wall.
- **Dust sheets:** to protect floors and furniture from paint.
- **Masking tape:** to protect light switches, skirting boards, architrave etc.
- **Decorator's brushes** or **paint pads** and **paint rollers:** to apply primer and emulsion (latex) paint.

Scaling and Transferring Images

Whether you begin with your own designs, or with those in this book, they will need to be scaled up. New technology has made this aspect of the work much easier, as photocopier or computer scanners provide a very quick and easy method of copying drawings, templates and other pictorial references, scaling them up (or down) to the size you require. However, if you don't have ready access to either of these, other techniques can be used.

For the step-by-step projects in this book, the main lines of the design can be drawn straight on to the wall using the dimensions in the diagrams. When you gain more confidence in your painting you may also wish to plan landscapes straight on to the wall without first drawing them on transfer paper.

Scaling

Photocopier or computer scanner
Most photocopiers allow you to enlarge or reduce an image, setting the size in terms of a percentage of the original. A computer with a scanner and image manipulation software will give you even more control over the size of the image: an excellent feature, which I have found invaluable, is the facility to enlarge an image greatly using a method called 'tiling'. The result is printed on numerous sheets of paper, which can then be taped together like a jigsaw.

Projection
The image can be projected straight on to the wall, using either an overhead projector or an enlarger. An overhead projector requires the image to be drawn on an acetate sheet, so you

will have to trace off the template first. This is not necessary with an enlarger, which is therefore less time-consuming.

Although it appears to be the most straightforward, this method does have a few hitches. First, you need to have darkness or very subdued light in the room to be able to see the projected image clearly enough to draw it. The projector must face the wall squarely, otherwise the image will be distorted, and adjusting the size of the image usually involves moving the projector further away or closer to the wall. It is advisable to project the image on to transfer paper at the size you require it, and then trace it on to the wall. Although I own an image enlarger, I rarely use it.

Grid method
This is the method that you will need to fall back on if all else fails. It involves drawing a grid over the image you wish to scale. To enlarge the image, draw a second grid to the larger scale, making sure it contains the same number of squares across the height and width as the smaller grid. Then draw the image to the larger scale, using the grid as a guide (see below).

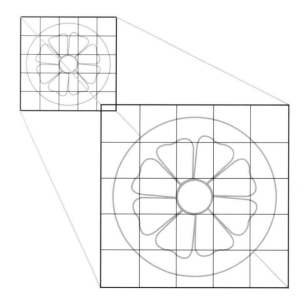

Transferring

Once you have produced your scaled-up template, either on a sheet of semi-transparent transfer paper or on ordinary photocopier or printer paper, it needs to be transferred to the wall. If you are using transfer paper, simply rub a soft graphite pencil on the back behind the outlines, then tape the sheet in place on the wall and trace over the outlines using a harder graphite pencil, to leave an imprint of the design on the wall.

This method also works with ordinary paper, although it can be difficult to see the outlines from the back of the sheet: simply rest the paper against a window in daylight so that the lines are visible. Alternatively you can use sheets of non-wax carbon paper between the design and the wall, and trace the design using a graphite pencil.

Transferring symmetrical designs
Planning and drawing objects such as a wine glass and bottle on the wall may seem a daunting task, but the template examples throughout this book have been designed to make things easier for you. If a template is symmetrical, you need only scale up half the image. Transfer this half on to the wall, then flip the paper over, line it up and trace the other half.

With symmetrical designs such as bottles and urns, you need to ensure that the images are square with the horizontals and verticals of the mural, otherwise they will appear to be leaning over. To help with this, lightly draw in a vertical guideline using a spirit level where you want the image. Align the symmetry line on the template with this vertical before tracing each side.

Rub over the back of the design with a soft pencil before taping the transfer paper in position, then draw over the outlines to leave a tracing on the wall.

Equipment

- **Tape measure:** for making accurate measurements; a steel or plastic **ruler** is useful where a tape measure would be too cumbersome, and doubles as a straight edge.
- **Spirit level:** for drawing accurate horizontals and verticals. Some levels have rotating bubbles, so that you can accurately draw angled lines. A small carpenter's level is useful for the more detailed planning; a larger level can also act as a straight edge when drawing and painting.
- **Protractor:** for measuring angles.
- **Right-angled triangle/set square:** for drawing 90° and 45° angles and for checking horizontals against verticals.
- **Charcoal and graphite pencils:** for drawing on the wall. Charcoal can be wiped off with a damp cloth; graphite is more difficult to remove, but graphite pencils have a finer point so are essential for accurate marking.
- **Eraser or putty rubber:** for removing pencil lines.
- **Semi-transparent transfer paper:** for planning designs and copying templates before transferring them to the wall; household greaseproof (waxed) paper is an alternative.
- **Carbon paper:** for transferring photocopies to the wall. If possible use a non-wax variety.
- **Masking tape:** to hold transfer paper in position.
- **Calculator:** for scaling up templates and dividing up a wall space.
- **String:** for drawing large circles and curves.
- **Pens** for drawing on **acetate:** for use with an overhead projector.

Paints and Painting

I use both good quality emulsion (latex) paint and artist's acrylics for painting murals. As both are water-based, mixing them is not a problem. Both are durable and have little odor. They also dry quickly, allowing you to build up your design gradually in layers without having to wait hours for a previous coat to dry. To paint a whole wall using purely artist's acrylic paints would be very costly, so I use matt emulsion, generally in white, to mix with the acrylic paints.

Artist's acrylic paints

These are very resilient and versatile paints. As they are water-based, thinning colors and cleaning brushes is very straightforward. The pigments are bound with polymer resin, as opposed to oil or gum: this means that the paints are very durable, do not yellow in the way that oil paints do, and as they are more porous than oil paints they are less prone to blistering.

Acrylic paints can be used thick, straight from the tube, to emulate the texture of oil paint, or thinned down with water to make a translucent wash almost like watercolor. As you will be working on vertical surfaces, it is important not to overload the brush when working with thinned paint, as it may run.

The first color I use when starting to paint a mural is Red Oxide acrylic. After you have planned out the mural in pencil, use Red Oxide, slightly thinned with a little water, and a No. 3 or No. 5 round pointed brush to paint over all the outlines. This will ensure that you can still see the lines of the design as you start to build up the layers of color.

Matt emulsion (latex) paint

Household matt emulsion can be used both as a base coat on the wall, and to mix with acrylic colors. Make sure you use a good quality brand of paint – buying cheap paint is a false economy, as it will generally not have the same coverage and you will need to add further coats.

Although I mainly use white emulsion, the choice of colors available in modern paint ranges is mind-boggling. Thanks to computer technology the colors do not have to be held in stock – the paint can be mixed up for you on the spot. This is very useful if your mural uses a lot of the same color (for instance, in a blue sky) and can save you labor as well as money.

Varnish

As well as protecting the surface of the mural and prolonging its life, varnish will even out the varying lustres of acrylic and emulsion paints. I use both a satin and a flat matt acrylic varnish. First apply one or two coats of satin varnish to seal the surface. When dry, apply two to three coats of matt varnish, letting each coat dry out thoroughly before applying the next. Thin the first coats slightly with water. Apply varnish using a paint pad, as it gives a flatter, more even coating than a brush, and avoids brush marks.

Use scrunched-up plastic to create texture in wet paint (above). Build up colors in a distant view (below) starting with blues and blending into greens, intensifying the colors toward the foreground.

Equipment

- **Decorator's brush:** 13cm (5in) wide, for applying base coats, colorwashing and painting large areas such as skies.
- **Nylon artist's brushes:** range from round pointed tips for more detailed work, to wide flat shapes for blocking in colors. These are relatively inexpensive and of a reasonable quality; sable brushes are more expensive, but will long outlive nylon brushes if looked after properly.
- **Hog-hair varnishing brushes:** for blending in larger areas of color (rather than applying varnish). Also excellent for stippling in foliage effects. They eventually become worn and chiselled, but are still useful for stippling effects.
- **Paint pad:** for applying varnish smoothly and evenly.
- **Plastic cups:** for mixing and holding paint. If possible, use cups with lids to stop paints drying out when not in use. Use plastic spoons to spoon emulsion paint out of its tub. Use old artist's brushes to mix the paint.
- **Permanent maker pen:** to label plastic cups containing mixed colors. Useful when using various shades of the same color (such as graduating sky blues). It can be difficult to see whether one color is darker than another until they have dried on the wall.
- **Low-tack masking tape:** for painting crisp straight edges. I do not advocate excessive use of masking tape for this purpose, but when painting subjects such as trellis or railings it would be difficult not to use it. The paint surface must be sound as, if it is not, some paint may be lifted when the masking tape is removed later. Use short brush strokes, working out from the tape to avoid paint seeping underneath.
- **Plastic bags:** used to create a rough stony texture. Try dabbing, rolling and rubbing a bag over the wet painted surface to achieve different effects. When the bag gets overloaded with paint, discard it and use a fresh one.

Understanding Perspective

Creating the perception of a real three-dimensional space on a two-dimensional surface is the challenge for all trompe l'oeil artists. Filippo Brunelleschi, a 15th-century architect, formulated mathematical laws that can be applied to spatial relationships, and these allow us to create believable illusions of space beyond a flat surface.

An understanding of the basic rules of perspective is vital for creating convincing three-dimensional trompe l'oeil on a two-dimensional surface. When planning a mural it is vital that you work out the correct perspective first, as a mistake at this stage can be very difficult to rectify when you are halfway through the painting. It quickly becomes obvious if the perspective is not correct: for example, a patio in the foreground of a garden scene might look as if it is going uphill, rather than lying level. Slight errors are difficult to spot while you are working on the wall, as your eye becomes adjusted to them. Try looking at the reflected image of the mural in a mirror – this will give you a fresh view, and instantly show up any areas that need attention.

One-point perspective

Imagine standing in the middle of a straight level railway track (do not try this for real!). Looking along the track, you will notice that the two rails seem to move closer and closer together the further away they are. The railway sleepers also appear closer to each other (see diagram above right). When the two rails reach the horizon, they appear to meet – the point where they meet is referred to as the vanishing point. Imagine a line of trees running parallel to the track – they will also diminish in size as they near the vanishing point.

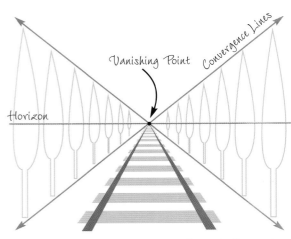

One-point Perspective

The horizon line and eye level

In general, the vanishing point is located on the horizon line. Imagine looking out across the sea to the distant horizon (below), where the sea and sky meet. This line will always appear to be at your eye level, whether you are standing or sitting, are on the beach or on a cliff top.

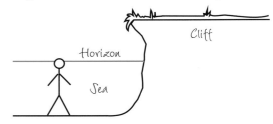

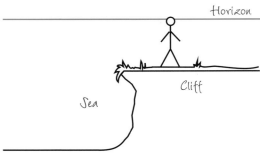

The Horizon Line and Eye Level

Establishing the horizon line is one of the first steps when planning a mural. To foster the illusion that you are looking into the distance, it needs to be placed on the wall at around the actual level of your eyes. My own eye level is at a height of about 173cm (5ft 8in), but because my murals will also be viewed by shorter people I plan a compromise horizon line to accommodate lower eye levels. If you are painting a mural that will normally be viewed from a sitting position, an even lower horizon line may be more effective.

The horizon line is the starting point for planning a distant landscape – any mountains or highlands will be above the line. However, there will be occasions when using the true horizon line would mean that little room would be left for an area of sky. In such cases, a degree of compromise is again required, and the rules may have to be bent slightly in favor of aesthetics.

Drawing convergence lines

The lines of the railway track are convergence lines: when parallel lines run away from the viewer, they will always meet at the vanishing point on the horizon. Similarly, if you stand in a room and face the far wall squarely, you will see that the edges of the floor and ceiling appear to be at an angle and to be leading toward the same point.

To help plan these converging lines in your mural, the first step is to establish the vanishing point. Once you have done this, a piece of string will suddenly become one of the most invaluable tools at your disposal. Simply fix a suitable length to the vanishing point using masking tape. Use three pieces of tape for this: the first piece holds the string in place, and two further pieces immediately to each side of the vanishing point stop the string slipping or the first piece of tape lifting away. You should be able to move the string in all directions without it slipping from the vanishing point, otherwise your measurements will be inaccurate.

The string can now be used to plan all the one-point perspective convergence lines in your mural, such as the edges of paving slabs, the inside edges of archways, windows and doorways, and other

architectural features in your design. Hold the string firmly so it is taut (but not so taut that it is pulled from the wall) and mark off points along the string with a pencil. Draw each convergence line along these points using a straight edge.

In this picture the converging lines of the doors, louvers and patio slabs would all meet at the vanishing point on the distant horizon. See page 41 for another example of convergence lines.

Use three pieces of tape to hold one end of the string at the vanishing point, so that you can move it in any direction without pulling it away from the wall. Hold the other end firmly while you mark the convergence lines.

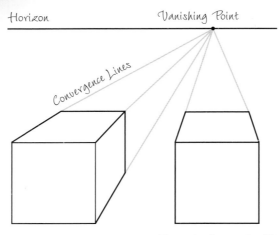

Horizon · Vanishing Point

Convergence Lines

Two-point Perspective (A)

Two-point perspective

Imagine a cube-shaped block. If it is directly in front of you, and below the vanishing point, you will be able to see the top of the block, with the sides converging toward the vanishing point, but the edges of the front face will be horizontal and vertical (see diagram A, above). If the block is moved to the left of the vanishing point, you will see some of the right-hand side, but the front face will still be square.

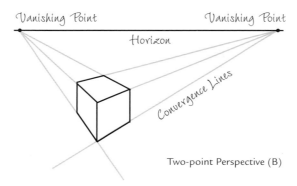

Vanishing Point · Vanishing Point

Horizon

Convergence Lines

Two-point Perspective (B)

Now imagine that the block is turned round slightly (see diagram B, above). The top and bottom edges of the front, which were horizontal, will now appear as converging lines, with a vanishing point on the horizon line to one side of the block. The other visible face has a separate vanishing point, again on the horizon line. The block no longer has a center vanishing point.

While the vanishing point for one-point perspective is straightforward to establish, two-point perspective can present problems. The vanishing points may be at quite a distance along the horizon line, and you will often find that there is not enough wall space to mark one of them in. In the Provençal Landscape project (page 334), the front edges of the louvered doors each have a separate vanishing point, but rather than try to establish these, which would be a fair distance from the mural, I simply drew the short converging lines by eye.

Three-point perspective.

If the block were extremely tall, like a skyscraper, the vertical sides would also appear to be converging toward a third vanishing point above it. However, it is very unlikely that you would ever need to resort to using three vanishing points, unless you need to exaggerate a great height or depth in your mural – generally, all your vertical lines will stay vertical.

Reflections

If an object is reflected in water, the reflection will share the same vanishing points as the object, and the depth of the reflection should equal the height of the object. If the reflected object is actually in the water (such as a boat) or right at its edge, the reflection will begin at the foot of the object.

An object such as a building or a tree is more likely to be standing further away from the water's edge. However, the line of reflection remains at the foot of the object and the depth of the reflection should still be measured from here. If the object is situated higher up – on a river bank, for instance – there will be a vertical distance between its foot and the surface of the water. The depth of the reflection will equal this vertical height plus the height of the object.

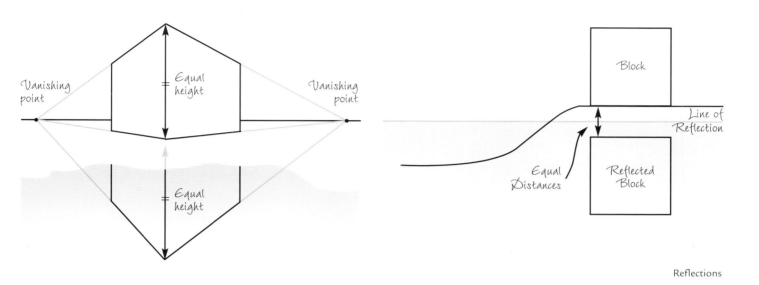

Vanishing point

Equal height

Vanishing point

Equal height

Block

Line of Reflection

Equal Distances

Reflected Block

Reflections

Equipment

· **Spirit level:** for establishing horizontals and verticals.
· **Charcoal pencil:** for marking guidelines that can be easily erased.
· **Straight edge:** for ruling lines.
· **String:** for marking convergence lines.
· **Masking tape:** to secure string at the vanishing point.

Using Color

Entire books have been written concerning color theory, but only brief notes are possible here. Sir Isaac Newton, who used a prism to separate daylight into its constituent colors, developed the color wheel in 1704, and a basic understanding of the wheel is helpful when choosing and mixing colors.

The three primary colors are red, yellow and blue. In theory, using these three colors in their purest form, any color in the spectrum can be produced. Secondary colors, shown between the primaries on the wheel, are produced by mixing two of the three primary colors together. Mixing red and blue produces violet, blue and yellow together produce green, and yellow and red produce orange.

Complementary colors

The use of complementary colors is a visual trick that artists have been playing for centuries. Colors that are opposite each other on the color wheel have the effect of enhancing each other. For example, a ripe tomato will appear a more vibrant red if it is placed on a green cloth, an orange will seem more striking against a blue sky, and so on.

As an experiment, paint two small areas of color – one in blue and one in red. Now paint an orange circle in the middle of each. The orange circle in the blue area will look much sharper and bolder than the circle in the red area, even though the strength of the orange is the same in both (see left, top and bottom).

Mixing two complementary colors will tend to give browny-grey tones, because opposite colors neutralize each other. This can be useful for mixing shadow tones, and is more effective than adding black to create a shadow, as this will only dirty the color. (As an exception to this rule, I do sometimes add a little black, or even Paynes Grey, to Chromium Oxide Green to make a deeper green.)

Harmonious colors

These are the colors that sit next to each other on the color wheel, such as the greens and blues, or the yellows and oranges. They can be used to create a more relaxing scene, in which the colors do not have the effect of pulling you in opposite directions.

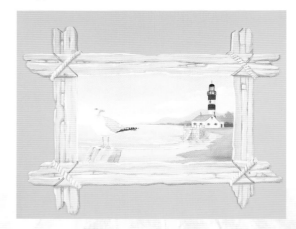

This painting uses mainly cool blues and greens. The red lighthouse offers the only striking visual element to complement the harmonious colors.

Warm and cool colors

Red, orange and yellow, on one side of the color wheel, are the warm colors that we associate with fire, while green, blue and violet on the other side are the cool colors that we associate with snow. However, if you compare different tones of any color, you will see that there are warm and cool versions of it.

Greys and neutrals

If you mix the three primary colors together in equal strengths you will get a true grey. In unequal strengths, they give a colored neutral. These neutrals and greys are much more versatile than the grey obtained by mixing Black and White. When painting skies, I usually mix Cobalt Blue with White for a general sky blue; by adding some Flesh Tint I can create a subtle pinky grey that is ideal for adding shadows to clouds.

Aerial or color perspective

The use of color can help to suggest distance in a mural. If you look over a landscape you will see that the distant hills and foliage take on a hazy bluish tinge, and may appear only a shade darker than the sky. This is due to the moisture and dust particles present in the atmosphere. The more distant an object, the more atmosphere you have to look through to see it, and the more faded its color will appear. A tree in the foreground will be a more vibrant green, with more visible detail, than one in the distance. If the distant elements in your mural look too defined, try painting over a light blue colorwash to 'knock back' the colors and blur the edges.

The color palette

If you flick through this book, you will see that I generally use the same basic paint colors for every project. This is the palette I have grown used to and as a rule I can use it to mix any color I need, rather than using a different tube of paint. Using a limited palette is a good discipline, and it has the effect of harmonizing the whole painting, because the acrylic color used to mix the sky tones, for example, will be the same one that was used to mix the colors for the mountains and trees. Over time you will build up your own personal palette of colors that you feel comfortable working with.

The rich colors and strong contrasts used in this mural help to evoke the brightness and warmth of a summer's day.

Tips on mixing colors

· If you are likely to need a lot of a particular color, mix more than you think you will need and keep it in an airtight container to stop it drying out. Mixing exactly the same shade again is nearly impossible. Alternatively, mix up a tester shade of the color you need, paint some on to a card and take it to a paint supplier to get as close a match as possible.

· When mixing very dark colors, like Paynes Grey or Cobalt Blue, into a lighter color, put some of the dark color in a separate pot and gradually mix in about 3–4 parts water. Gradually add this to the lighter color in another pot, mixing the paint as you go, until you get the desired color.

· When testing colors on the wall, bear in mind that the color will alter slightly as the paint dries, and will generally be darker when wet. A hair dryer can be useful to dry paint quickly.

· If you need to match a color on the wall, cut a square hole in the center of a small piece of white card. Mix the color you think will fit and paint it over the card. When the paint has dried, hold the card up to the wall and look at the two shades – this should give you a indication of how close your color match is and how to amend it.

Applying Light and Shadow

When light is cast on to an object, the shadows, highlights and tonal values that are created describe the object's form. In trompe l'oeil, the use of light and shadow has a vital role in rendering believable three-dimensional objects.

Light source

Before you can model an object using highlights and shadows, you need to establish the direction of the light source. If the wall you are working on has a window to the left or right then it makes sense to use this as the light source for your painting. If the mural depicts an open window, the main source of light will be from the perceived daylight coming through the window. This will have the effect of highlighting the inside return of the window frame – even the top. Do not feel that as the sun is high in the sky the top return of the window should be in shadow: it will be highlighted by reflected light – if in doubt, look at a real window in daylight from inside to see what I mean.

Cast shadows

If you are painting a trompe l'oeil scene, such as an urn in a garden, think about the time of day you are trying to recreate and therefore what the sun's position in the sky would be. At midday in the summer, the sun would be high in the sky so the cast shadows would be short and sharply defined. Early or late in the day, the light would be weaker and the shadows longer. They would be more defined near the base of the urn, softer and more blurry toward their ends.

The best way to appreciate how light affects an object is through observation: look at objects at different times of the day, and even in artificial light. It is equally important to observe

Subtle shading on the terra cotta pot contrasts with the sharp highlights on the glazed vase.

the colors in the cast shadows – they are seldom grey. Shadows on white surfaces, for example, can take on a subtle blue-grey color, or may sometimes even be pinkish. Sometimes you can use some of the complementary color of the object in its cast shadow – for example, adding a purple tinge to the color of the shadow cast by a bunch of bananas.

If the surface on which the shadow falls is a different color, such as red, you will need to add its complementary color, green, to make a shadow tone. Look at the real shadows cast on the wall and try to match the color – this involves a lot of trial and error so I suggest experimenting on another part of the wall until you feel the color is right.

Conveying the solidity of a subject such as this urn and pedestal depends entirely on the depiction of light and shadow playing on the stone.

to look at a black and white photograph. In the absence of color, you can see how the light is affecting the tonal values of different objects. You will also notice how different shapes and surfaces are affected by the light, and the transitions between tones. For example, a spherical object will have smoother gradations of tone than an angular object, and a polished surface has sharper highlights than a matt surface.

When painting these tones, you can simplify them down to a medium tone, or base color, a shadow tone and a highlight tone. Both the shadow and highlight tones should be mixed from the base color.

The smooth, curved surface of this ball (above) calls for subtle gradations of tone, while sharp highlights and shadows define the angular contours and hard, shiny surfaces of a child's toy bucket and spade (left).

Tone

Tonal values are the different grades of a single color that come about when light is cast over an object. If you look at a yellow ball in sunlight, you will see that on the part of the ball facing the light the yellow is almost white. As the ball's surface curves away from the light, the color deepens. A very bright light would give dramatic changes in tone, and a more diffused light would give a more subtle gradation of tone. The best way to appreciate this is

Clouds can be added, with the flat brush, by using some of the lighter blues and painting the top edge of the color, then blending downward. Repeating this and overlapping the cloud shapes will give the sky a feeling of depth. A little white can be added to the cloud tips as a highlight.

Special Painting Techniques

The detailed instructions for the projects in this book include plenty of hints on achieving realistic-looking textures and effects in trompe l'oeil, but some elements crop up in many different contexts, and it is well worth mastering some of the tried and tested techniques that will turn your paintings into really convincing illusions. Expert sky, cloud and foliage effects will give depth to landscapes, while ageing techniques are applied to give interest to the painted surface itself.

Skies

If you look at the sky on a clear day you will see that the blue is deepest in the highest part, and lightens toward the distant horizon, to a very pale blue that is almost white. Early in the morning the sky may be a light ochre yellow near the horizon, while a subtle pinky tinge to the horizon will suggest the end of the day.

I use Cobalt Blue and Coeruleum Blue mixed into White to make sky blues. Mix at least three shades, graduating them from light to dark, and thin them slightly with water to help the colors blend together more easily. Using a flat brush, paint the sky in horizontal strokes, working from the top down to the horizon. Begin with the darkest shade, and work through to the lighter shades, blending the colors as you go.

Foliage

The different colors and textures of leaves are very useful in suggesting depth in a mural. The trees and shrubs in the foreground will show the strongest colors and highest contrasts, and clumps of foliage can be indicated by stippling with a flat brush. Further away, the colors will appear softer and bluer, until they almost merge with the distant hills or the sky.

To reproduce a warm late afternoon sky, White mixed with a little Flesh Tint is blended up from the horizon into the lighter blues, and is also used to tint the bottom of the clouds.

Depth is created in this hazy landscape by stippling in the mid-ground foliage and distant trees in a range of blue tones. Further forward in the mural more greens are added, so that the bold foliage stands out against the subtle blues and jades of the distant trees.

This olive tree has been built up in stippled layers. The tree trunk and branches are painted using Raw Umber mixed with Paynes Grey. The green base color is Chromium Oxide Green with a little Paynes Grey. Mid-green, a mixture of White, Chromium Oxide Green, Flesh Tint and a little Cobalt Blue, is first stippled along the top edge of the tree and then blended down. This can be repeated to highlight other prominent parts of the foliage. Further highlights can be picked out in light green, mixed from White, Chromium Oxide Green and Naples Yellow, which is then blended into the mid-green. If the effect begins to look too dense, patches of the background colors can be stippled between the foliage to break it up slightly.

Ageing effects

Ancient frescos, like the leaping dolphins that adorn the walls of the Queen's Apartment in the Cretan Palace of Knossos, hold a great fascination. Much of their charm lies in their fragility, as the passing centuries have crumbled away parts of the the fresco surface. If you want to echo the soft colors and pitted surface of an ancient wall you can either leave your mural to age naturally for the next few thousand years – or try a few shortcuts to achieve the impression of age.

Vandalizing your work in such a manner may seem daunting, but the results will be worth it. It is a good idea to practice the techniques first on a sample board or another wall, particularly those that involve painting over your mural.

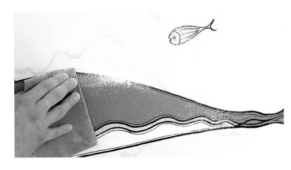

1 First distress the surface of the mural in random areas, using medium-grade sandpaper – use different motions to see what effects can be achieved. Try rubbing away a small area of solid color, then painting over it again in one light coat – this will give a subtle patchy effect to the color.

2 Make up a wash using 1 part Raw Umber and 7 parts water. Brush this color over random areas of the wall using a large decorator's brush, ensuring that you brush out any paint runs. This will have the effect of dirtying the mural, so do not overdo it. Use a wet cloth to rub off some of the color in a few areas. Repeat this as desired, and above all experiment.

3 Mix Naples Yellow with White and add a small amount of Raw Umber and Paynes Grey. Add little or no water, as the paint needs to be reasonably thick. Using a 15mm (^{5}/$_8$in) flat brush, paint a diagonal crack, adjusting the pressure and angle of the brush to control the width of the line. As you reach the edge of the mural, open the crack out so that it forks, creating little islands of broken fresco. Keep the edges sharp and angular, occasionally rounding the odd edge here and there. The 'missing' parts of the mural need to be completely blotted out, so keep building up the layers of paint.

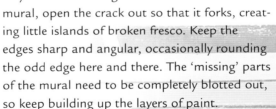

4 Add a little more Raw Umber and Paynes Grey to some of the color to make a shadow tone. Using a No. 5 round pointed brush, pick out the sharp cast shadows in the areas you have painted out, to create the illusion that the areas of missing fresco are recessed into the wall. In some areas, the edges where the light would fall can be slightly highlighted using Naples Yellow and White with a No. 3 round pointed brush.

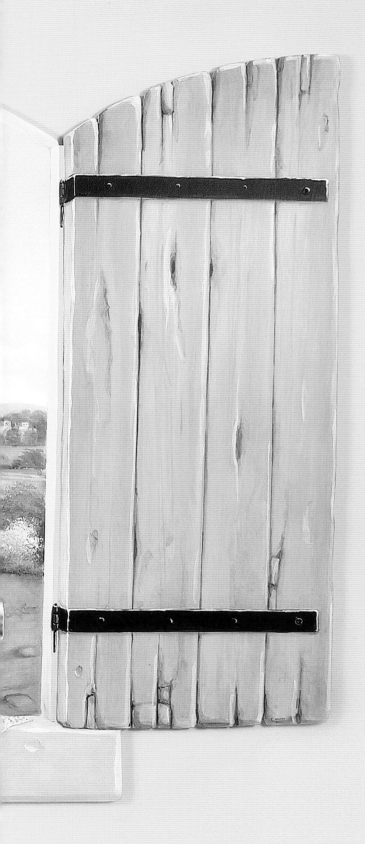

Country Views

Thoughts of the countryside can summon up a host of different images: we might envisage a vibrant carpet of bluebells, with their delicate scent wafted on the spring breeze, a babbling brook, a crumbling villa flanked by cypress trees, the vivid greens and sky blues of a lazy summer, or the golden browns of fallen leaves as the end of the year approaches. Even a countryside scene frozen under a covering of snow can fill us with warmth.

A view of open space and natural beauty is a constant pleasure, providing an escape from towns and cities, steel and concrete, into a simpler way of life away from the pressures of modern living. But if you don't have the countryside just outside your window, a painted view of your favorite rural scene can lift your spirits even on the dullest days.

For the best effect, link the scene outside to your own interior by framing it in a doorway or window, softened with curtains or shutters, or perhaps a trailing plant – even a grapevine. If you are painting a windowsill, add a vase of country flowers that look as if you have just picked them in the fields outside.

Provençal Landscape

THE DIVERSE LANDSCAPE of this region of southern France has a rich palette of colors, blending fields of golden wheat with rows of lavender, vineyards and orchards growing cherries, peaches and apricots. These beautiful, sunlit vistas inspired Van Gogh and his contemporaries to capture the essence of the Provençal landscape on canvas.

The feeling of depth in this mural is created by the use of perspective on the window shutters, the receding rows of lavender, the cool blue of the hills and the pale jade greens of the distant trees. Bold colors are used for the foreground elements – the terra cotta-washed wall, yellow shutters and purple lavender – helping them to leap forward in the mural. Sunlight is suggested by the strong shadows cast by the shutters, and the contrast between the sunlit and shaded walls of the distant farmhouse.

Experiment with variations of the scene and colors (see pages 346–349 for inspiration). You might prefer a sand-colored wall, with green or jade shutters, or you could change the scene entirely, perhaps to a view of Tuscan, Basque or Scandinavian countryside.

Palette

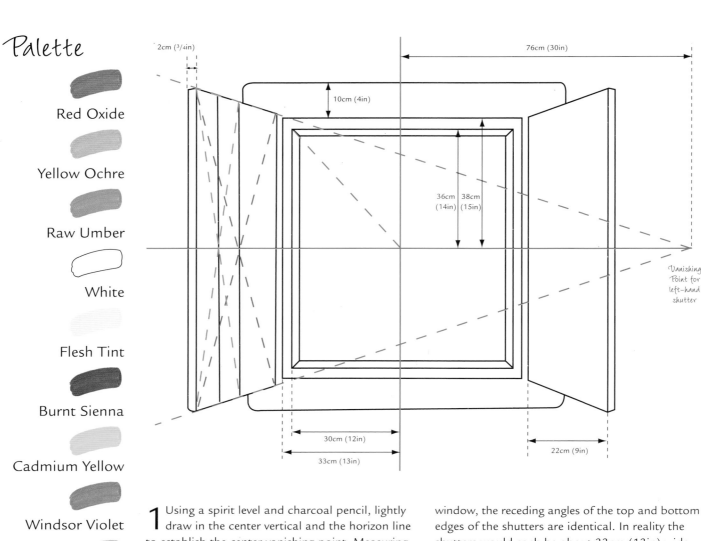

2cm (³/₄in)

76cm (30in)

10cm (4in)

36cm (14in) 38cm (15in)

Vanishing Point for left-hand shutter

30cm (12in)

33cm (13in)

22cm (9in)

Red Oxide

Yellow Ochre

Raw Umber

White

Flesh Tint

Burnt Sienna

Cadmium Yellow

Windsor Violet

Raw Sienna

Cobalt Blue

Coeruleum Blue

Chromium Oxide Green

Paynes Grey

Leaf Green

1 Using a spirit level and charcoal pencil, lightly draw in the center vertical and the horizon line to establish the center vanishing point. Measuring from these guidelines, draw the rest of the window frame referring to the diagram. To draw the short receding lines at the inner corners of the frame, position a straight edge so it intersects the center vanishing point.

Draw the inner edges of the shutter doors about 1.5cm (⁵/₈in) from the window frame to allow space for the hinges, which should be about 10cm (4in) from the top and bottom of the shutters. Different vanishing points are needed to draw the shutters as they are open at an angle to the wall. Measure 76cm (30in) from the center along the horizon on each side. Fix a length of string to the first point to mark the positions for the top and bottom edges, and the hinges, of the opposite shutter, then repeat on the other side. As the horizon line passes through the middle of the

window, the receding angles of the top and bottom edges of the shutters are identical. In reality the shutters would each be about 33cm (13in) wide, but as they are viewed at an angle they appear foreshortened and are drawn at about 22cm (9in) wide. Use a length of masking tape to help establish the position of each outer edge, standing back to check it by eye, then draw in the vertical to meet the two diverging lines. Draw parallel verticals for the edges of the shutters, which are 2cm (³/₄in) thick; the lines at the top and bottom of the edges should slope slightly from the horizontal.

To divide each shutter into planks, draw diagonals from the corners and draw a vertical where they intersect. Repeat with each section to divide the shutter into four. When drawing in the hinges, ensure that they extend over all the planks and follow the same vanishing point used for the door.

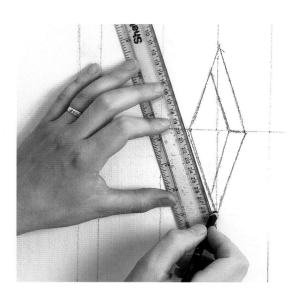

2 Position the diamond cutouts in the center of the shutters by measuring 8cm (3in) above and below the horizon line for the top and bottom of the diamond. Mark the two side points in the middle of the width of each plank, and join the points to make the diamond. Draw a 2cm (³/₄in) line horizontally from the inner corner of the diamond, then draw the two inner diagonal lines parallel to the outer lines, to represent the thickness of the shutter.

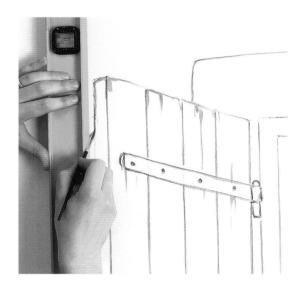

3 Paint in the outlines of the frame, shutters and hinges, using dilute red oxide paint and a No. 5 round pointed brush. Use a spirit level to guide the brush. Indicate some ageing and random splitting of the wood. Divide the stone frame into three at the top and bottom, and paint in the joints, kinking the vertical lines inward on the inner part of the frame in line with the center vanishing point.

4 Attach a sheet of transfer paper to the area inside the window and draw in the horizon line established in step 1. Draw the main elements of the design using the illustration, or your own preliminary sketches, as reference. Keep the distant highlands above the horizon line and the foreground below. To help with the perspective of the lavender rows, use string taped halfway between the center vanishing point and the right hand side of the window on the horizon line, but avoid drawing the lines too straight. When you are happy with the composition transfer the design on to the wall.

5 Paint in the land-scape outlines in Red Oxide, using Nos. 3 and 5 round pointed brushes, and adding further details as you go. Mix up a color-wash using Yellow Ochre, Raw Umber and White mixed with about 4–5 parts water. Test the wash on a small area to ensure you are happy with the color, then wash it over the whole mural using a large decorator's brush. Leave to dry and repeat if necessary.

6 Mix up a terra cotta color using Flesh Tint, Burnt Sienna and White, mixed with about 2 parts water. Using a 25mm (1in) hog-hair brush, paint the area outside the window frame (use the large decorator's brush if you are carrying this color over a large wall area). Aim to achieve the effect of an aged terra cotta wall, applying the color unevenly and thinning it in places with the wash used in step 5. The effect can be finalized with further coats later.

7 For the shutters, mix Cadmium Yellow Deep Hue with a little White and 1 part water. For a deeper shadow tone, mix some of this color with a little Windsor Violet and Raw Sienna. Use a 25mm (1in) hog-hair brush and a 15mm (⁵/₈in) flat brush to block in the doors using vertical strokes. Leave the paint patchy in places to give a weathered effect. As the light source is to the right, the left-hand door will catch more light than the right, so paint this lighter, with the edge in shadow. The right-hand door should be painted in the slightly darker tone.

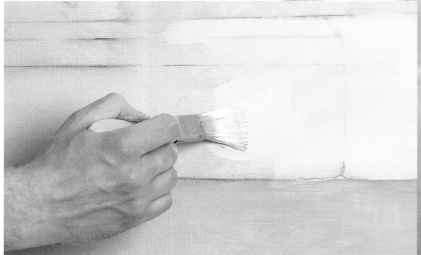

8 For the window frame, mix Raw Umber and White with 1 part water. Add some Flesh Tint to make a second, warmer stone color. Use a 25mm (1in) hog-hair brush and a 15mm (⁵/₈in) flat brush to brush and stipple the two colors to create a stone effect.

9 Mix Cobalt Blue, Coeruleum Blue and White, with 1 part water, to give three varying shades of blue (the lightest blue should be nearly white). Using a 15mm (5/8in) flat brush, paint the sky, starting from the top with the deepest blue, and working downward using horizontal strokes. Switch to the lighter blues as you work down toward the mountains, blending the colors as you go. Repeat until you get a smooth gradation of color.

10 Loosely block in the distant mountains using a 15mm (5/8in) flat brush and a mix of Cobalt Blue, White and a little Burnt Sienna, with 1 part water. Allow the yellow wash to show through slightly, to give the color a pleasing texture. Try also mixing in some of the sky blue colors to vary the tones.

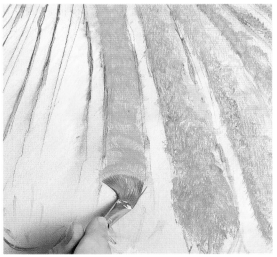

11 Mix two shades of jade green using Cobalt Blue, Chromium Oxide Green and White, with 1 part water. Use Nos. 3 and 5 round pointed brushes to block in the mid-ground trees and foliage, again leaving a patchy texture. Build up the shade on the farmhouse using some of the terra cotta wall color and the deeper sky blue. Leave the walls facing the light source unpainted, to give the buildings form.

12 Mix two shades of lavender using Windsor Violet and White. Use a 15mm (5/8in) flat brush to stipple the color down each row of lavender, pushing the brush into the wall so that it fans out. As the light is coming from the right, keep the darker shade to the left of the rows. Note that where you see the lavender rows head on, the gaps between them are visible, but they are gradually obscured as you look across the rows.

13 Returning to the stone window frame, mix a dark stone color using Flesh Tint, Cobalt Blue, Paynes Grey and a little White, with 1 part water. Using Nos. 3 and 5 round pointed brushes, pick out the deep shadows in the joints between the stones, next to the shutter and in the inner recess of the frame. Mix White with a little of the original stone color mixed in step 8 to pick out the highlights at the top of the frame, and around the recess. Create chips in the stone by smudging the darker tone in places and adding a highlight to the bottom left of the smudge.

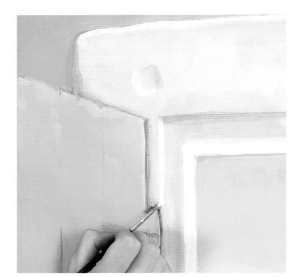

14 Boldly defined shadows cast by the shutters suggest strong sunlight. With the light source from the upper right, the shadows are cast toward the bottom left. The shadow cast by the right-hand door is shorter, but the bottoms of both shadows should line up horizontally, as both doors are open at the same angle. Use masking tape lightly to help you plan where the shadows should fall, re-applying it until you are happy with their angle and length. Sketch in the edge of the shadow and remove the tape.

15 Mix up a shadow tone by adding Cobalt Blue to some of the wall color mixed in step 6, and paint it on using a 25mm (1in) hog-hair brush and a 15mm (5/8in) flat brush, not forgetting to paint inside the diamond cutouts. Paint the shadow over the window frame using the dark stone color mixed in step 13.

16 For the shadows on the shutters, mix a deeper yellow with Cadmium Yellow and Windsor Violet, with a small amount of White and a little water. Use a No. 3 round pointed brush to pick out the deep shadows between the planks. Paint shallow shadows underneath the hinges and bring out the detail by adding highlights at the top, using White mixed with a little Cadmium Yellow. Pick out highlights on the tops of the doors and along the planks. Deeper yellows can also be used to suggest a woodgrain effect.

17 Mix Chromium Oxide Green with a little Paynes Grey, and use Nos. 3 and 5 round pointed brushes to strengthen the greens of the mid-ground trees, darkening the color toward the bottom. Mix in some Leaf Green and stipple some more vibrant foliage using a 10mm (³/₈in) flat brush. Mix some of the deep sky blue color with a little more Cobalt Blue, and use this to add some deep blue foliage behind the trees, to build up the feeling of depth.

18 Sketch the large tree on the right lightly in charcoal. Mix Raw Umber with Paynes Grey, with 1 part water, and use Nos. 1, 3 and 5 round pointed brushes to build up the structure of the tree, with the trunk splitting into branches and then into smaller branches and twigs. Keep a suitable reference nearby.

19 Use 15mm (⁵/₈in) and 10mm (³/₈in) flat brushes to stipple the foliage of the tree. First use Chromium Oxide Green to flesh out the skeleton, leaving random gaps in the foliage. Paint in the trunk and branches again where necessary, before stippling on a lighter color using a mixture of Leaf Green, Chromium Oxide Green and White. Leave some of the deeper green visible to help create depth in the foliage.

20 Use the yellows of the shutters and shadow tones to build up layers of grass in the foreground, to obscure the ends of the lavender rows. Using a 15mm (⁵/₈in) flat brush, apply the paint in short upward sweeps. Blend in some of the greens in places to break up the yellow. Look over the whole mural again and tweak the details or build up the colors where necessary.

Wisteria Trellis

TREILLAGE, OR THE ART OF TRELLISWORK – using a latticework of wooden struts to create elegant garden features – has been around since the fourteenth century. It has been used to erect elaborate structures that echo grand architectural forms, but these days trelliswork is most often used more simply, fixed to a wall to act as a support for climbing plants.

In this mural, the trellis provides a well-structured yet light and airy support for the climbing wisteria, providing a delicately colored setting for the dangling flowers. Its open center allows a clear view of the blue sky, and through the structure can be seen a tantalizing glimpse of the landscape beyond. The wall to be painted can be white or off-white.

This small-scale project looks effective on its own, but it could also be combined with other ideas: a trellis archway with climbing plants could lead into an idyllic country garden, or a trellis frieze could be painted along the top of a wall, with a climbing plant weaving in and out of it, such as the ivy or grapevines on pages 350–351.

Palette

Raw Umber

White

Flesh Tint

Naples Yellow

Windsor Violet

Cobalt Blue

Coeruleum Blue

Chromium Oxide
Green

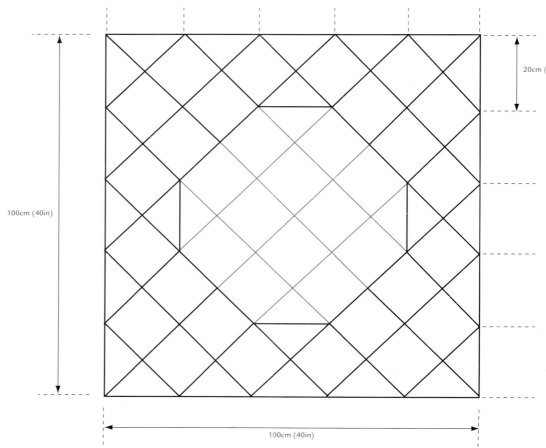

100cm (40in)

20cm (8in)

100cm (40in)

1 Using a spirit level and charcoal pencil, measure out a 100cm (40in) square at about window height on the wall. Divide each of the four sides into five 20cm (8in) sections. Lightly join up the points with diagonal lines, following the diagram, to form the grid pattern for the trellis.

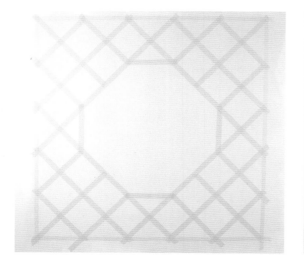

2 Using low-tack masking tape 2.5cm (1in) wide, tape over the diagonal charcoal lines, leaving a window in the center. Also mask off the four sides of the outer square. Be careful not to lift flakes of paint when you remove the tape. Test an area first, and if the painted surface is unsuitable for masking tape, paint the design onto a panel which can be mounted onto the wall when finished.

3 Mix three or four sky blues, using varying proportions of White, Cobalt Blue and Coeruleum Blue. Keep the paint reasonably thick, adding only a small amount of water, if any, to avoid paint seeping under the tape, and use a 25mm (1in) hog-hair brush, working outward from the tape in short strokes. Blend the colors from darkest at the top to lightest at the bottom, and repeat this step two or three times to get the desired effect. Finally, add some simple clouds in the middle, using the lighter blue and blending the color downward.

344 Country Views

4 Mix one shade of green using Chromium Oxide Green and a little White, and a second, darker shade using Chromium Oxide Green, Cobalt Blue and a little White. Using a 15mm (^{5}/$_8$in) flat brush and the darker green, loosely paint some foliage along the bottom and a little way up the sides of the trellis. Gradually blend this color upward into the paler green, and then into the deeper sky blue. Create vague leaf shapes using simple, short brush strokes.

5 Mix two greeny browns, using Raw Umber, Chromium Oxide Green, Naples Yellow and a little White. Using Nos. 5 and 7 round pointed brushes, paint the wisteria stems coming in from about a quarter of the way up each side and winding up and over the trellis, gradually tapering the stems.

6 Use a No. 3 round pointed brush to add the smaller stems that will bear the leaves, curving them slightly downward. Add even smaller stems growing out equally on each side, again curving down. Using the greens mixed in step 4 and a No. 5 round pointed brush, paint the long

7 Paint similar fine stems for the flowers, about 18cm (7in) long, hanging down from the main stem and slightly curved. Mix two shades using White, Windsor Violet and Coeruleum Blue, and paint the flowers using Nos. 3 and 5 round pointed brushes. Follow a simple inverted teardrop shape for each flower panicle, wide at the top and tapering at the bottom, curving it to follow the shape of the stem. Use simple short brush strokes for the individual flowers.

8 Work over the mural again to enhance any areas that need bringing out more, such as deepening some of the foliage at the bottom. When the paint is completely dry, carefully remove the masking tape and wipe off the charcoal guidelines. Mix a pinky grey shadow tone using White, Flesh Tint and Cobalt Blue. Using a No. 3 round pointed brush, paint thin cast shadows to the lower right of each intersection so that it appears that the trellis is overlapping. A small blob of shadow tone in the middle of each intersection gives the appearance that the trellis is nailed together. Add more leaves and flowers hanging in front of the trellis (mix some slightly lighter greens and vio-

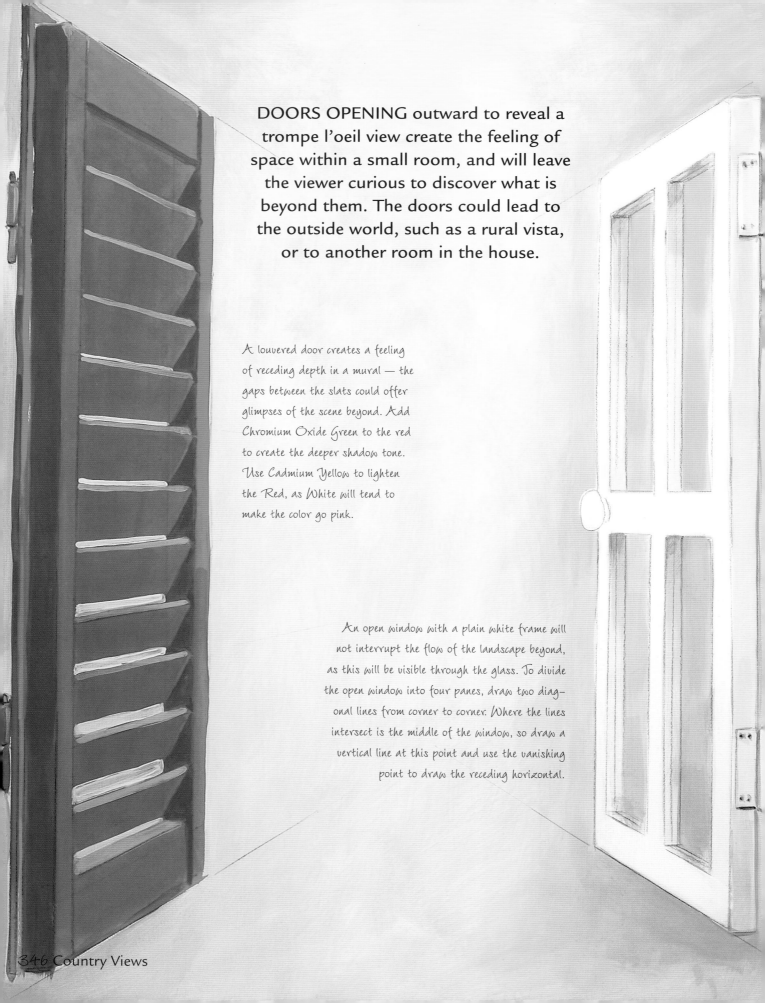

DOORS OPENING outward to reveal a trompe l'oeil view create the feeling of space within a small room, and will leave the viewer curious to discover what is beyond them. The doors could lead to the outside world, such as a rural vista, or to another room in the house.

A louvered door creates a feeling of receding depth in a mural — the gaps between the slats could offer glimpses of the scene beyond. Add Chromium Oxide Green to the red to create the deeper shadow tone. Use Cadmium Yellow to lighten the Red, as White will tend to make the color go pink.

An open window with a plain white frame will not interrupt the flow of the landscape beyond, as this will be visible through the glass. To divide the open window into four panes, draw two diagonal lines from corner to corner. Where the lines intersect is the middle of the window, so draw a vertical line at this point and use the vanishing point to draw the receding horizontal.

This design demonstrates clearly the use of one-point perspective. The horizon line of the sea is the same as the eye-level line. The vanishing point is shown in the middle of this line. Note how the receding lines of the floor tiles and the louvered doors all converge at this point.

This rustic window, above, opens on to a view of a vineyard in Tuscany, and a bottle and glass of red wine, from the Chianti region, sit on the windowsill to bring the theme into the foreground. Pages 356—357 show how to paint realistic glasses and bottles.

A simple piece of fabric draped over a curtain pole will soften the edges of an otherwise stark window frame (see page 355). The pot of flowers in the foreground brings the window to life, and provides opportunity for detail that looks so real it will keep the viewer guessing.

WHAT COULD be more relaxing than the view of fields, trees and distant hills? The ideas here bring a sense of space and light into any room of the house. You may want to embellish the window frames with ivy or rustic accessories (see the next few pages for ideas) depending on which room you have chosen.

For a garden scene with perspective, try a pergola surround, framing an archway cut in a hedge, leading to a vista further beyond. This is a simple way to create an interesting view-beyond-a-view.

Here is a twist on the trompe l'oeil window — you could almost peer through the window into a rustic cottage! This would be effective in a conservatory or other extension — the 'original' window appearing to still be intact. The glass of wine and napkin add depth to the windowsill.

A GRAPEVINE growing up the side of a wall and then along the top of an arch or doorway makes a fantastic framing element for a landscape mural, especially if the view includes a distant vineyard. Intertwine ivy with classical stonework (pages 370–379) for a soft, aged look; twist it through trellis in a kitchen or conservatory (see page 342) or use it as a backdrop for real plants to merge reality with illusion.

The vine leaf shape is easy to sketch. First, lightly draw a rough circle using a charcoal pencil, then sketch a line dividing the circle in two. From about a third of the way along this line, draw four slightly curved lines to form the structure or skeleton of the leaf. It is now a simple task to flesh out the leaf shape, adding the crinkly edges. This leaf is flat, but the basic technique can be adapted to draw the leaves at different angles. Build up the color using Chromium Oxide Green, Leaf Green and White.

A trained ivy plant in a plain terra cotta pot would make a simple feature in the foreground of a mural. A matching pair could perhaps be placed on either side of a doorway. Paint the basic shape of the twisting plant in Chromium Oxide Green using a 15mm (⁵/₈in) flat brush. Mix a lighter green using Chromium Oxide Green, Leaf Green and White, and use a No. 3 round pointed brush to paint the lower edges of an individual leaf, then smudge the color upward to blend into the deep green. Repeat this all over the plant, and add a few straggly leaves breaking away from the clipped shape. Mix some Paynes Grey into the Chromium Oxide Green to pick out some deeper shadows, especially on the side of the plant that is further from the light source — in this case, the left-hand side.

Ivy leaves can be planned out in a very similar way to the vine leaves opposite. In this case, the leaf is more pointed. Ivy leaves are quite dark: use Chromium Oxide Green with a little Paynes Grey. The veins and edges of the leaves have been picked out with White mixed with the leaf color.

A SIMPLE arrangement of flowers, or even a single stem, makes an excellent foreground subject, for instance on a windowsill, when you are painting a country view, linking the painted frame with the landscape. You could also paint a vase of flowers on a real or trompe l'oeil shelf or table, such as those on the next few pages.

Use Permanent Rose for pink rose flowers, lightening the color by adding White to pick out the upper surfaces of the petals. This will define the form of the flowers.

Outline a clear glass bottle in a mix of Paynes Grey and White, blended out toward the middle. Add a little of the background color. The color of the water is deepened at the top, to emphasize the contrast with the light reflected on its surface. The stem of the rose is also shown slightly refracted as it passes through the water surface. A subtle green wash glazed over the water area gives a slightly murky look.

These white daisies would also work very well if painted against a deep background color to give a strong contrast. .

The part of the tulip I love the most is not the flower but the wonderfully expressive leaf, which unfurls from around the stem as it grows. The leaves here are a little more stylized than real. The flower is painted in Cadmium Orange and Cadmium Yellow, and gives a bold, contemporary feel suitable for a modern sitting room.

These geraniums have very rounded leaves: use a paler green to delineate their crisp edges and contrast with the deeper green veins, then blend it in toward the middle of each leaf. The flowers are simply painted as a cluster of blobs, using a mixture of Permanent Rose and White.

For a collection of china that is both
unbreakable and never requires dusting,
a row of willow pattern plates would be
ideal, mounted onto a real or trompe
l'oeil shelf.
Transfer the willow pattern design for
the plate on to the wall. Use Cobalt
Blue and White with Nos.1 and 3
round pointed brush to pick out the
details, although do not try to copy the
willow design to the exact last detail.

A lace effect is easy to achieve, and is a subtle way to enhance a bare
wall or plain shelf. Photocopy or scan a piece of lace and use this to
trace the design on to the wall. Paint in the design with Red Oxide
before painting on the background colors. Then use Nos.1 and 3 round
point brushes to pick out the lace work with White paint.

EVEN THE simplest of embellishments can add country charm to a kitchen or dining room. Create a collection of teapots by experimenting with different colors and patterns. For a believable effect, everything in the collection should be lit from the same direction. In addition, a stark kitchen window that has only a blind would benefit from a pair of checked curtains to soften the window frame and add color and movement.

The use of a pattern on fabric helps to suggest form through the folding and bunching, as seen with the blue and white checked curtain opposite. In the case of the red and white curtain (right), the pattern has been used to suggest movement as it blows in the breeze from an open window. To re-create this effect, first block the curtain in with base color, in this case an off white, then build up highlights and shadows to suggest folds. Very lightly plan out the pattern on the curtain using a charcoal pencil — note how the pattern follows the shape at the bottom of the curtain. Finally, use a suitable round or flat brush to paint in the design using a deeper shade to suggest the folds and shadow.

Highlights and shadow suggest the smooth curves of an object, such as this teapot. A touch of highlight on the spout, lid and handle bring the surface to life, while the highlight on the body of the teapot suggests a reflected window.

A HALF-FILLED glass of wine and a half empty bottle provide a relaxed focal point in a mural, and are simple to add to a window sill or table. Why not paint them on a dining room sideboard, or on the wall at the back of the kitchen work surface?

The wine bottle is built up with a mixture of Leaf Green, Chromium Oxide Green and White — the highlights emphasize the curvature of the bottle. The red wine color is a mixture of Red Oxide and Chromium Oxide Green, which deepens the red for the shading.

For the edges of the glass use Paynes Grey, Raw Umber and White with Nos. 1 and 3 round pointed brushes. Note the white highlights, the way the wine color is reflected down the stem of the glass and the colors of the tablecloth, visible through the base of the glasses.

The champagne bottle uses the same greens as the wine bottle, but add some Paynes Grey to the mix for the deep tones along the edges, to accentuate the curvature. Yellow Ochre, Raw Umber and White have been stippled on for the gold colored foil. Simply suggest the lettering on the label, and turn the bottle so the label is off-center and partly obscured.

Use Raw Sienna mixed with White for the champagne in these flute glasses — add a little Raw Umber to blend in a deeper tone around the edges. Dab on some bubbles with White and a No. 3 round pointed brush, and repeat for the fizzing along the surface of the champagne.

THE CONTENTS of a country kitchen offer lots of potential to enhance your mural with extra details, such as a notice board with postcards, cookery books, utensils and cooking ingredients on kitchen shelves. Why not paint the doors of plain kitchen cupboards to give the illusion that they are stocked with homemade preserves or pots and pans?

Various interesting wall surfaces are shown here, including a crumbling brick wall, cracked plaster, and tongue-and-groove paneling. The bunch of lavender would also look effective hanging from a window frame or shutter framing a rustic landscape.

Wherever possible, use the real objects for reference. Use different textures to create visual interest: here the sharp reflective highlights on the bottles and grater contrast with the subtle shading on the eggs and terra cotta jar.

Classical Details

The architecture of classical Greece left an enduring legacy, which can still be seen in building styles today. The classical orders were embraced by the Romans, who built upon the beauties of Greek architecture by introducing rounded arches in their desire to build on a larger scale. Their influence spread throughout the western world with the growth of the Roman empire, and the architects of the Renaissance returned to the grace and proportions of classical style, which could still be seen in the buildings that had survived since ancient times. It remains an essential part of the fabric of our modern environment, forming an architectural link with a culture of 2,500 years ago.

The decorative details of 18th- and 19th-century homes, which we love today for the charm and elegance they add to period interiors, often drew on classical conventions. Trompe l'oeil techniques allow you to add architectural distinction of this kind to a plain interior, by creating the illusion of carved pediments above doorways, or by adding pillars, paneling and moldings. You can also incorporate classical details in a painted vista, such as a balustrade to frame the view, or a crumbling ruin in the distance.

Stone
Rosette Panel

THIS IS A SIMPLE architectural ornament that could be used effectively as a detail in a larger scheme incorporating decorative stonework, or to enhance a trompe l'oeil architectural feature such as a decorative door frame or faux paneling. In a large-scale project this kind of motif might be repeated, but a single rosette would make an attractive decoration for a chimney piece, a cupboard door or perhaps a plinth supporting an urn — either real or painted in a mural.
Pages 370–373 show further intricate stonework features that could be isolated and used as embellishments in the same way.

The three-dimensional form is quickly achieved by adding shadow and highlight tones to the simple design, and you can apply this technique to almost any carved shape. Since the relief effect depends entirely on light and shade, it's important to establish the direction of the light source, and this must be consistent if you are painting more than one motif. In this example, the light is coming from the upper left, so the shadows are cast down to the right. Keep standing back to view the effect – you will soon see if it is working.

Stone Rosette Panel 363

Palette

White

Flesh Tint

Cobalt Blue

Naples Yellow

1 Trace and scale up the rosette on transfer paper. The example shown here is 16cm (6¹/₂in) in diameter. Decide on the position for the center of the motif on the wall, and use a spirit level and charcoal pencil to draw horizontal and vertical guidelines intersecting at this point. Draw guidelines on the design to help you line it up, and transfer the design to the wall.

2 Remove the transfer paper, and use compasses to draw in the circle around the design (stick some masking tape over the center point to protect the wall, and to stop the compasses from slipping).

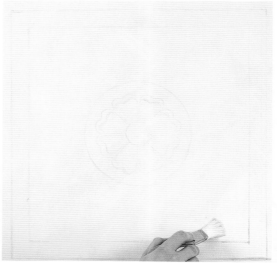

3 Ensuring that the rosette is centrally placed, lightly draw the lines for the square panel using a spirit level and charcoal pencil. In this example the inner panel is 40cm (15¹/₂in) wide and the outer panel is 46cm (18in). Mix some Flesh Tint, Cobalt Blue and a little White with a small amount of water. Use a No. 3 round pointed brush to paint over all the outlines, using a straight edge for the panel lines.

4 Mix three light colors for the stone, using White and Naples Yellow, White and Flesh Tint, and White and Cobalt Blue. Mix 1–2 parts water into each color. Using a 25mm (1in) hog-hair brush, paint over the whole design, building up a subtle stone effect by alternating between the three colors (use the White and Naples Yellow color sparingly). You should still be able to see the outlines. Use the brush in all directions and stipple the color in places, perhaps adding a little white if it is getting too dark.

5 The outline color mixed in step 3 can be used as a shadow tone. Using Nos. 3 and 5 round pointed brushes, pick out the shadows cast by the relief carving, using the colors from step 4 to soften the shadow edges. As you paint the shadow around the circular base, gradually increase the pressure to thicken the line, then decrease to taper it. Paint a crescent-shaped shadow on the center on the rosette, then blend the color toward the other side. Because the square panel is recessed, the top and left-hand edges are painted in the shadow tone.

6 Highlight the edges catching the light, in this case the top left edges all around the molding, using White and a No. 3 round pointed brush. Again use the colors from step 4 to blend it down. Highlight the bottom and right-hand side of the panel, using a straight edge if necessary.

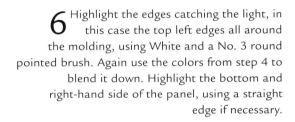

7 Use the colors from step 4 with a 15mm (⁵⁄₈in) flat brush to deepen the stone color adjacent to the highlights. This will provide a bolder contrast to emphasize the highlights. Blend in a little of the shadow color from step 5 as well if necessary.

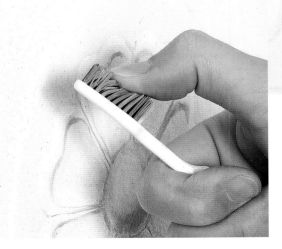

8 To add a subtle texture to the stone effect, dip the bristles of an old toothbrush into a little of the outline color from step 3. Spatter the paint at random on to the wall, using your thumb to flick the bristles. Vary the distance between the brush and the wall for slightly different effects.

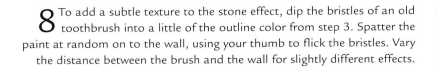

Doorway Pediment

IF YOU WANT TO ADD an architectural flourish to a plain door, a trompe l'oeil pediment painted above it can dramatically enhance its appearance, providing a grand entrance to the room beyond.

When designing a pediment to fit the top of your doorway, you need to ensure that the pitch you use suits the space available between the top of the architrave and the ceiling. The pitch will probably need to be lower if you are planning a pediment over a double door. Remember that you need only scale up half the pediment on transfer paper, as it is symmetrical.

The pediment could be painted on its own, on a plain or colorwashed wall, or could form part of a larger trompe l'oeil scheme, incorporating other architectural features such as stone blocking, balustrading and columns, perhaps with views over an Arcadian landscape. Pages 370–379 offer plenty of ideas that will allow you to bring a classical feel to any room of the house.

Palette

Raw Umber

White

Flesh Tint

Windsor Violet

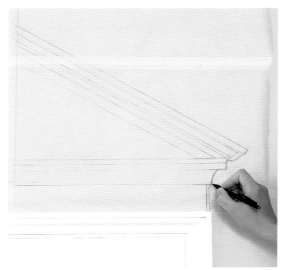

Paynes Grey

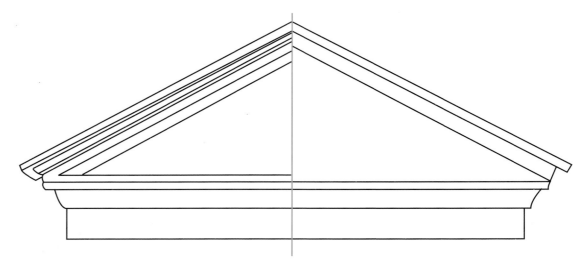

1 The diagram above includes the design for the pediment described in this project (left) as well as a simplified version (right). You will need to adjust the design to fit your doorway, before scaling up one half of the pediment on to transfer paper.

2 Measure the top of the doorway to find the center, and draw a faint vertical line from it using a spirit level and charcoal pencil. Position the scaled-up drawing on the wall so it lines up with the top edge of the architrave and the center vertical. Transfer only the outline of the image to the wall, then flip the paper and repeat for the other half of the pediment. Remove the drawing and retain for later.

3 Using White thinned with a little water and a 15mm (5/8in) flat brush, carefully cut in the line of the pediment around the edges. (You may wish to use low-tack masking tape to achieve crisper edges.) Use a larger decorator's brush to fill in the middle, and repeat until you have a reasonably even covering.

4 Mix three subtle colors: White with a small amount of Paynes Grey, White with Flesh Tint, and White with Flesh Tint and a small amount of Paynes Grey. Add a little water to each color. Using a 25mm (1in) hog-hair brush, stipple the colors over the pediment to create a subtle pinky/grey stone effect. Repeat if necessary, then leave to dry. Position the transfer paper again, and trace off all the pediment detail for both sides.

5 Add a little more Paynes Grey and Flesh Tint to the colors mixed in step 4, to create a shadow tone. Pick out the detail and shadows using a No. 7 round pointed brush. Use a spirit level as a guide to keep the lines straight. If the light source is above right, the cast shadows will be more pronounced on the right-hand side.

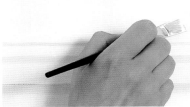

6 Mix a darker shadow tone and use Nos. 3 and 5 round pointed brushes to pick out the deeper shadows on the underside of the moldings. Do not paint the cast shadows in this darker tone. Paint the highlights on the pediment in white – especially along the top edge of the molding forming the bottom of the triangle.

7 Using a 15mm (⁵⁄₈in) flat brush, blend White thinned with a little water over the pediment near the cast shadows (do not paint over the shadows). This will sharpen the contrast at the edge of the shadow. You can also use a stone color slightly darker than those used in step 4 to deepen the pediment color next to a highlight, making the highlight more prominent.

8 Mix the color for the shadow cast on the wall. In this example, a little Raw Umber, Paynes Grey and Windsor Violet were added to the yellow emulsion (latex) paint. Using a 15mm (⁵⁄₈in) flat brush, paint a cast shadow to the lower left of the pediment, roughly copying the shape of the pediment edge. You may need to use some of the original wall color to sharpen the edge of the shadow.

COLUMNS ARE very versatile when used in a trompe l'oeil scene. They can be part of the land-scape, or may be used as architectural elements flanking a view. Use the examples on these pages, which show the various decorative orders intro-duced by the Greeks, scaling them up to fit your measurements. Establish the center vertical on the wall before lightly marking in the outlines. The col-umn shaft should be slightly wider at the bottom than at the top. It may be helpful to fix two lengths of string on the wall (held with masking tape) to represent the sides of the column before you start drawing, to give you an idea of the effect.

The Tuscan style has no orna-ment and would be ideal to try first. Note that the top and bottom of the shaft are curved where they meet the capital and base, to suggest the curvature of the column.

The Corinthian order has a cap-ital richly decorated with acan-thus leaves and scrolls, which is shown below in more detail. You could also decorate the plain shaft of the column with a mar-ble effect.

The Doric order is the most massive of the four columns shown here. It has no base: the shaft sits directly on the platform. The shaft is grooved but, unlike the Ionic column, the grooves meet in a sharp ridge and are not separated by a flat band.

The Ionic order has a scroll-like capital and a tall shaft, with decorative fluting separated by flat bands, as can be seen in the detail below. When you are planning the fluting, ensure that the grooves appear closer together toward the edges to suggest the curvature of the column. The fluting can also be picked out with shadows and fine highlights.

AN URN on a pedestal can provide a central focal point for a trompe l'oeil scene – for instance, it might be viewed through a trellis archway and backed by a formal garden. You can also inject extra color and interest by filling it with flowers or foliage (see opposite). Use the ivy shown on page 351 to soften the stonework, trailing it over the edges of the pot, or creeping around the base.

These designs for urns and plinths can be scaled up to suit your needs. You need only trace and enlarge half of each design, because they are symmetrical. Flip the tracing paper over to transfer the opposite side of the design.

Pay careful attention to the light source when depicting the decorative moldings. You should mix at least three stone colors: a base color (mid-tone), a shadow tone and a light tone, although I recommend using more variations. The Stone Rosette Panel project gives an example of a stone color mixed using Flesh Tint, Cobalt Blue, Naples Yellow and White.

The shading on the urn is subdued, suggesting the rounded stone surface, while the highlights and shading on the pedestal are much sharper, to help emphasize its angular form.

ELEGANCE, BALANCE and rhythm are important in a classical mural, and balustrading adds all three. Balustrades can be used as an attractive yet subtle boundary. Painted in the foreground of a mural, they create a sense of perspective without dominating the overall scene.

If you are using a row of balusters as the foreground to a trompe l'oeil view, they should be scaled up to a height of about 60cm (24in), with a rail along the top about 9cm (3¹/₂in) deep, and a plinth about 11.5cm (4¹/₂in) high. I usually space balusters so that the gaps between them are about a half to three-quarters of the width of the base.

Combining a row of balustrading with an obelisk, or an urn set on a plinth can be very effective. This kind of feature can be the main focus in the middle of a mural, or a pair could frame a view into a classical garden.

Because the balusters are rounded they look the same seen from the front, to the left or the right. However, the tops and bases are angular and there will be variations as you look down a row of balustrading, because you will begin to see the sides as well as the front faces. An understanding of one-point perspective can help here. Because there is no ornament on the bulbous part of the baluster it is important to use light and shade to define the form. In these examples the light is coming from the upper right, so the color deepens toward the bottom left. The color lightens slightly along the left edge as this will be picking up reflected light bouncing off other objects.

An alternative to balustrading is a parapet wall with a decorative screen. Architectural features like these are effective in dividing the background from the foreground without interfering too much with the view (see page 360). Glimpses of the landscape through balustrades and pierced walls contrast effectively with the stonework, emphasizing its shape.

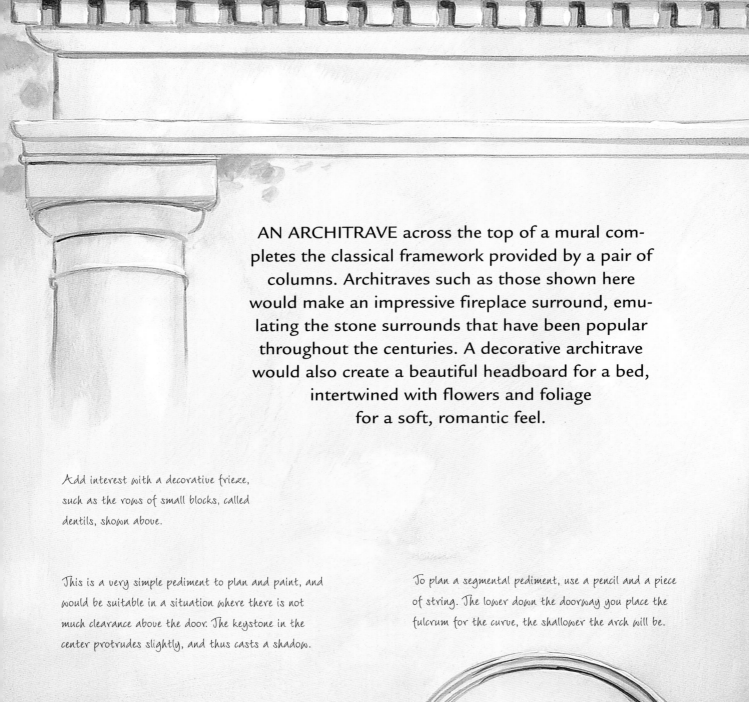

AN ARCHITRAVE across the top of a mural completes the classical framework provided by a pair of columns. Architraves such as those shown here would make an impressive fireplace surround, emulating the stone surrounds that have been popular throughout the centuries. A decorative architrave would also create a beautiful headboard for a bed, intertwined with flowers and foliage for a soft, romantic feel.

Add interest with a decorative frieze, such as the rows of small blocks, called dentils, shown above.

This is a very simple pediment to plan and paint, and would be suitable in a situation where there is not much clearance above the door. The keystone in the center protrudes slightly, and thus casts a shadow.

To plan a segmental pediment, use a pencil and a piece of string. The lower down the doorway you place the fulcrum for the curve, the shallower the arch will be.

The simple fluted design of this frieze is similar to that used for the shaft of an Ionic column (page 371).

There are many possible variations of the Doorway Pediment project on pages 366—369, using the same planning and painting techniques. You could even add quirky details like a perched bird or a butterfly to the design — the injection of color against the stonework would contrast well. Remember that the amount of space between the top of the doorway and the ceiling will dictate the kind of design you are able to paint.

This design is known as a broken pediment and is similar to that used in the Doorway Pediment project (pages 366—369), except that a circular break has been cut out of the top.

This pediment was inspired by the Wisteria Trellis project (pages 342—345). A little trailing greenery could be added to complete the rustic effect.

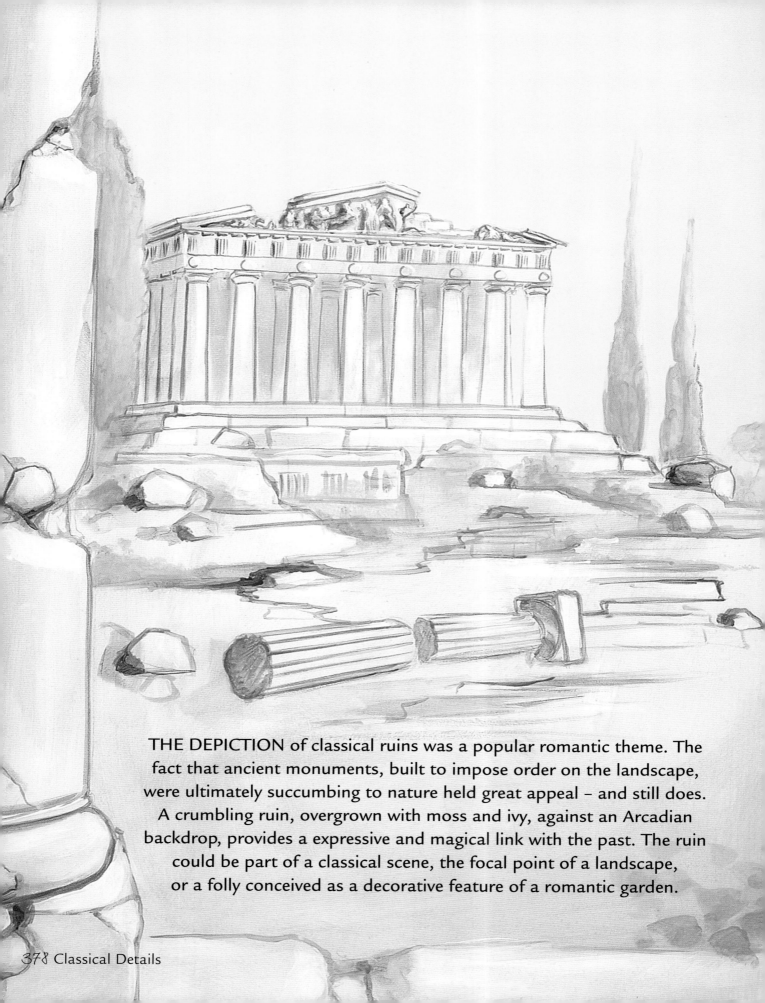

THE DEPICTION of classical ruins was a popular romantic theme. The fact that ancient monuments, built to impose order on the landscape, were ultimately succumbing to nature held great appeal – and still does. A crumbling ruin, overgrown with moss and ivy, against an Arcadian backdrop, provides a expressive and magical link with the past. The ruin could be part of a classical scene, the focal point of a landscape, or a folly conceived as a decorative feature of a romantic garden.

Ruins can be fun to paint but be careful not to overdo it — the brush is a powerful tool and your once magnificent temple could be reduced to a pile of rubble in a few strokes. To paint cracks, first paint and smudge in the direction of the crack in a deep tone, then add a finer line using a No. 1 or 3 round pointed brush and a very deep tone. Highlights can be added corresponding to the light source. Experiment and keep the painting fluid and random, to help the effect look more natural.

The Water's Edge

For mural painters, the theme of water is an almost limitless resource for inspiration, from waterfalls and raging rapids, to serene lakes reflecting distant mountains; from rivers meandering through the countryside, to waves breaking on a tropical shore; from ships sailing across vast oceans to the mysteries of the deep ocean – and it is said that we know more about the surface of the moon than we do about our oceans and the life contained there.

Water is a vital element for the survival of all plants and animals, but it is not only essential to our physical wellbeing. The sight of a sparkling stream raises the spirits, while gazing over a sheet of placid water with its rippling reflections induces a deep sense of calm.

A mural with a watery theme can help to instill that same sense of peace in your home. It is an ideal subject for an area where you relax, such as a sitting room or a bathroom, where a vista of golden sand lapped by gentle waves will transport you far from mundane chores and chilly weather.

Seagull and Lighthouse

THE SEA HAS BEEN AN INSPIRATION for many artists – most notably J. M. W. Turner, whose fantastical stormy seascapes captured the sheer ferocity of crashing waves and heaving seas. This mural opts for a calmer approach, with gentle waves lapping on the sandy shore and a seagull stopping for a rest in the salty breeze. The lighthouse is a reassuring element, in case the calm weather takes a turn for the worse.

The colors – cool blues, greys and greens – are subtle and harmonious. The red lighthouse, in sharp contrast, provides visual interest, and the seagull in the foreground appears to be looking back at the lighthouse, forming a link between the two. The subdued colors sit well with the faded driftwood frame, bound with rope.

This mural on a marine theme (see the Design Library for more ideas) would work well in a bathroom, or even in a bedroom, where the emphasis is on relaxation. As it is painted on a board, it can be moved into its final position after completion, but remember to note where the light source will ultimately be, so you can relate it to the painting.

Seagull and Lighthouse 383

Palette

Red Oxide

Raw Umber

White

Burnt Sienna

Cadmium Yellow

Windsor Violet

Cobalt Blue

Coeruleum Blue

Chromium
Oxide Green

Paynes Grey

Phthalo Turquoise

Black

Flesh Tint

Cadmium Orange

Naples Yellow

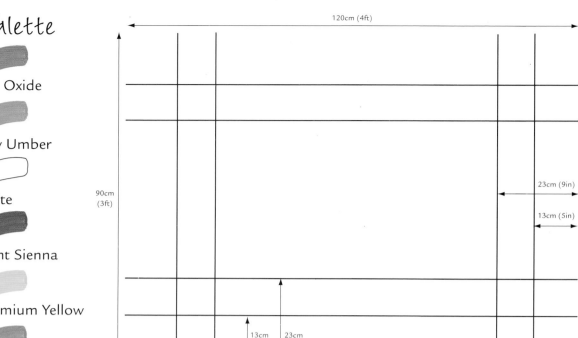

120cm (4ft)

90cm (3ft)

23cm (9in)

13cm (5in)

13cm (5in)

23cm (9in)

1 Take a sheet of 9mm (³/8in) or 12mm (¹/2in) medium density fiberboard approximately 120 x 90cm (4 x 3ft). Lightly rub down the surface to provide a key, then build up successive layers of white matt emulsion (latex), diluting the paint slightly with water. Leave to dry, then measure 13cm (5in) and 23cm (9in) in from each edge and draw the eight lines that form the basis of the driftwood frame, following the diagram above.

2 Draw the frame, varying the thickness of the planks and adding weathered splits to the ends. Plan this first using a charcoal pencil, or go straight into Red Oxide paint with a No. 3 or No. 5 round pointed brush: the latter will give a more fluid line. Do not use a straight edge, as the lines need to look soft and weathered. Suggest splitting and pits, using your fingers to smudge the line in places. Note that the horizontal planks overlay the vertical planks. Add another line about 6mm (¹/4in) in from each inside edge, to suggest the thickness of the wood.

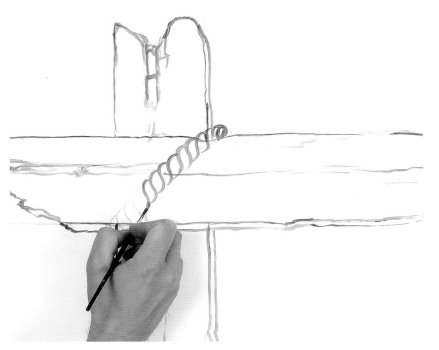

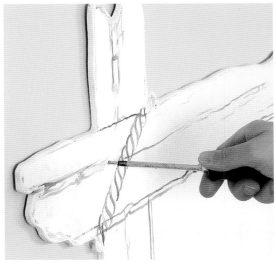

3 Sketch in the ropes at the corners using simple repeated S-shaped strokes. One diagonal rope binds each corner of the frame. The top left rope goes diagonally up from left to right, and the top right rope goes diagonally down from left to right. The ropes in the lower corners should mirror those in the top corners.

4 Wearing a protective mask to avoid inhaling sawdust, cut around the outer edge of the frame using a jigsaw. Sand all the cut edges thoroughly, smoothing over the corners, then paint them as in step 1. Drill a hole in each corner to take suitable fixings, positioning them to give the impression that they are holding the planks together: do not put the fixings through the ropes as this will spoil the illusion. Attach the panel to a wall.

5 Tape transfer paper to the panel and plan the landscape. Sketch in the horizon line about 29cm (11½in) from the bottom of the panel. Draw the lighthouse, cliff and sea wall. The horizon line cuts though the lower half of the house, and the wall sits below the horizon. Suggest the water curving along to the left of the panel and the distant hills. When you are happy with the design, transfer it to the panel and paint in the outlines using Red Oxide and a No. 3 round pointed brush.

6 Attach another sheet of transfer paper and sketch the seagull and its perch, using photographic references if you wish. Transfer the design to the wall and outline in Red Oxide.

7 Mix up a wash using White, Raw Umber and Naples Yellow with 3–4 parts water. Using a 25mm (1in) hog-hair brush, wash the color over the whole panel. When painting the driftwood frame, keep the brush strokes in the direction of the grain. Leave to dry and repeat.

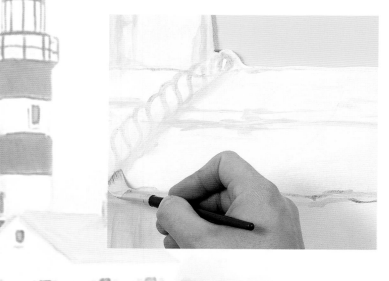

8 Mix a similar color to the wash, adding only a little water and mixing in more Raw Umber and a little Cobalt Blue. Using a 15mm (5/8in) flat brush, loosely paint in some of the grain and splitting detail along each plank. Vary the angle of the brush to open and close the splits and gaps. Add some cast shadows on the vertical planks where the horizontal planks cross them, and add the small shadows cast by the ropes. The light in this case is coming from the top left.

9 Mix White with a little Raw Umber. Using a No. 7 round pointed brush paint the rope, following the S-shape and applying more pressure to the middle of the brush stroke so the line thickens and then tapers. Mix some more Raw Umber into the paint to pick out the deeper shadows in the twists of the rope.

10 Add more Raw Umber and a little more Cobalt Blue to some of the color mixed in step 8. Using Nos. 1 and 3 round pointed brushes, pick out the finer, deeper shadows in the wood splits. Also use some of the original color from step 8, blending and smudging with your fingers to achieve the desired effect.

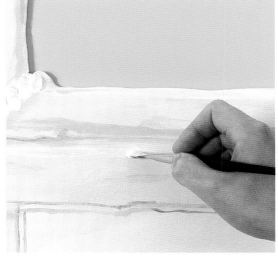

11 Mix a color similar to the wash used in step 7, adding more White and only a little water. Use a 15mm (⁵⁄₈in) flat brush to pick out some of the highlights along the tops of the planks and the wood splits. Where there is a horizontal split in the wood, the area immediately below is highlighted; along the vertical splits the highlight is to the right.

12 Mix three gentle shades of sky blue using White, Coeruleum Blue and Cobalt Blue, adding a little water to each. Paint the sky with a 15mm (⁵⁄₈in) flat brush, starting with the deepest blue at the top and gradually blending down to a very pale blue on the horizon. Add a small amount of Burnt Sienna to some of the deepest blue, and block in the distant hills. Start building up the shadow tones on the seagull using some of the colors used for the frame.

13 Using the lightest blue and a 15mm (⁵⁄₈in) flat brush, build up some loose clouds behind the lighthouse and thinner ones along the horizon. Use a little water on the brush to blend the bottom of the clouds, and a little white to pick out highlights on the tops. Mix White with a little Windsor Violet and 2 parts water to add purple shadows to the bottom of the clouds, again using a little water on the brush to stop the colors becoming too defined.

14 Mix White, Chromium Oxide Green and Cobalt Blue with a little water. Using a 10mm (³/₈in) flat brush, stipple in some foliage behind the lighthouse, tapering it out along the coastline to the left. Mix a slightly deeper shade by adding more Chromium Oxide Green and Cobalt Blue, and stipple along the bottom of the foliage, blending it into the lighter color.

15 Mix four colors for the sea and sand, adding a little water to each: 1. White and Cobalt Blue, to a slightly deeper shade than the deepest sky color; 2. White, Cobalt Blue and Phthalo Turquoise; 3. White, Naples Yellow and Raw Umber; 4. White and Naples Yellow. Starting at the horizon and using a 15mm (⁵/₈in) flat brush with color 1, paint with horizontal strokes, blending the paint down into color 2 and then into color 3 where the waves break, then into color 4 up to the edge of the frame. Repeat until there is a reasonably smooth transition of color. Paint a thin strip of color 4 under the distant foliage to look like a faraway beach, tapering the color out to the left.

16 Add a little water to some White and with a 10mm (³/₈in) flat brush, loosely paint some gentle lapping waves along the area where colors 2 and 3 blend together. Use slightly curved horizontal strokes, with a little water on the brush to blend out the top of the wave, keeping the bottom edge defined. Do not overdo this – the trick is to keep it simple. Using color 4 mixed in step 15, add a fine cast shadow under the lapping waves in the foreground.

17 Start blocking in the lighthouse using Cadmium Orange and Red Oxide. For the house, use White and a mix of White with a little Paynes Grey and Flesh Tint. Note that the right-hand side of the house is in shadow. Use this shadow color for the right-hand side of the white bands of the lighthouse. Add a little Chromium Oxide Green to the lighthouse red for the shading on the red bands. Using a No. 6 flat brush, pick out the the detailing on the windows and doors with the grey shade, adding a little more Paynes Grey if necessary. Mix some White, Burnt Sienna and Raw Umber for the roof. Use the driftwood frame colors to block in the sea wall. For the grass on the clifftop, mix some Chromium Oxide Green into some of the sand color 4 mixed in Step 15. Block in the color using a 15mm (⁵/₈in) flat brush.

18 Pick out the fine detailing on the sea wall with a No. 1 round pointed brush, using the deepest frame color mixed in step 10. Loosely suggest pebbles on the beach, using your finger to smudge the line of the reflection in the water. Build up the colors on the lighthouse, mixing Chromium Oxide Green into some of the red to add a shadow down the right-hand side. Pick out the railings with a No. 3 round pointed brush, highlighting with a little White. Add window shutters to the house using the roof color mixed in step 17 and a No. 6 flat brush.

19 Mix a warm light grey using White, Flesh Tint and a little Paynes Grey with a little water, and block in the seagull's wings using a 15mm (5/8in) flat brush and a No. 10 flat brush. For the seagull's breast, mix White with a little Flesh Tint. Blend in some of the wing color to shade under the head and beak, and where the legs join. Add a little more Paynes Grey to some of the wing color and pick out the deeper color on the tail. Mix some White, Flesh Tint and Cadmium Yellow, and paint the legs and beak with Nos. 1 and 3 round pointed brushes.

20 Using a No. 1 round pointed brush, or finer, pick out the final details on the seagull. Deepen the shadow above the eye and under the beak. Colour the eye with White and Cadmium Yellow, using a few coats to build up a vibrant color. Once dry, add a small pupil with Black and, when this has dried, add a small blob of white to the top left of the pupil so that it overlaps the yellow. This simple highlight has the effect of bringing the eye to life. Pick out some of the feathers to suggest the plumage, using a slightly deeper grey than that used to paint the wings and some White. Use White to pick out some of the feather tips – especially along the tail. Use some of the deeper grey to give more definition to the details on the beak.

Fish Mosaic

Mosaic is an ancient and enduring method of creating pictures or abstract designs by embedding tiny pieces of stone or marble, called 'tesserae', in cement. The Romans, who learned the skill from the ancient Greeks, created designs of great subtlety using stone and colored glass cut into small squares.

Viewed from a distance, a mosaic may itself be a trompe l'oeil, and the illusion is doubled when the little colored squares are in fact painted on a flat surface. The subtle variations of color and texture that characterize mosaics give them great visual appeal, and this quality is easy to replicate in paint. The painted mosaic can be given an aged effect, as here, by leaving a few pieces missing from the design.

This simple fish design could be developed into a frieze, using it as a repeating motif or adding different fish and sea shells. Both the marine theme (extended in the Design Library pages) and the mosaic style would be appropriate for a bathroom, or even for a kitchen, where the fish could be accompanied by lobsters, crabs and other seafood.

Palette

Raw Umber

White

Flesh Tint

Naples Yellow

Cobalt Blue

Coeruleum Blue

Burnt Sienna

Paynes Grey

1 The mosaic design is applied using square stamps, which can be cut from high density foam (such as upholstery foam) using a craft knife. The decorative checkerboard stamp shown here was found in a craft shop and simply cut into separate squares. Mix the paint on a plate to make it easy to pick up on the stamps.

2 Mix a warm grey base color using White, Naples Yellow, a little Raw Umber and a little Paynes Grey. You will need enough for at least two coats, plus some spare for touching up later. Paint the wall and leave to dry, then lightly draw a horizontal guideline using a spirit level and charcoal pencil. Scale up the outline of the fish on the previous page on to transfer paper and trace it on to the wall. This fish is 59cm (23in) long, and the stamps are 14mm (¹/₂in) square.

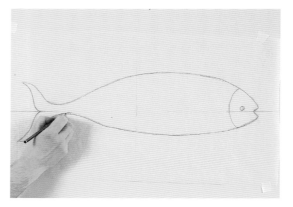

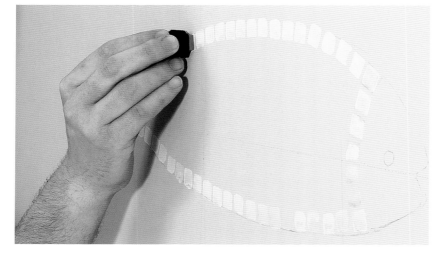

3 Mix White with Naples Yellow and use to stamp the outline of the fish, being careful not to overload the stamp with paint. Leave a small gap between each square, and keep the squares to the inside of the outline. The squares will overlap in places – especially when you are painting the tail – but you can use some of the base color later to redefine the mosaic pieces. Instead of stamping very small pieces, such as the pointed end of the tail, paint them in with a No. 1 or 3 round pointed brush.

4 For the body of the fish mix Flesh Tint, Burnt Sienna and White. Starting around the edges, keep the mosaic rows following the arched shape of the fish. You can print small pieces by using only part of the stamp if you wish, or use a paint brush. Mix two shades of blue using White and Cobalt Blue, and White and Coeruleum Blue. Outline the fish, alternating the blues here and there for variation.

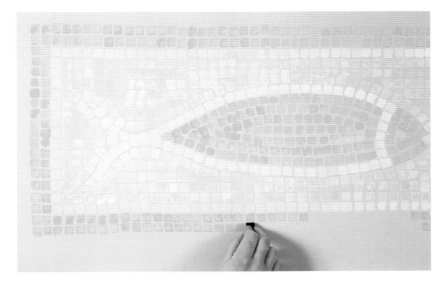

5 Lightly sketch in horizontal and vertical guide-lines around the fish, using a charcoal pencil and a spirit level. Build up the blue area by stamping horizontal rows of squares, up to and in places overlapping the blue outline painted in step 4. The rows should be reasonably straight, but slight variations of level add to the attraction of this design. Add a simple border design using the colors used in steps 3 and 4.

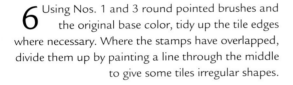

6 Using Nos. 1 and 3 round pointed brushes and the original base color, tidy up the tile edges where necessary. Where the stamps have overlapped, divide them up by painting a line through the middle to give some tiles irregular shapes.

7 Using the base color and a No. 10 flat brush, block out one or two of the mosaic squares in random areas, to suggest that the pieces have fallen away. Be careful not to overdo this.

8 Mix in a little more Raw Umber and Paynes Grey with the base color. Using a No. 1 round pointed brush, pick out fine shadows along the bottom and right edges of some of the squares. Use your finger to smudge the shadow in places – smudging the color over some of the squares can help the aged effect. Make some shadows thicker than others and leave some squares with no shadow, to give the impression that the surface is slightly uneven. You can also add highlights to the top and left edges of a few tiles using the tile color mixed with a little more White, but don't overdo this.

WHAT COULD be more relaxing then a white sandy beach, the sound of the sea lapping at the shore and palm trees swaying in the breeze? Recreate your favorite holiday memories in any room where you like to unwind. This complete scene would look stunning along the wall of a bedroom, allowing you to wake to a tropical beach scene every day. For a children's room, the sandcastle, bucket and spade from page 397 could be incorporated. The palm trees themselves would add a touch of dramatic greenery to a bathroom.

A tropical beach scene can be framed with palms and other exotic plants. On the horizon, add simple palm trees with a No. 1 or 3 round pointed brush, using some of the sea and sky blues mixed with a little Chromium Oxide Green. When building up a lot of foreground foliage, mix a darker green using Chromium Oxide Green and a little Paynes Grey. Use this dark tone to paint around the profile of the leaves, to make them stand out and give the foliage more depth.

When painting palm leaves try not to be too fussy. Lightly sketch in the spine of the leaf, curving downward, then paint the fronds using a 15mm (⁵⁄₈in) flat brush. Work from the spine outward in bold strokes, tapering off at the ends. Use Chromium Oxide Green, and Chromium Oxide Green mixed with Cadmium Yellow for the deeper greens (darkening the color near the spine by adding a little Paynes Grey). For the lighter greens use Leaf Green, and Leaf Green mixed with White. Use a finer round brush to paint in the sharp ends of each frond. Add a mix of Yellow Ochre and White to the leaf in places, to vary the color.

This simple sea shell effect on a piece of driftwood could be used with the Seagull and Lighthouse project (pages 382—389).

The base color for the starfish shape is a mixture of Burnt Umber, White and a little Cadmium Orange. The details have been picked out with Nos. 1 and 3 round pointed brushes, using Burnt Umber and Raw Umber, and the high-lights are White with a little Burnt Umber.

I have kept the colors of the shells very faded and washed out, concentrating on their form.

A SANDCASTLE or two can add foreground interest to a mural on a seaside theme, leading your eye toward the beach beyond. The sandcastles could also be decorated with sea shells, like those shown opposite. This subject is a natural and popular choice for the bathroom, and a collection of sea shells, driftwood and starfish would add a sophisticated beach atmosphere.

To create sandcastles, use Raw Sienna and White for the basic sand color, mixing in some Raw Umber for the shading. Use White mixed with a little Raw Sienna for the highlights. To get the sand effect, stipple the paint on with a 25mm (1in) hog-hair brush, using a 15mm (⁵/₈in) flat brush to stipple along the edges. You can also vary the texture by using a toothbrush to spatter the paint, as described in the Stone Rosette Panel project.

TROPICAL FISH are some of the most eyecatching animals in the world, and this amazing tropical scene would add a splash of color to any room of the house. It could be the aquarium you have always longed for, or you may want to gaze at the exotic fish as you laze in the bath. Children are enchanted by underwater scenes, and would welcome a friendly dolphin on their bedroom wall.

For the background to an underwater scene, blend White at the top into a mix of White, Cobalt Blue and Coeruleum Blue. The sunken ship and distant coral are painted using two mixes of Cobalt Blue, White and a little Burnt Sienna. These deep blues help to push the ship and coral into the distance.

The dolphin is painted using the same colors as the ship and distant coral, again helping to push it further into the distance.

Sketch in the shapes of the foreground coral very lightly before painting the forms freehand in bright colors, which contrast sharply with the deeper, cooler blues to enhance the feeling of depth. Use a 15mm (⁵/₈in) flat brush and Nos. 3 and 5 round pointed brushes to paint in the various forms, using Cadmium Yellow, Orange and Red, White and Leaf Green.

Trace the outlines of the fish and fill in the shapes with two or three coats of White, to cover the deep blue background. When dry, trace on the final details and block in the colors with White mixed with Cobalt Blue, and Cadmium Yellow.

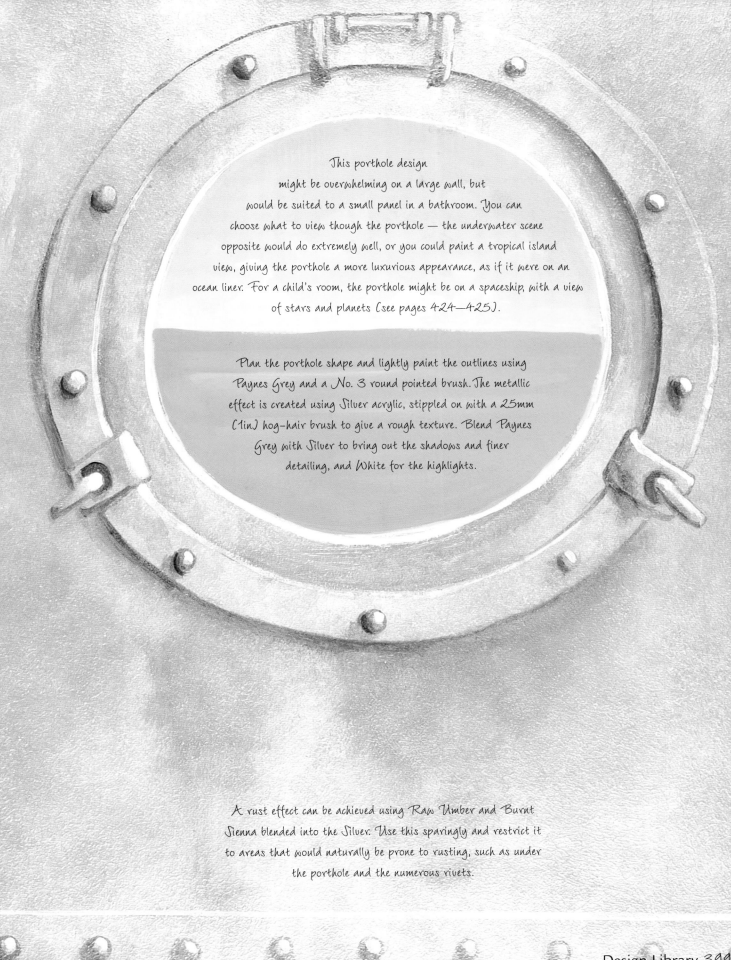

This porthole design
might be overwhelming on a large wall, but
would be suited to a small panel in a bathroom. You can
choose what to view though the porthole — the underwater scene
opposite would do extremely well, or you could paint a tropical island
view, giving the porthole a more luxurious appearance, as if it were on an
ocean liner. For a child's room, the porthole might be on a spaceship, with a view
of stars and planets (see pages 424—425).

Plan the porthole shape and lightly paint the outlines using
Paynes Grey and a No. 3 round pointed brush. The metallic
effect is created using Silver acrylic, stippled on with a 25mm
(1in) hog-hair brush to give a rough texture. Blend Paynes
Grey with Silver to bring out the shadows and finer
detailing, and White for the highlights.

A rust effect can be achieved using Raw Umber and Burnt
Sienna blended into the Silver. Use this sparingly and restrict it
to areas that would naturally be prone to rusting, such as under
the porthole and the numerous rivets.

THE REFLECTIVE quality of water immediately instills a sense of calm and peace into even the busiest of people, so these scenes will add serenity wherever you choose to paint them. You may like to dine looking out over the water to a classical urn or temple, by framing the scene with a window frame or louvered doors. The boat scene would appeal to a sailing fanatic, and look charming on a child's bedroom wall. Use reflections to suggest still or moving water – the boat's reflection is distorted and fragmented, suggesting the movement of the sea.

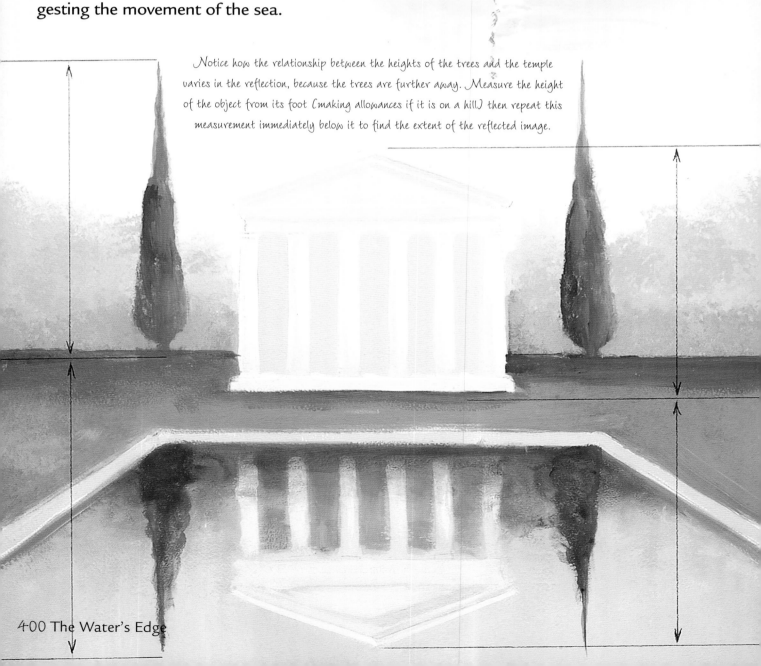

Notice how the relationship between the heights of the trees and the temple varies in the reflection, because the trees are further away. Measure the height of the object from its foot (making allowances if it is on a hill) then repeat this measurement immediately below it to find the extent of the reflected image.

The foliage effect is easily achieved by stippling with a 25mm (1in) hog-hair brush. First stipple the distant foliage with a mix of White, Chromium Oxide Green and a little Cobalt Blue. Block in the main area of the foliage arch with Chromium Oxide Green, stippling the edges. Block in the urn and plinth with white. Stipple the flowers in a range of colors. Finally, pick out the detailing on the urn and plinth using White mixed with Paynes Grey and Flesh Tint in various shades. Using Chromium Oxide Green and a little Paynes Grey, darken the area behind the urn to help define the edges.

Use the same colors for the reflection in the still water. Stipple the paint again but use another brush loaded with a little water to drag the color down slightly while the paint is wet — have a cloth handy to catch any runs.

Children's Worlds

Although trompe l'oeil often uses realistic scenes in its attempts to trick the eye, there is no need to restrict your mural painting to what is present in the physical world. You can delve into the limitless realms of fantasy, while still using your skills in conveying depth and solidity to create the illusion of a three-dimensional scene.

Children's rooms are obviously the prime location for murals of this kind, and most of the subjects in this chapter have been designed with children in mind. Large-scale murals can transform children's bedrooms into their own fantasy kingdoms, and the themes you choose will naturally depend on their own interests, from enchanted castles and fairyland scenes, to an adventure in space. For a nursery wall, there are also some bright, friendly toys.

Fantasy murals can enchant adults as well as children. The castle walls and turrets shown on the following pages could be adapted to decorate a dining room or hall in gothic style, while theatrical red curtains could create a dramatic bedroom setting.

Magic Castle Window

IF YOU ASK A CHILD what they would most like to see outside their bedroom window, a fire-breathing dragon could well be high on the list. If such mythical beasts do not frequent your neighborhood, you can always paint one, complete with a stony castle window through which to view it safely. For a young alchemist, you can also provide the necessary basic equipment: a pestle and mortar, a bottle of magic potion and the obligatory book of spells.

This mural works well on its own, but you could go further, giving the whole room a mythical medieval theme, with crumbling castle walls, turrets, battlements, drawbridges, hanging tapestries and jousting knights on horseback. The idea need not be restricted to decorating children's rooms – for a dining room with an ancestral feel, picture instead a castle window with a dramatic view across the calm waters of a lake, to dense forests and distant highlands. Use the stonework on pages 416–417 to create these amazing scenes.

Magic Castle Window 405

Palette

Red Oxide

Raw Umber

White

Flesh Tint

Burnt Sienna

Cadmium Yellow

Winsor Violet

Raw Sienna

Cobalt Blue

Coeruleum Blue

Chromium Oxide Green

Paynes Grey

Yellow Naples

Cadmium Orange

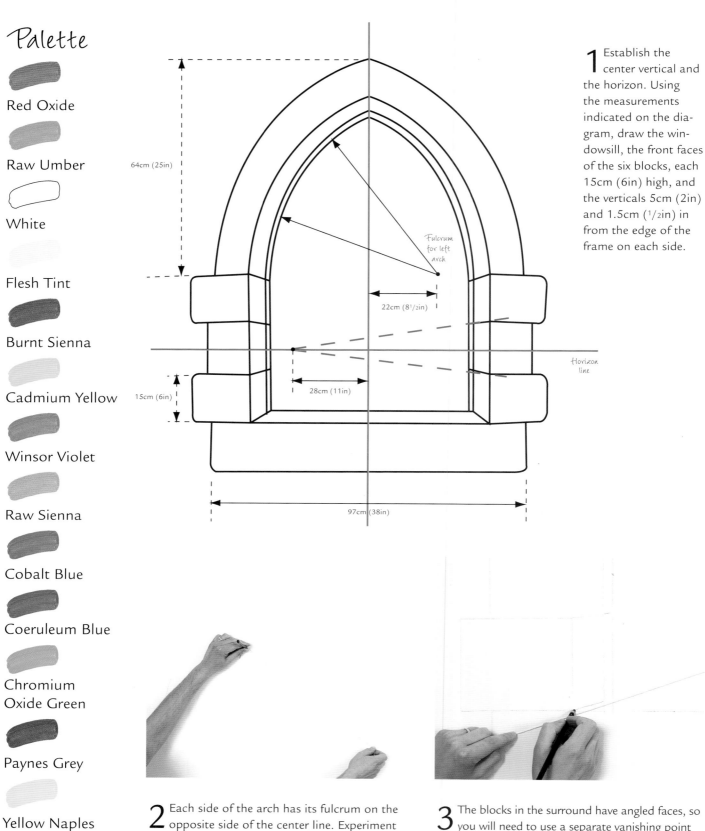

64cm (25in)

Fulcrum for left arch

22cm (8¹/₂in)

28cm (11in)

Horizon line

15cm (6in)

97cm (38in)

1 Establish the center vertical and the horizon. Using the measurements indicated on the diagram, draw the windowsill, the front faces of the six blocks, each 15cm (6in) high, and the verticals 5cm (2in) and 1.5cm (¹/₂in) in from the edge of the frame on each side.

2 Each side of the arch has its fulcrum on the opposite side of the center line. Experiment with different points to see the effect it has on the shape of the arch, but both fulcrums must be equidistant from the center and at the same horizontal. Fix a length of string, with a pencil tied to the end, to each fulcrum to draw the curves.

3 The blocks in the surround have angled faces, so you will need to use a separate vanishing point for each side. Measure 28cm (11in) to either side of the center along the horizon line. Use the vanishing point to the right to draw the receding lines of the blocks on the left, and the center vanishing point to complete the lines of the inside return of the blocks. Repeat on the other side.

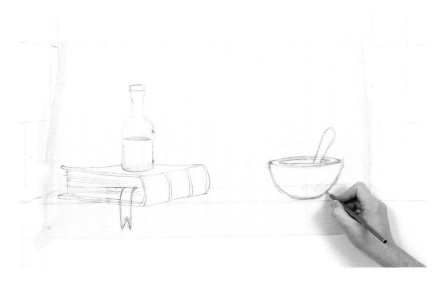

4 Fix transfer paper over the lower half of the window to plan the book, potion and pestle and mortar on the windowsill. To ensure the bottle and pestle are symmetrical, it may help to draw one half of each shape on a separate sheet, then fold it vertically to trace the second half. Once you are happy with the design, transfer it to the wall.

5 Paint over all the outlines in Red Oxide using a No. 3 round pointed brush. Mix up a wash with White, Naples Yellow and a little Paynes Grey, with about 4 parts water, and paint over the whole design using a large decorator's brush. Repeat when dry. The outlines will remain visible.

6 Mix up four stone colors, adding a very small amount of water to each but keeping the paint reasonably thick: White, Flesh Tint and Raw Umber; White, Flesh Tint and a little Paynes Grey; White, Burnt Sienna and a little Paynes Grey; White, Raw Sienna and a little Paynes Grey. Using a 15mm (⅝in) flat brush, cut in around the edge of the window surround, alternating between the different colors. Paint the rest of the area liberally using a 25mm (1in) hog-hair brush, blending the colors in and out of each other. Dab and roll a scrunched-up plastic bag over the wet paint to create a rough stony texture.

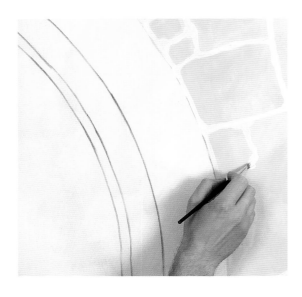

7 Mix a mortar color using White and a little Raw Umber, adding a little water. Using a No. 10 flat brush, paint in the mortar lines, keeping the block sizes irregular. Start around the arch area, siting the stones so that they follow the arch shape, and then work outward. You may wish to sketch the mortar lines first with a light charcoal pencil before painting them. At least two coats will be needed as you are painting a lighter color over a darker color. Don't worry about neat, even lines or crisp edges, as you want to achieve a rough look. Touch in some of the stones with the colors from step 5 to vary their colors.

8 Mix White, Naples Yellow and a little Paynes Grey to give the same stone color used for the wash, but of a much thicker consistency. Mix some of this color with more Paynes Grey and some Raw Umber to make a shadow tone, and some with White to make a highlight tone. Using a 15mm (5/8in) flat brush, block in the window surround using the mid-tone. Depending on your light source (in this case, above left), paint the angled face of the arch and blocks in the highlight tone on one side and in the shadow tone on the other side. Paint the inside return edge of the window lighter on both sides.

9 Mix a range of shades of sky blue using White, Cobalt Blue and Coeruleum Blue. Use a 15mm (5/8in) flat brush to cut in around the window, and a 25mm (1in) hog-hair brush to blend the sky blues down from dark to light. You will need two or three coats to achieve a smooth gradation of color.

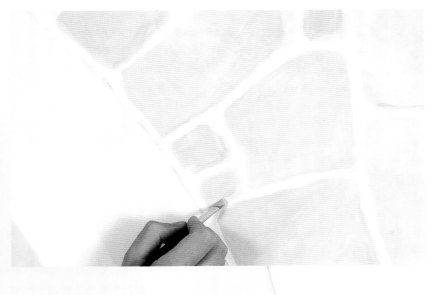

10 To some of the mortar color mixed in step 7, add some more Raw Umber and a little Paynes Grey to make a shadow tone. Use a No. 10 flat brush to add a cast shadow on the mortar, along the bottom and right edge of each block, to give the impression that the stones are standing out from the mortar. Use your finger to smudge the shadows in places.

11 Mix some Raw Umber and a little Paynes Grey with a little water. Using this and the shadow color mixed in step 10, and Nos. 3 and 5 round pointed brushes, add chips and cracks to the mortar, even painting out some areas, to suggest it has crumbled away. Use your finger to smudge some areas and blend the colors together, so that the lines do not become too defined.

12 Using the shadow color mixed in step 10 and a No. 3 round pointed brush, paint along the top of the mortar lines in the window surround. Use a straight edge as a guide. Paint the shadow tone to the left of the mortar joint at the top of the arch, as the light source is on the left.

13 Using White and a No. 3 round pointed brush, add sharp highlights to the blocks underneath the joints. Highlight the angled edges to give the corners more definition.

14 Using the dark color mixed in step 11 and a No. 1 round pointed brush, pick out the fine joints in the surround, again using a straight edge as a guide.

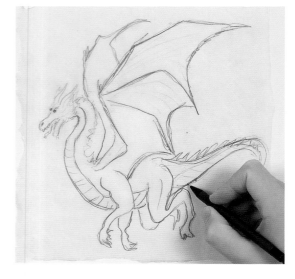

15 Draw the dragon on transfer paper, and transfer the image to the wall. Paint the outlines with Red Oxide and a No. 3 round pointed brush.

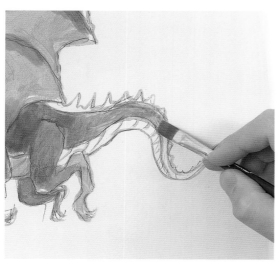

16 Build up layers of color on the dragon using Red Oxide and Cadmium Orange (adding little or no water) with a No. 10 flat brush.

17 For a bold color you will need to apply three or more coats, allowing each to dry thoroughly. Mix a little Chromium Oxide Green into the red to make a shadow tone and use this color with Nos. 1 and 3 round pointed brushes to pick out the finer detailing and shadows, blending the shadow color into the red. Paint the far wing in the shadow tone to create a feeling of depth. Use Naples Yellow to paint the dragon's belly, and pick out the detailing in Raw Umber with a No. 1 round pointed brush.

18 Block in the objects on the windowsill, using Chromium Oxide Green for the book and mixing White with a little Raw Umber for the pages, Red Oxide and Cadmium Orange for the potion, and the stone colors mixed in step 6 for the pestle and mortar.

19 Mix three or four colors for the dragon's smoke, using White, Flesh Tint and Windsor Violet in varying quantities and adding 1–2 parts water to each color. Using a 15mm ($^5/_8$in) flat brush and the darker colors, stipple a stream of smoke from the dragon's mouth toward the bottom left corner of the window, widening the stream as it goes down. Use a 25mm (1in) hog-hair brush in a circular motion to build up the billows of smoke in the lower part of the window. Alternate between the colors, making the color deeper at the edge of the window. With the flat brush, cut in around the window edges and the objects and blend into the smoke.

20 Mix White with Cadmium Orange and use Nos. 3 and 5 round pointed brushes to pick out a stream of fire in the center of the smoke issuing from the dragon's mouth. Deepen the color of the smoke around the fire to create a bolder contrast. Add some white highlights to the smoke, using the 25mm (1in) hog-hair brush and the same circular motion, and use a No. 5 round pointed brush to pick out the lightest highlights along the top edges of the smoke clouds. Smudge and blend the colors together with your fingers.

21 Add the final details to the book, potion and pestle and mortar. Mix Chromium Oxide Green and Red Oxide to make a shadow tone for the spine of the book. Pick out the gold detailing in Cadmium Yellow using a No. 3 round pointed brush. Use Raw Umber and a little Paynes Grey to define the pages. Use White to pick out the sharp highlights on the potion bottle – the deep smoke color behind the glass should make them appear quite bold. Build up the pestle and mortar colors so that they are deeper along the bottom and right-hand sides, and inside the bowl. Using some of the stone shadow tone mixed in step 8, paint cast shadows on the windowsill to the bottom and right of the objects.

Carved Toy Chest

THE TOYS FILLING this lovely chest will never clutter up a child's bedroom – at the end of the day they will still be neatly stored away in the box, with all the other playthings of which we can see only tantalizing glimpses.

This is an ideal mural to personalize for a child. You could paint his or her favorite toys peeking out from the top of the box, and instead of the teddy bear relief on the front panel, it could be decorated with the child's own name in carved letters.

The toy chest is painted on the wall, but it is an ideal subject to paint on a panel of medium density fiberboard if you want to be able to change its location. The overall shape of the box can easily be cut out using a jigsaw, and the fixings used to secure it to the wall could be disguised as nails on the hinges.

Carved Toy Chest 413

Palette

Red Oxide

White

Yellow Ochre

Raw Umber

Chromium
Oxide Green

Cadmium Yellow

Cadmium Orange

Cobalt Blue

Paynes Grey

Black

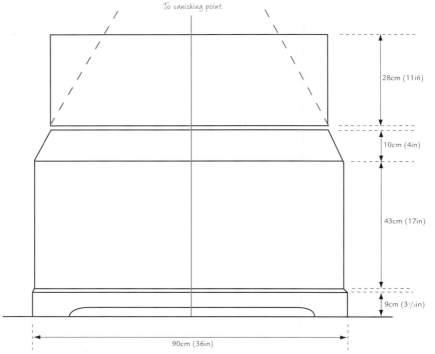

To vanishing point

28cm (11in)

10cm (4in)

43cm (17in)

9cm (3½in)

90cm (36in)

1 Draw the center vertical using a spirit level and charcoal pencil. Using the dimensions on the diagram, draw the front face of the chest. Locate the vanishing point, about 150cm (5ft) from the floor on the center vertical.
Fix some string at the vanishing point and use it as a guide to draw the receding sides. Draw the back of the chest and the lid, using the spirit level.

2 Build up the detailing, adding the framework to the front, the two metal hinges and the curved base. Divide the lid into three planks. Stand back to check that the chest looks correct to the eye. Once you are satisfied, paint over all the outlines in Red Oxide, using a No. 3 round pointed brush.

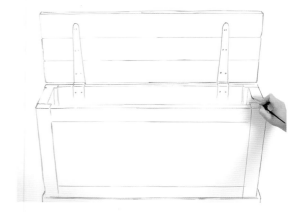

3 Draw one half of the carved teddy on transfer paper, so that the height will fit the front panel of the chest. Transfer the design to the wall, lining it up with the center vertical, then flip the paper over and trace the other half. Add a few simple star shapes, which can be sketched freehand. Sketch the toys in the chest very loosely on transfer paper, then transfer them to the wall. Try to keep the arrangement balanced – in this case the teddy in the chest is balanced by the boat. Paint over all the outlines in Red Oxide.

4 Mix three colors for the wood. The palest is a mixture of White and Yellow Ochre; add some Raw Umber for the mid-tone, and more Raw Umber for the deepest shade. Mix 2–3 parts water into each, then use a 25mm (1in) hog-hair brush to paint the whole design, alternating between the colors. Use a 15mm (⅝in) flat brush to paint along the edges of the chest.

5 Mix some Raw Umber and Yellow Ochre with about 1 part water. Using a 15mm (5/8in) flat brush, loosely pick out some graining. Add a few knots here and there and then curve the graining around them. Keep the grain running horizontally on the box and lid, but vertically on the sides of the frame. Use the shape of the brush to vary the graining – twisting it slightly to widen or taper the lines. Use some of the colors mixed in step 5 to blend the graining, and do not overdo it – add more later if necessary.

6 Using the graining color from step 6, pick out the shading and cast shadows – especially on the carved teddy bear and stars. The light source is above left, so the shadows fall to the right and below the relief. Use a No. 10 flat brush for the larger shadows, blending them in slightly using the base wood colors used in step 5. Use a No. 3 round pointed brush to pick out the finer detailing on the teddy's face and paws, and to indicate the stitching. Pick out the shadows cast by the left and top of the frame, and deepen the color inside the chest around the toys.

7 Block in the toys using a No. 10 and a 15mm (5/8in) flat brush. Mix White, Yellow Ochre and Raw Umber for the teddy and stipple this color on to suggest a furry texture. Use White for the sail and the teddy colors for the hull of the boat. The ball is painted in stripes of Chromium Oxide Green, Cadmium Orange, Red Oxide and Cobalt Blue – some colors can be used as they are but some will need to be lightened by mixing in some White. Block in the hinges with Paynes Grey and a little White.

8 Mix White with a little Yellow Ochre and Raw Umber, and a little water, to make a highlight tone. Use a No. 10 flat brush to add the highlights to the left side and bottom of the teddy relief and the stars, and a No. 3 round pointed brush to pick out the detailing. Use the same color to pick out the other highlights on the chest, such as the tops of the planks and the edges of the frame. Mix Raw Umber with a little Paynes Grey and use a No. 3 round pointed brush to pick out the wood joints and a few splits and chips. Build up the colors and forms of the toys, adding cast shadows to the lid. Finally, use blobs of Black to add nail heads to the hinges, and highlight them with White mixed with a little Black, using a No. 3 round pointed brush.

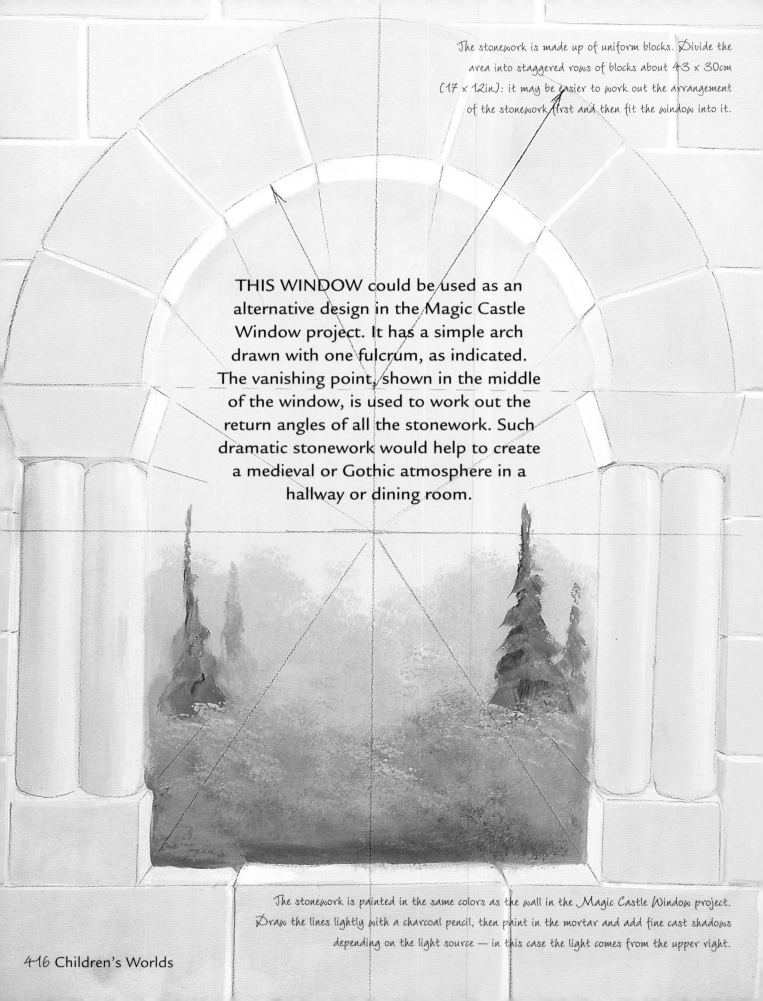

The stonework is made up of uniform blocks. Divide the area into staggered rows of blocks about 43 x 30cm (17 x 12in): it may be easier to work out the arrangement of the stonework first and then fit the window into it.

THIS WINDOW could be used as an alternative design in the Magic Castle Window project. It has a simple arch drawn with one fulcrum, as indicated. The vanishing point, shown in the middle of the window, is used to work out the return angles of all the stonework. Such dramatic stonework would help to create a medieval or Gothic atmosphere in a hallway or dining room.

The stonework is painted in the same colors as the wall in the Magic Castle Window project. Draw the lines lightly with a charcoal pencil, then paint in the mortar and add fine cast shadows depending on the light source — in this case the light comes from the upper right.

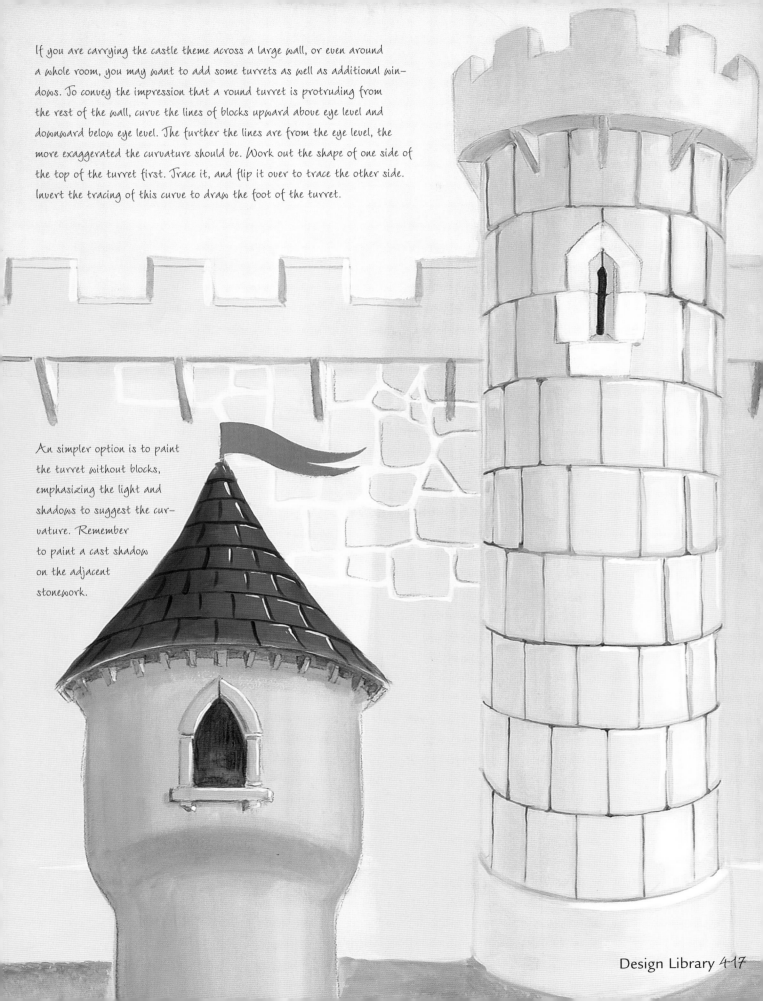

If you are carrying the castle theme across a large wall, or even around a whole room, you may want to add some turrets as well as additional windows. To convey the impression that a round turret is protruding from the rest of the wall, curve the lines of blocks upward above eye level and downward below eye level. The further the lines are from the eye level, the more exaggerated the curvature should be. Work out the shape of one side of the top of the turret first. Trace it, and flip it over to trace the other side. Invert the tracing of this curve to draw the foot of the turret.

An simpler option is to paint the turret without blocks, emphasizing the light and shadows to suggest the curvature. Remember to paint a cast shadow on the adjacent stonework.

THIS FAIRYLAND scene is ideal for younger children, as most of the detail and interest is low down at their eye level. The trees form an excellent framing element, with the branches and roots running along the top and bottom of the wall. If you are continuing the scene around more than one wall, the tree trunks can be painted in the corners of the room.

For the tree trunks use a wash mixed from White, Raw Sienna and Raw Umber, deepening the color toward the edge of the tree to suggest the curvature. Using a No. 3 round pointed brush, pick out the details of the bark, and define the outline, with Raw Umber. You can also blend in a little green in places to bring the tree surface alive.

Paint flowers and toadstools in a very naïve way. You can even paint outlines with a fine round pointed brush to emphasize the individual elements.

The background foliage is stippled on with a 25mm (1in) hog-hair brush, using a light green mixed from White, Chromium Oxide Green and a little Cobalt Blue. Mix in some Leaf Green for the foliage in the middle ground, and more Chromium Oxide Green in the foreground. Deepen the green around the base of the trees and toadstool by adding a little Paynes Grey. For the shoots of grass in the foreground, use a No. 3 round pointed brush with Leaf Green and White, painting short tapering strokes from the bottom up.

Fanciful details like a front door and a window in a tree trunk will help to bring the scene alive, as children imagine who might live inside.

The colors used for the red squirrel are Burnt Sienna, Raw Umber and White.

DRAMATIC DRAPERY creates a theatrical feel for a fantasy landscape. The effect could be carried across a wider wall by adding a few more swags at the top. Such heavy, velvet drapes would also add a passionate touch to a bedroom, or a medieval feel to the window of a dining room.

Sketch one side of the drape first, trace it and flip the tracing to draw the opposite side. Outline the curtains in Red Oxide. Paint a few base coats of Cadmium Red and Red Oxide, or use a red matt emulsion (latex). Mix a little Chromium Oxide Green with the red to paint the shadows in the folds. Mix Cadmium Yellow into the red to pick out the slight highlights on the fabric.

Add the gold fringe using a No. 3 round pointed brush with Naples Yellow. Use short downward strokes, trying to keep them all of a uniform size, and leave some of the deep red showing through the tassels to help define them. Retouch the red later if necessary. You could also add touches of Gold acrylic on top of the Naples Yellow.

If you have an interest in calligraphy or a good handwriting style, you can use it as part of a mural scene. The elements in this scene frame an unrolled scroll, on which you could inscribe a nursery rhyme, lines from a fairytale or a suitable quotation.

Use various mixes of White, Yellow Ochre, Raw Sienna and Raw Umber for the scroll. Water the colors down and build up layers of washes to give the look of old parchment.

Add highlights using lighter colors and White — the highlights on the book spines can be painted using a small flat brush and stippling horizontally down the side of each spine.

Both shelves, and the books on the upper shelf, have the same vanishing point. Plan these first, before adding the toy images. Outline the whole design in Red Oxide using a No. 3 round pointed brush.

A TROMPE l'oeil shelf is an ideal solution if the available wall space is limited and the wall is painted in a plain color. You may wish to give the wall a fresh coat of paint before you start. The toys shown here are ideal for a child, but the shelf could be painted in any room of the house, and hold books (see left), flowers (page 352), a collection of sea shells (page 396) and any number of trompe l'oeil items. Flick through the design libraries for more inspiration.

To begin, block in the main areas of color, watering down the paint only slightly, and using suitable bright colors. Paint all the areas of the same color simultaneously (such as the red on the soldier and the wooden train) to help knit the painting together. As you build up the colors, begin to differentiate between the light and shadowed sides of each toy to bring out their forms. Deepen the shadows where the toys sit on the shelf.

You will need to include cast shadows behind a trompe l'oeil shelf, so you will need some of the color used to paint the wall to mix the shadow colors: you may wish to give the wall a fresh coat of paint before you start. For this light yellow wall, the shadow tone is made by adding very small amounts of Windsor Violet and Paynes Grey. Use some of the original wall color to diffuse the edges of the shadows so they do not become too harsh. Mix some white with the original wall color and blend in a little of this up to the shadows to emphasize them.

You can trace the toys on these two pages, or sketch real toys belonging to the child for whom you are painting the mural.

THIS STYLIZED space scene is inspired by 1950s science fiction, and is perfect for budding young astronauts. The starry sky would also be fitting for a bedroom ceiling.

Sketch the large planet using a pencil tied to a piece of string taped low on the wall. Mix three colors for the sky: Black and Windsor Violet, Black and Cobalt Blue, and plain Black. Alternate between the colors and blend them into each other on the wall. You will need at least two coats to achieve the dark, rich color of the sky. To create the hazy nebulae, mix Cobalt Blue with a little White, and Windsor Violet with a little White; thin with 2—3 parts water. Use a large decorator's brush to stipple some faint cloudy shapes, fizzling them out towards the edges. Keep stippling to soften the color and remove any obvious brush marks.

To create the eclipse, a rare phenomenon that appeals
to astronomers young and old, draw round a circular object
(a plate is ideal) and paint in the white crescent with a No. 5 round
pointed brush, blending it out into the dark sky and stippling in more of the cloudy
effects. Redraw the circle and paint it in pure Black, using a 15mm (⁵/₂in) flat brush.
The stars are blobs of White, very slightly watered down and applied with Nos. 1 and 3 round
pointed brushes. Keep the spacing random and try to cluster stars in places, especially inside the nebulae.
Paint the planet in the foreground using mixtures of Chromium Oxide Green, Burnt Sienna and White.

Suppliers

UK

Craig and Rose
Halbeath Industrial Estate
  Road
Dunfermline
Fife KY11 7EG
tel: 01383 740 011
www.craigandrose.com
dead flat varnish and other specialist paints and brushes

Daler-Rowney Ltd
Bracknell
Berkshire RG12 8ST
tel: 01344 461000
www.daler-rowney.com
artists' materials including acrylics, oils, gouache and brushes

Polyvine Limited
Marybrook Street
Berkeley
Gloucestershire GL13 9AA
tel: 0870 787 3710
www.polyvine.co.uk
flat and satin varnish and other clear coats, decorative paints, woodcare products and industrial coatings

Royal Brush Manufacturing (UK) Ltd
Unit K2, Peartree Industrial Estates
Crackley Way Off Peartree Lane
Dudley
West Midlands
tel: 0138 425 8188
www.royalbrush.com
artists' brushes and paints

Winsor & Newton
Whitefriars Avenue
Harrow
Middlesex HA3 5RH
England
tel: 0208 427 4343
www.winsornewton.com
artists' materials including acrylics, oils, gouache and brushes

US

Daler-Rowney
2 Corporate Drive
Cranbury
New Jersey 08512
tel: 609 655 5252
www.daler-rowney.com
artists' materials including acrylics, oils, gouache and brushes

Polyvine Inc
500 Palm Street #22
West Palm Beach
Florida 33401
tel: 561 820 1500
www.polyvine.com
flat and satin varnish and other clear coats, decorative paints, woodcare products and industrial coatings

Royal & Langnickel Brush Mfg Inc
6707 Broadway
Merrillville
Indiana 46410
tel: 800 247 2211
www.royalbrush.com
artists' brushes and paints

Winsor & Newton
PO Box 1396
Piscataway,
New Jersey 08855
tel: 800 445 4278
www.winsornewton.com
artists' materials including acrylics, oils, gouache and brushes

Online
Muralsplus, developed by Martin Alan Hirsch, is an online resource for faux painting enthusiasts, muralists, and decorative painters looking for ideas or wanting to increase their level of expertise.
www.muralsplus.com

por siempre jamás

Cover designer: Clare Finney
Production Editor: Jennifer Ziegler
Production Coordinator: Kristen Heller